digital tectonics

edited by

Neil Leach
David Turnbull
Chris Williams

WILEY-ACADEMY

All illustrations are courtesy of the contributors.

Cover and title page: Study for sculpture by Chris Williams

A RIBA Future Studies Project with the University of Bath supported by the Happold Trust.

Published in Great Britain in 2004 by Wiley-Academy, a division of John Wiley & Sons Ltd

Other Wiley Editorial Offices

John Wiley & Sons Inc., 111 River Street, Hoboken, NJ 07030, USA

Jossey-Bass, 989 Market Street, San Francisco, CA 94103-1741, USA

Wiley-VCH Verlag GmbH, Boschstr. 12, D-69469 Weinheim, Germany

John Wiley & Sons Australia Ltd, 33 Park Road, Milton, Queensland 4064, Australia

John Wiley & Sons (Asia) Pte Ltd, 2 Clementi Loop #02-01, Jin Xing Distripark, Singapore 129809

John Wiley & Sons Canada Ltd, 22 Worcester Road, Etobicoke, Ontario, Canada M9W 1L1

ISBN 978-0-470-85729-8 (P/B)

Design and Prepress: ARTMEDIA PRESS Ltd, London

Printed and bound in Italy by Conti Tipocolor

CONTENTS

INTRODUCTION

Digital Tectonics – this volume has a seemingly contradictory title. For how can the digital be tectonic? And how – for that matter – can the tectonic be digital? Surely, most would argue, the digital belongs to a completely immaterial world of computer algorithms, and the tectonic, by contrast, to a resolutely material world of construction. So what can the term mean?

The term digital tectonics is being used here to refer to a new paradigm of thinking in architectural culture. From the moment when computers first made a significant impact on architectural design, a critical counterculture began to emerge. This counterculture championed the tectonic, and claimed that those who were producing seductive computer imagery failed to understand the intrinsic nature of architectural production. It was argued that architecture was born not of the algorithmic potential of computer programs, but of the tectonic capacities of actual materials. Critics of the computer included figures such as Kenneth Frampton, whose book, *Studies in Tectonic Culture*, could be read as a polemic against the fast evolving digital culture.[1] With time, however, computer technologies have infiltrated almost every aspect of architectural production, and are now being used to offer insights even into the realm of the tectonic. In particular, they are allowing us to model – with increasing sophistication – the material properties of architectural components. This volume, then, marks a particular moment in the history of architecture when the old opposition between the digital and the tectonic has begun to collapse, and the digital is beginning to be used increasingly in the service of the tectonic. A new tectonics of the digital – a *digital* tectonics – has begun to emerge.

But, importantly, the term digital tectonics also evokes a further paradigm shift within architectural culture, a shift that is in part facilitated by – but not totally dependent upon – the technological possibilities afforded by the digital realm. For one of the dominant trends emerging within architectural culture at the beginning of the twenty-first century is a renewed interest in the structural logic of buildings. What we are beginning to witness is a 'structural turn' within architectural culture. It is clear that a significant number of progressive architects are seeking to step beyond a certain Postmodern sensibility which celebrates scenographic properties and surface effects, and focus instead on the structural integrity of buildings.[2]

This 'structural turn' has inaugurated a new spirit of collaboration between architecture and engineering, which looks set to influence the production of buildings for some time to come. New dialogues are beginning to emerge, as these two professions, which have often been perceived as quite separate areas of concern, are coming together within a culture of mutual respect. This may lead to new hybrid formations, interdisciplinary practices that exist within the space between the two professions. We are even seeing the emergence of a new hybrid practitioner – a kind of architect-engineer of the digital age.

Digital Tectonics, then, addresses this new sensibility within the building industry, and explores its dependence upon digital technologies. Yet this emerging culture of digital tectonics has remained hitherto without any theoretical commentary. The task of this volume is to put this right, by assembling a body of significant work, and situating it within a landscape of theoretical ideas which serve to define and articulate its objectives. In short, the task of this volume is to provide a manifesto for a new culture of digital tectonics.

The Structural Turn

The whole history of architecture could be understood as a dialectic between two alternative – yet by no means mutually exclusive – ways of thinking, a distinction that could be described as that between the Gothic and the Classical. Broadly speaking, the Gothic is based primarily on understanding architecture in terms of materiality and structure, while the Classical is based primarily on understanding architecture in terms of visual composition. The Gothic is concerned more with process, the Classical more with representation. This volume concerns itself with the former. It tracks the genealogy of a certain Gothic spirit in architecture, a tradition based not on the formal appearance of the Gothic – as in the case of neo-Gothic – but on a certain process-orientated approach towards architectural design, that recognises the importance of structural forces and material composition.

In his contribution to this volume, 'Material Complexity', Manuel DeLanda looks at the development of the science of metallurgy within an empiricist tradition of material experimentation as a lens through which to consider a new paradigm of thinking about the materiality of structure. We need to entertain the possibility of understanding the behaviour of materials, DeLanda maintains, not in terms of fixed and static rules, but rather in terms of processes of dynamic adaptation. Hence we need to look beyond the laws of physics established by eminent figures of the 'major' state sciences – figures such as Isaac Newton – to embrace also the findings of experimental practitioners of what Deleuze terms the 'minor' sciences – relatively unknown figures such as Robert Hooke – in order to understand the possibilities of material formations that 'emerge' from the complex dynamic behaviour of their components. 'We may now be in a position,' DeLanda concludes, 'to think about the origin of form and structure, not as something imposed from the outside on an inert matter, not as a hierarchical command from above as in an assembly line, but as something that may come from within the materials, a form that we tease out of those materials as we allow them to have their say in the structures we create.'[3]

This Gothic spirit has a genealogy that extends well beyond the Gothic period itself, and manifests itself in certain later incarnations, notably the work of Antonio Gaudí, an architect with an acute understanding of structural concerns. Gaudí's work is itself situated within a creative fusion of past and present, in that the construction of his Sagrada Familia Church in Barcelona is being completed several years after his death in 1926, using technologies that were unavailable in his lifetime. Gaudí had left behind a number of physical studies of forms proposed for the building, alongside the examples of work already undertaken, but the problem has been that he left behind no accompanying description to explain these forms. Mark Burry, acting as a consultant on this project, is attempting to use modern digital techniques to analyse and understand Gaudí's individual, highly sophisticated approach to design. In his article, 'Virtually Gaudí', Burry outlines a parametric approach towards the use of the computer which can generate a language of form not inconsistent with Gaudí's own analogue technique. Such operations suggest new ways of reconfiguring Gaudí's approach, that open up fresh formal possibilities.

In 'Gaudí's Hanging Presence', Mark Goulthorpe offers a brief reflection on the reception of Gaudí's ideas within the contemporary architectural arena. Goulthorpe has coined the term, 'post-Gaudian praxis', to refer to his own practice, which also relies heavily on the use of digital technologies. While there were many discourses at work within Gaudí's design methodology, his innovative use of simple string and lead tensile models to define in reverse the compressive forces in his proposals, stand out as a clear manifestation of the Gothic spirit. Goulthorpe outlines how Gaudí's structural experiments have acted as a 'hanging presence' to influence his own work.

Frei Otto is one of the next major protagonists of the Gothic spirit within architecture. Otto established research links with Professor Ted Happold of the University of Bath in the late 1960s. The legacy of this collaboration can be found in the firm Buro Happold, which continues to act as consultants for various innovative engineering problems, often involving membrane structures. Mike Cook of Buro Happold outlines the thinking behind this research, illustrating in particular the debt that Otto owed to forms in nature. Otto's practice was based less on the digital than the analogue, and indulged in a certain measure of 'biomimetics', seeking to learn lessons from material formations in nature that could be redeployed within the modern highly technological world of contemporary construction to provide efficient solutions to various questions. Indeed the whole notion of 'efficiency' lends this work a certain environmental spin. The soap bubbles and other physical models favoured by Otto, have now been displaced – to some extent – by the computer, although the computer does not always lead to greater efficiencies. We should therefore remain mindful, Cook warns us, of the lessons about efficiency that can be learned through analogue modelling.

Otto's influence lives on in the work of Lars Spuybroek, an architect as well known for his theoretical writings as he is for his innovative design work. Spuybroek readily acknowledges the inspiration that Otto has provided him with. Here Spuybroek describes SoftOffice inspired by Otto's material machines for form-finding. Otto's own technique for reconfiguring tensile structures by loosening their members, and then soaking them so that the fibres start to merge and divide in new ways while maintaining their original structural integrity, is redeployed to provide an analogue computer to define the forms of both projects.

At first sight, Greg Lynn's interest in the 'ornamental' appears somewhat incongruous in a volume devoted largely to the question of structure. Yet if we inquire further we can see from the interview, 'The Structure of Ornament', that far from being out of place in this volume, Lynn's own work points towards an important corrective that serves to counter a potentially undialectical attitude towards structure and ornament in contemporary avant-garde circles. Lynn's approach stands out in particular in an architectural culture dominated by a fascination with processes, which tends to champion process over representation. One result of this tendency has been a marked reluctance within a broadly Deleuze-inspired avant-garde of today to address questions of beauty and ornamentation, even if those aspects still constitute an important consideration within architectural design.[4]

Yet if we think through the matter closely, a true Deleuzian position would always entertain a discourse of representation. Indeed, although for Deleuze it is an important theoretical conceit to champion one over the other, as a necessary corrective to existing practices, we must understand that these terms are locked into a mechanism of reciprocal presupposition. Process always folds into representation, and vice versa. As such, Lynn's attempts to inscribe a discourse of ornamentation within a discourse of structuration appears in fact to be more Deleuzian than other positions within the avant-garde. In his process-based exploration of ornamental treatment, Lynn seeks to understand ornamentation as related to internal organisational structures, rather as the patterning on the surface coat of an animal skin relates to the armature of bone and soft tissue beneath. This highlights the need to think of ornamentation structurally, but so too to think of structure ornamentally.[5]

Digital Operations

How then might one begin to place the theory of the significance of the digital within this new concern for structure? In 'Swarm Tectonics' Neil Leach makes connections between a Deleuzian understanding of an architecture of the Gothic spirit and a theory of the digital, by means of the scientific discourse of 'emergence'. One of the interesting aspects of the discourse of 'emergence' that has become extremely popular within certain architectural schools is that it makes connections between various 'populational' behaviours – between the operations, for example, of ants or termites and human populations, right through to the operations of the computer itself. For the computer – as its name implies (*computare* is the Latin verb for to think together) – is itself made up of the operation of smaller components working together. This can also be understood in terms of 'swarm intelligence' – the way that a flock of birds, swarm of bees or shoal of fish begins to develop a certain group intelligence which is greater than the sum of its parts. This 'swarm intelligence' can also be extended to describe the way that structure operates as a self-organising mechanism. A link between the operations of the computer and structural behaviour can therefore be established and a theoretical paradigm can be set up for thinking about the possibility of understanding structural behaviour through computer simulations.

Any theoretical overview of the potential of the computer to simulate structural performance must, however, depend on the actual programs written to perform these operations. In 'Design by Algorithm' Chris Williams outlines the role that algorithms may play in structural design, illustrating his argument with an analysis of the design for the glass roof over the courtyard of the British Museum in London, designed by the architects Foster and Partners, and the engineers Buro Happold. The particular challenge for this design was to find a solution that could be positioned as a 'lid' over the space, without exerting any external thrusts on to the surrounding fabric. Acting as a consultant for this project, Williams initially wrote an algorithm that defined the form of the roof in outline, and then applied the 'dynamic relaxation technique', pioneered within the realm of engineering by Mike Barnes, in order to define the precise position of the nodes. This relaxation process involved the shifting of nodes within a numerical grid until each node was the 'weighted average' of surrounding nodes, a process that was repeated exhaustively until the grid reached a form of equilibrium.

In contrast to this very precise use of the computer to understand structure, Alisa Andrasek presents a highly idiosyncratic and poetic account of the use of L-systems in the architectural design studio. Her take on what could otherwise be a realm of dry science opens up the possibility of using digital technologies in a highly inspirational way, using sampling, hacking and other such tactics. Andrasek belongs to a new sensibility, a group of highly computer-literate experimental practitioners, who have discovered within the digital realm new forms of expression and new design methodologies.

L-systems, cellular automata, genetic algorithms, and other similar programs have all been used within architectural culture for generating novel forms. These programs represent a significant development within the evolution of the design process. Here the designer is recast not as some demiurgic figure who imposes form on the world, but rather as the controller of processes who allows formations to emerge. The designer, moreover, is using the computer not merely as a tool of representation but as a 'collaborative partner' within the design process itself, to such an extent that our whole notion of design needs to be reconfigured.

Much of the inspiration for this work has come from the realm of nature. Yet these programs remain simulations of natural processes of growth, and do not incorporate the full performative character of these processes. For example, many of the forms generated have no structural integrity. The challenge of proposing a program that would generate structural form has been taken up by Kristina Shea. The eifForm research software that she devised offers a generative design methodology based on a combination of a search algorithm for a structural shape grammar and an optimisation procedure for simulated annealing. This is a non-deterministic search process which does not generate any single optimised solution, but yields a variety of equally valid alternatives.

In 'Directed Randomness' Shea describes her first collaborative venture in constructing a full-scale physical model of a form generated by eifForm, using decidedly low-tech techniques of construction to realise a design produced by the most hi-tech of programs. The project for a temporary structure in Amsterdam is an experimental one that does not address the full range of architectural concerns, such as durability, weather proofing, environmental control and so on. Yet it nonetheless raises some provocative questions as to how such similar programs might be devised for the future. For while Shea's program is a structural one, we could imagine the development of a range of other programs which might exploit the potential of the computer to act as a search engine seeking out efficiencies within other domains, such as environmental, constructional or programmatic concerns.

A further facet of this new culture of digital tectonics has been the use of machinic processes. These have been introduced into the design laboratory as a means of fabricating material components through digitally informed techniques, ranging from the use of Computer Numerically Controlled (CNC) milling operations to Rapid Prototyping processes. What these techniques facilitate is the possibility of exploring physical form at stage one of the design process. Their use is now widespread within product design, and although their potential contribution to architectural design has yet to be fully realised, they represent an important development in architectural production. Just as the drawing board and set square have been all but superseded by the computer, so too, where resources allow, the use of scalpels, balsa and cardboard for model-making is being replaced by more sophisticated modelling techniques, which provide immediate material feedback on the digital designs being undertaken. These machinic processes are not limited to study models. Their introduction into the actual process of construction has become increasingly common. CNC milling allows a high degree of accuracy in the manufacture of component parts, and is especially useful where complex forms are involved. What we are witnessing throughout the building industry is a shift towards more advanced techniques of modelling and construction facilitated by the introduction of the computer into the whole process of design and construction.

One of the early exponents of these techniques has been Bernard Cache, an architect who has been a pioneer in many arenas. Cache has been responsible for setting up a highly innovative production company, Objectile, for the fabrication of experimental building components. In his article Cache describes how he devised his own state-of-the-art software, as part of a move towards fully associative design and manufacture, in which modifications can be incorporated within a design without entailing the wholesale redrafting of designs. This associativity needs to be comprehensive. In the case of his small Philibert de L'Orme pavilion, this entailed the establishment of a 'seamless set of relations between a few control points and the 765 machining programs needed to manufacture it on a numerical command router'. We can only speculate about the forms that will be produced in the future through digital technologies, but, according to Cache, a crucial concern is sure to be the development of software that can respond flexibly to the new demands of design and construction.

The collaborative office SERVO has established a highly unusual form of practice. Working as a co-operative network, the office is based in several different cities. Not only this, but the office collaborates with other design studios, and operates itself at the interface between different techniques and practices. Its *Lattice Archipelogics* project is at once an exercise in machinic processes of construction and also an exercise in interactive design. Designed in conjunction with smart studio, the lattice structure is constructed of translucent plastically deformed lattice cells modelled using techniques of stereolithography. These are lit up interactively with LED illuminators through audience participation. The lattice structure therefore begins to delineate a three-dimensional responsive space that is choreographed by the movements of the audience.

OCEAN NORTH is a practice that also works as a design co-operative based in different cities, and straddles different disciplines. Its work uses digital technology not through some 'self-indulgent fascination', but in order to 'inject performative potential into the built environment'. The *Extraterrain* furniture project is derived through digitally sampled sectional geometries that are reconfigured to provide landscapes of occupation, in which users are invited to find their own body positions, without any particular position being prescribed. The thinking behind all of the practice's work is based on Umberto Eco's notion of the 'open work'. Architecture should not prescribe precise patterns of occupation. Rather it should be left ambiguous, encouraging a broad range of occupations. It is therefore up to the user to invent programmatic uses for any structure. Yet while its work involves the digital domain in both the generation of forms and their fabrication using CNC milling, OCEAN NORTH defines the whole notion of 'computing' not as some distinction between the digital and analogue worlds, but rather as one that straddles both, and incorporates the performativities of the human body in order to generate fully inclusive design scenarios.

New Dialogues
These new developments have prompted new forms of collaboration, and opened up new modes of operation. The final section is composed of discussions and interviews that outline the new approaches that are being adopted.

If we were to look for an emblem of this new spirit, it would be the temporary pavilion designed by Toyo Ito and Cecil Balmond for the Serpentine Gallery in London. This is a project designed not by the architect with the subsequent technical assistance of the engineer, but by the architect and engineer working in tandem, with neither party having any preconceived notion of how the eventual design would turn out. In his article Balmond describes the generation of the design of the Serpentine Pavilion. Eschewing 'beam or column in the conventional sense', they devised an algorithm that set a square diagonally within a square, a pattern that is folded back, so that it provides 'a continuous zigzag tracing over the three-dimensional form'. In so doing they construct 'a cubic space made only out of vanishing lines', 'a capsule of drifting space'.

One of the challenges for a volume concerned with structure is the problem of creating a theory for a discipline such as engineering that has little history of any text-based theory of structure, and whose discourse is based primarily in scientific calculations and material experimentations. How might we write a philosophy of structure? Yet the possibilities are there if we consider how we might extend DeLanda's thinking on the performativity of materials, inspired by the writings of Gilles Deleuze, to the work of many of the engineers covered in this volume. Indeed it is perhaps no coincidence that terminology which emanates from a structural engineering background – terms such as 'connectivities' and 'nonlinearity' – echo terms used by Deleuze himself. For even if engineers have not read Deleuze's own writings, they manifest a similar set of preoccupations. Nor need they have read any books on philosophy, because their very work – in keeping with DeLanda's observations – is a form of material thinking, or thinking through materials. Engineers could therefore be described as exponents of a certain 'material philosophy'.

For Balmond there is an urgent need to question the traditional discourse of post-and-beam structure in architecture. Not only does the whole Gothic tradition suggest that trabeated architecture is seldom the most efficient from a structural point of view, but new engineering possibilities emerge alongside the exploration of new forms – especially curvilinear ones. 'What you have got to realise,' notes Balmond, 'is that every point of curvature is a structural possibility.' What are required are new strategies for recognising structural possibilities: 'A point becomes a zone, a line becomes surface, plane becomes volume etc' so that engineering moves beyond its traditional methodologies.

UN Studio have established themselves as one of the pre-eminent network practices having reorganised their office as an increasingly open 'flexible platform' through which they can fulfil the role of what they call the 'public scientist'. In this way they have recast the office as an infrastructure. Dialogue and collaboration are central to this formulation of a practice in which they put themselves in the situation where the outcome of the exchange of ideas is manifestly a joint 'product'. The term product is important here because however loosely it may be used it suggests that architecture needs to be rethought as a form of product design. Product design is never overwhelmed by a heavy sense of rooted specificity or semiotic depth. It is joyful, light and passion inspiring and, in a profound sense governed by the way that products behave in time. It recognises its problematic position in relation to ecological questions, and can respond to new imperatives in an agile manner. In 'Live It - Love It', Ben van Berkel and Caroline Bos explain the motivation for UN Studio's design for the Mercedes Benz Museum in Stuttgart.

Finally, various contributors to this volume take part in a round table discussion chaired by David Turnbull, 'An Aesthetics of Calculus' which is simultaneously an opportunity for reflection and a social event that reminds us that architecture and engineering require social as well as technical action. In social terms the shift from what Cecil Balmond calls the assumption of a Linear Space, in which Architecture leads and Engineering follows because it is imagined to be inherent in Architecture's catalogue of types – post and beam, arch, vault and so on, to a Non Linear Space of risk and experiment, has extraordinary ramifications. Non-linear thinking and action is reorganising every aspect of contemporary life. Recognised by the RAND Corporation in the USA as a symptom of a fundamental change in social practices, it is the operative mode of the terrorist organisation as much as it is the underlying structure of the rave, the flash-mob or the anti-globalisation demonstration, the key to the strategic reorganisation of the workplace as well as the restructuring of the urban-rural continuum. So, what is being staged here is the contemporary reformulation of the disciplines of architecture and engineering and a new articulation of professional categories. This raises a number of pressing concerns for both education and practice.

A predominant theme throughout this volume is the need to rethink the relationship between architect and engineer. The theme is developed here to address how this relationship is figured within both architectural and engineering education. Burry comments on the emphasis on being 'hip and creative' over possessing technical ability in the admissions policies to certain schools of architecture. This is a symptom of a culture in which 'stress' and 'strain' have become dirty words for architects, just as 'aesthetics' has become a dirty word for engineers. What we need, notes DeLanda, is a means of enthusing architecture students with technical concerns and engineers with aesthetic ones. This does not mean the literal teaching of various technical operations, such as calculus, so much as the need to inculcate architecture students with an understanding of the *point* of these operations. This would help to produce, perhaps, a hybrid discipline, an 'architecture-engineering' of the digital age. As Balmond comments, 'There are fantastic opportunities ahead to have a *new* discipline.' But this must be grounded in a radically new approach to design within our educational system. What we need, according to Balmond, is a 'fundamental revolution in how we approach teaching, both in engineering schools, and in architectural schools'.

The volume concludes, then, with the sort of productive discussion between architects and engineers that is emblematic of a new synergetic approach towards design which has begun to appear. It is an approach which seeks to break down the received opposition between architecture and engineering, and which also looks to digital technologies as a means of facilitating that process. The future of the profession, and indeed the very good health of the discipline of architecture, surely depends on a more open-minded approach not only to collaboration with other professionals – especially structural engineers – but also to the possibilities afforded by new digital technologies.

Notes

1 Kenneth Frampton, *Studies in Tectonic Culture*, (Cambridge, Mass: MIT Press, 1996).
2 This tendency to divorce structural concerns from aesthetic ones reached its culmination in Frank Gehry's Guggenheim Museum in Bilbao, Spain. Although this building has received almost universal critical acclaim, some have found fault with it for the approach towards structure. It is as though the primary concern of the building was to achieve certain sculptural effects, and the structural support for these effects was treated as a secondary issue.
3 p.23
4 The work of architects such as Foreign Office Architects can be contrasted with the work of architects such as Frank Gehry. There may appear to be certain formal similarities between the end products, but, as Foreign Office Architects would themselves always stress, their working methods are quite different. Whereas Gehry would privilege elegance of form, Foreign Office Architects would concern themselves with processes of formation. As a consequence, although their final designs may appear very beautiful – and few would deny that their Yokohama ferry terminal is indeed beautiful – somewhat disingenuously, it would seem, issues of formal beauty are never acknowledged.
5 In a pre-Ruskinian age ornament was thought of not as some surface-based decorative motif, but as part of structure. Indeed Alberti makes the claim that, while the column is the principal ornament in architecture, a row of columns is nothing other than a wall with a series of holes cut into it. As such, we should maybe revise the recent translation of Alberti's treatise on architecture. Ornament is not something 'attached or additional' but something 'impacted' [Latin: *impactum*] into the structure. LB Alberti, *On the Art of Building in Ten Books*, trans J Rykwert, N Leach and R Tavernor (Cambridge, Mass: MIT Press, 1988).

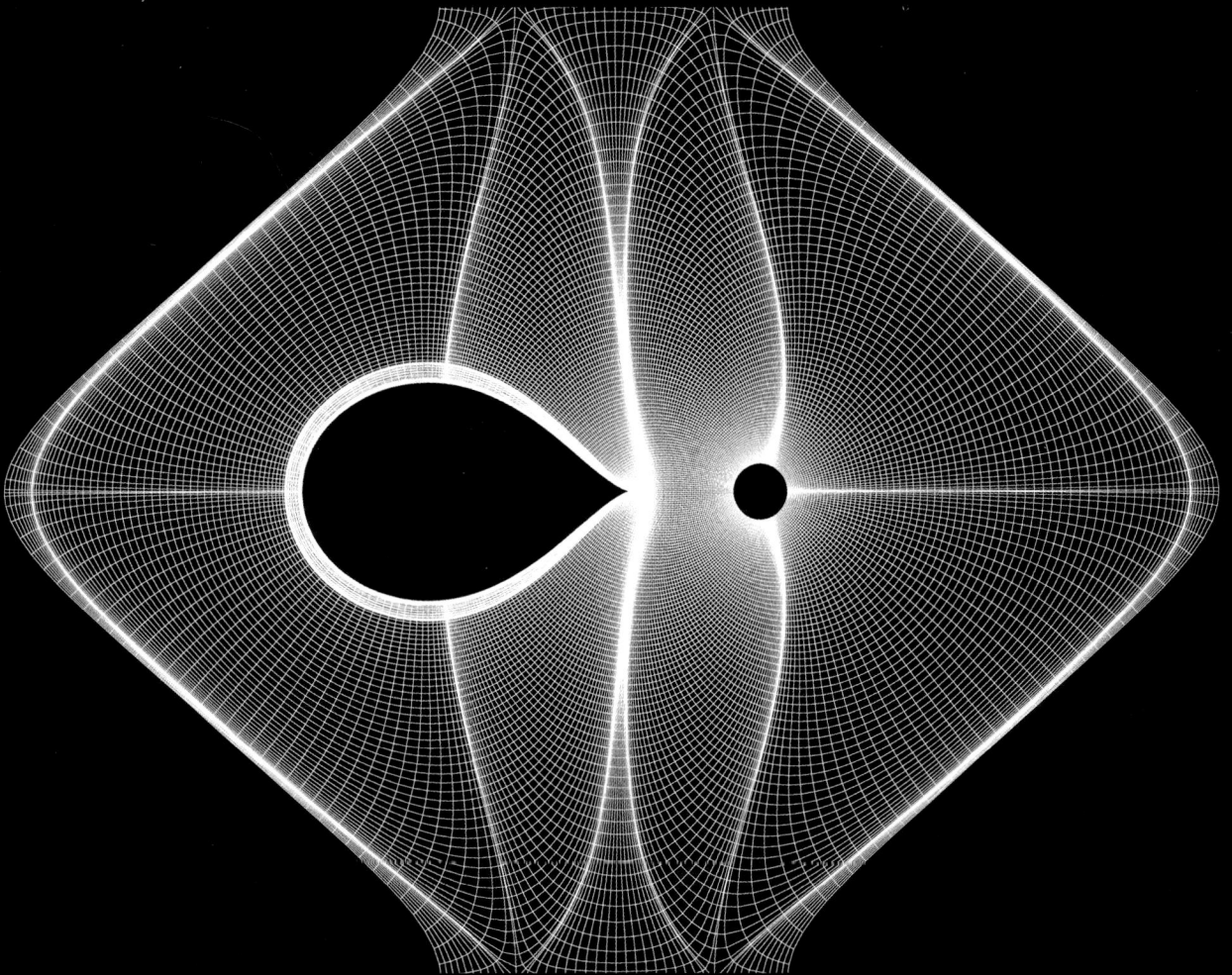

THE STRUCTURAL TURN

Study Shell Structure (Chris Williams for Buro Happold)

MATERIAL COMPLEXITY

Manuel DeLanda

For centuries the scientific study of the behavior of materials was performed in relatively obscure engineering or metallurgy departments, away from the highly prestigious centers of 'pure' science. For physicists, it seems, the only property of materials that carried any weight was their mass; their strength was relegated to the more peripheral fields of applied science. Today this has all changed and the study of the complex behavior of matter has acquired legitimacy and its own name: materials science and engineering. The long institutional struggle to gain respect, and the more sophisticated conceptual and technical tools that may be brought to bear on the study of material complexity, are full of lessons for the philosopher of science. Materialist philosophers, it is becoming increasingly clear, cannot afford to ignore the basic fact that the study of matter does matter.

Cyril Stanley Smith, a metallurgist and historian of materials, has explored the development of the philosophy of matter in the West and has concluded that for the most part the study of the complexity and variability of behavior of materials has always been the concern of empirically oriented craftsmen or engineers, not of philosophers or scientists. He argues that we may have inherited this generally condescending attitude from the Greeks, who admired the handcrafted products produced by the blacksmith but who despised his material activities and his apparent unwillingness to engage in verbal exchanges on political or philosophical questions. As he puts it:

> To those engaged in materials production and fabrication, it may be disconcerting to realize that for a fair fraction of human history their activities have been viewed with suspicion and downright distaste by social thinkers and the general public. The ancient Greek philosophers, who set the tone for many of the attitudes still prevalent throughout Western civilization, regarded those involved in the production of material goods as being less worthy than agriculturalists and others who did not perform such mundane tasks . . .Throughout ancient society the most menial tasks, especially those of mining and metallurgy, were left to slaves. Hence the common social attitude of antiquity, persisting to this day in some intellectual circles, was to look down upon those who work with their hands. Xenophon stated the case in this fashion, 'What are called the mechanical arts carry a social stigma and are rightly dishonored in our cities. For these arts damage the bodies of those who work at them or who act as overseers, by compelling them to a sedentary life and to an indoor life, and, in some cases, to spend the whole day by the fire. This physical degeneration results also in deterioration of the soul. Furthermore the workers at these trades simply do not have the time to perform the offices of friendship or citizenship. Consequently they are looked

upon as bad friends and bad patriots, and in some cities, especially the warlike ones, it is not legal for a citizen to ply a mechanical trade.'[1]

Despite this negative attitude, Smith argues that Greek philosophers like Aristotle may have learned much from visiting workshops, given that practically everything about the behavior of metals and alloys that could be explored with pre-industrial technology was already known to craftsmen and blacksmiths for at least a thousand years. Indeed, as he says, the early philosophies of matter may have been derived from observation and conversation with those 'whose eyes had seen and whose fingers had felt the intricacies of the behavior of materials during thermal processing or as they were shaped by chipping, cutting or plastic deformation'.[2] For instance, Aristotle's famous four elements – fire, earth, water and air – may be said to reflect an awareness of what today we know as energy and the three main states of aggregation of matter: the solid, liquid and gas states, all of which were very familiar to a metallurgist.

As metaphysical speculation gave special meanings to these four elementary qualities their original physical meaning was lost, and the variability and complexity of real materials was replaced with the uniform behavior of a philosophically simplified matter about which one could only speculate symbolically. It is true that sixteenth-century alchemists recovered a certain respect for a direct interaction with matter and energy, and that seventeenth-century Cartesian philosophers speculated intensely about the variable properties of different ways of aggregating material components. But these early attempts at capturing the complexity of physical transmutations and of the effect of physical structure on the complex properties of materials, eventually lost to the emergent science of chemistry and its almost total concentration on simple behavior: that of individual components (such as Lavoisier's oxygen) or of substances that conform to the law of definite proportions (as in Dalton's atomic theory).

There was, as Smith observes, an 'immense gain' in these simplifications, since the exact sciences could not have developed without them, but the triumph of chemistry was accompanied by a 'not insignificant loss'. In particular, the complete concentration of analysis at the level of molecules caused an almost total disregard for higher levels of aggregation in solids, but it is there where most complex properties of interest to today's material scientist occur.[3] As is usual in the history of science there were several exceptions, such as Galileo, who studied the strength of materials in the sixteenth century, but who may have derived his interest and even some insights from his visits to the Venetian arsenal, the largest military-industrial complex of its time and home to a large variety of craftsmen. How are we to theorise this ambivalent relation towards complex materiality within science? Deleuze and Guattari offer a possible solution when they contrast two types of science, or two modes of conducting scientific research, a major and a minor mode: *royal science* and *nomad science*, the science of the royal societies and academies at the service of the state preoccupied above all with the discovery of abstract general laws, and the humbler science of those who built the laboratory instruments and had the job of testing the validity of those laws in concrete physical situations.

Indeed, the distinction between royal and nomad science is drawn more widely so that it does not coincide with the distinction between pure and applied science. In its minor mode, science deals with complex material behavior, liquids not solids, heterogeneous not homogeneous matter, turbulent not steady-state (or laminar) flow. (It also includes a preference for non-metric, projective or topological spaces, as well as for problematic rather than axiomatic logical structures.)[4] Not surprisingly, Deleuze and Guattari classify ancient metallurgy as 'minor science in person'.[5]

Although the distinction between the major and minor modes does not neatly divide individual scientists into two sharply drawn categories, we may illustrate it with two historical characters: Isaac Newton and his contemporary archenemy Robert Hooke, who developed the first theory of material elasticity. As materials scientist James Edward Gordon has remarked, 'Unlike Newton, Hooke was intensely interested in what went on in kitchens, dockyards, and buildings – the mundane mechanical arenas of life . . . Nor did Hooke despise craftsmen, and he probably got the inspiration for at least some of his ideas from his friend the great London clock maker Thomas Tompion . . .'.[6] The point Gordon is trying to make is not that scientists may be divided into two separate classes since, after all, the same Newton who headed the Royal Society had also been an alchemist, but that in seventeenth-century England much more prestige was attached to scientific fields that were not concerned with the mundane mechanical arenas where materials displayed their full complex behavior. This may be one reason why conceptual advances in the study of materials, such as the key conceptual distinction between stress and strain (one referring to the forces acting on a material structure, the other to the behavior of the structure in response to those forces), were made in France where applied science was encouraged both officially and socially.

Indeed, although Hooke is a perfect example of a minor scientist – his law of elasticity linking stress and strain (or more accurately, since these concepts did not yet exist, the load a structure bears and the deformation it undergoes under that load) was of the type characterising major science. In other words, his law postulated a *linear relation* between load and deformation, or what amounts to the same thing: a simple, well-behaved, proportional response to a given cause. Although some materials do have a range of loads under which they respond linearly (a small increase in load producing a proportionally small deformation) and also reversibly (after removal of the load the deformation disappears), even these simple materials display a critical threshold beyond which their behavior ceases to be elastic and becomes plastic: any further small load causes a large deformation and, moreover, the change of shape becomes irreversible. Plastic behavior, such as a permanent dent or bend in a metallic beam, is but one example of *nonlinear behavior*. Indeed, many materials behave nonlinearly even without critical loads. Organic tissues, for example, display a J-shaped reaction curve: a small load causes a large deformation at first, but then even large loads cease to have much effect. Rubber and other materials display an S-shaped reaction: a load fails to have any effect at all up to a point beyond which rubber stretches linearly but only to stop reacting to further loads beyond yet another point. Since a material's capacity to bear loads is directly related to its capacity to deform, rubber's inability to further deform under heavy loads makes it very brittle in those conditions. At any event, J- and S-shaped reaction curves, as well as many others, are examples of nonlinear, complex material behavior.[7]

Material complexity, however, needs more than just nonlinearity to become expressed. In particular, one may linearize a nonlinear system by studying it only under conditions *near or at equilibrium*. One of the oldest examples of this linearization, going back to Galileo, is the simple pendulum. The mathematical model of a pendulum shows that the relationship between the amplitude and the period of its swing is in fact non-linear, that is, there is feedback or interaction between the two. But given that nonlinear equations were pretty much intractable until the advent of computers, this physical fact presented an obstacle to the modeling of this simple dynamical system. So what scientists did was to study the pendulum's behavior only for extremely small values of its amplitude, so as not to let the nonlinearities become too visible. As mathematician Ian Stewart puts it:

> Classical mathematics concentrated on linear equations for a sound pragmatic reason: it could not solve anything else . . . So docile are linear equations that classical mathematicians were willing to compromise their physics to get them. So the classical theory deals with *shallow* waves, *low*-amplitude vibrations, *small* temperature gradients [that is, it linearizes nonlinearities]. So ingrained became the linear habit that by the 1940s and 1950s many scientists and engineers knew little else . . . Linearity is a trap. The behavior of linear equations . . . is far from typical. But if you decide that only linear equations are worth thinking about, self-censorship sets in. Your textbooks fill with triumphs of linear analysis, its failures buried so deep that the graves go unmarked and the existence of the graves goes unremarked. As the eighteenth century believed in a clockwork world, so did the mid-twentieth in a linear one.[8]

Thus, nonlinear behavior needs *non-equilibrium conditions* to become manifest. Today's complexity theory depends as much on nonlinear mathematics as it does on far-from-equilibrium thermodynamics. The latter discipline studies systems which, unlike its nineteenth-century classical counterpart, are not closed to intense flows of matter and energy from the outside. While linear systems tend to be characterized by a single, global stable state, systems which are both nonlinear and non-equilibrium display *multiple stable* states and these may come in a variety of additional forms, not only steady-state but also periodic and chaotic. In addition, scientists have come to realize that these multiple stable states seem to characterize not only inorganic material behavior, but also organic and even social behavior. In other words, we are beginning to understand that any complex system, whether composed of interacting molecules, organic creatures or economic agents, is capable of spontaneously generating order and actively organizing itself into new structures and forms. It is precisely this ability of matter and energy to *self-organize* that is of greatest significance to the philosopher. This can be illustrated by an example from materials science.

Long ago, practical metallurgists understood that a given piece of metal could be made to change its behavior, from ductile and tough to rigid and brittle, by hammering it while cold. The opposite transmutation, from hard to ductile, could also be achieved by heating the piece of metal again and then allowing it to cool down slowly (that is, by annealing it). Yet, although blacksmiths knew empirically how to cause these metamorphoses, it was not until a few decades ago that scientists understood the actual microscopic mechanism. As it turns out, explaining the physical basis of ductility involved a radical conceptual change: scientists had to stop viewing metals in static terms, that is, as deriving their strength in a simple way from the chemical bonds between their composing atoms, and begin looking at them as dynamical systems. In particular, the real cause of brittleness in rigid materials, and the reason why ductile ones can resist being broken, has to do with the complex dynamics of spreading cracks.

A crack or fracture needs energy to spread through a piece of material and any mechanism that takes away energy from the crack will make the material tough. In metals, the mechanism seems to be based on certain line defects or imperfections within the component crystals, called *dislocations*. Dislocations not only trap energy locally but, moreover, are highly mobile and may be brought into existence in large quantities by the very concentrations of stress which tend to break a piece of metal. Roughly, if populations of these line defects are free to move in a material they will endow it with the capacity to yield locally without breaking, that is, they will make the material tough. On the other hand, restricted movement of dislocations will result in a more rigid material.[9] Both of these properties may be desirable for different tools, and even within one and the same tool: in a sword or knife, for instance, the load-bearing body must be tough while the cutting edge must be rigid to be capable of holding on to its sharply triangular shape.

What matters from the philosophical point of view is precisely that toughness or rigidity are *emergent properties* of a metallic material that result from the complex dynamical behavior of some of its components. An even deeper philosophical insight is related to the fact that the dynamics of populations of dislocations are very closely related to the population dynamics of very different entities, such as molecules in a rhythmic chemical reaction, termites in a nest-building colony, and perhaps even human agents in a market. In other words, despite the great difference in the nature and behavior of the components, a given population of interacting entities will tend to display similar collective behavior as long as the interactions are nonlinear and as long as the population in question operates far from a thermodynamic equilibrium. For materials scientists this commonality of behavior is of direct practical significance since it means that as they begin to confront increasingly more complex material properties, they can make use of tools coming from nonlinear dynamics and non-equilibrium thermodynamics, tools that may have been developed to deal with completely different problems. In the words of one author:

> . . . during the last years the whole field of materials science and related technologies has experienced a complete renewal. Effectively, by using techniques corresponding to strong non-equilibrium conditions, it is now possible to escape from the constraints of equilibrium thermodynamics and to process totally new material structures including different types of glasses, nano- and quasi-crystals, superlattices . . . As materials with increased resistance to fatigue and fracture are sought for actual applications, a fundamental understanding of the collective behavior of dislocations and point defects is highly desirable. Since the usual thermodynamic and mechanical concepts are not adapted to describe those situations, progress in this direction should be related to the explicit use of genuine non-equilibrium techniques, nonlinear dynamics and instability theory.[10]

An understanding of background is important in bringing the two strands of the argument together. The contemporary science of materials is an offspring of World War II and the Manhattan Project. While prior to the war the field constituted a collage of minor sciences, engineers and metallurgists who had participated in wartime government projects finally unified and gave this discipline the prestige that it deserved. The study of material complexity is now the rule, and a new awareness of the self-organizing capacities of matter is beginning to emerge in this field. In its more prestigious counterpart, royal or major science, on the other hand, the focus on linear and equilibrium behavior has led to a view of matter as *an inert receptacle for forms imposed from the outside*, a view with many similarities to Creationism and Platonism. Gilles Deleuze refers to this conception of the genesis of form as 'the hylomorphic model'. Artisans, craftsmen, and minor scientists in general, he argues, always had a different conception of the relation between matter and form, at least implicitly: they did not impose but teased a form out of an active material, collaborating with it in the production of a final product rather than commanding it to obey and passively receive a previously defined form. As Deleuze and Guattari write, the hylomorphic model:

> . . . assumes a fixed form and a matter deemed homogeneous. It is the idea of the law that assures the model's coherence, since laws are what submits matter to this or that form, and conversely, realize in matter a given property deduced from the form . . . [But the] *hylomorphic* model leaves many things, active and affective, by the wayside. On the one hand, to the formed or formable matter we must add an entire energetic materiality in movement, carrying *singularities* . . . that are already like implicit forms that are topological, rather than geometrical, and that combine with processes of deformation: for example, the variable undulations and torsions of the fibers guiding the operations of splitting wood. On the other hand, to the essential properties of matter deriving from the formal essence we must add *variable intensive affects*, now resulting from the operation, now on the contrary, making it possible: for example, wood that is more or less porous, more or less elastic and resistant. At any rate, it is a question of surrendering to the wood, then following where it leads by connecting operations to a materiality instead of imposing a form upon a matter.[11]

The term 'singularities' in this quote refers to the multiple stable states which characterize nonlinear systems. These may be singular points representing *endogenous tendencies* towards a steady state, or tendencies towards endogenous oscillations, simple or turbulent, represented by periodic and chaotic singularities, respectively. Since these singularities represent the state a system will tend to adopt in the long run, or the final state towards which it is attracted, they are referred to as 'attractors'. Singularity may also refer to the bifurcations or critical points at which a given attractor changes into another, such as the well-studied Hopf bifurcation which turns a steady state attractor into a periodic one. The term 'affects', on the other hand, refers not to tendencies but to *capacities*, the capacity of a material to affect and be affected. Bearing loads, for example, involves the capacity to be affected by a load, in the sense that a load-bearing structure must be capable of stretching if the loads are in tension, or of shrinking if they are in compression.[12]

Any material, no matter how simple its behavior, has endogenous tendencies and capacities, but Deleuze argues that if the material in question is homogeneous and closed to intense flows of energy, its singularities and affects will be so simple as to seem reducible to a linear law. In a sense, these materials hide from view the full repertoire of self-organizing capabilities of matter and energy. On the other hand, if the material is far from equilibrium (or, what amounts to the same thing, if *differences* in intensity are not allowed to be canceled) or if it is complex and heterogeneous (that is, if the *differences* among its components are not canceled through homogenization) the full set of singularities and affects will be revealed, and complex materiality will be allowed to manifest itself. In other words, the emphasis here is not only on the spontaneous generation of form, but on the fact that this morphogenetic potential is best expressed, not by the simple and uniform behavior of materials, but by their complex and variable behavior.

In this sense, contemporary industrial metals, such as mild steel, may not be the best illustration of this new philosophical conception of matter. While naturally occurring metals contain all kinds of impurities that change their mechanical behavior in different ways, steel and other industrial metals have undergone in the last two hundred years an intense process of uniformity and homogenization in both their chemical composition and their physical structure. The rationale behind this process was partly based on questions of reliability and quality control, but it had also a social component: both human workers and the materials they used needed to be disciplined and their behavior made predictable. Only then the full efficiencies and economies of scale of mass-production techniques could be realized. But this homogenization also affected the engineers that designed structures using these well-disciplined materials. In the words of James E. Gordon:

> The widespread use of steel for so many purposes in the modern world is only partly due to technical causes. Steel, especially mild steel, might euphemistically be described as a material that facilitates the dilution of skills . . . Manufacturing processes can be broken down into many separate stages, each requiring a minimum of skill or intelligence . . . At a higher mental level, the design process becomes a good deal easier and more foolproof by the use of a ductile, isotropic, and practically uniform material with which there is already a great deal of accumulated experience. The design of many components, such as gear wheels, can be reduced to a routine that can be looked up in handbooks.[13]

Gordon sees in the spread of the use of steel in the late nineteenth and early twentieth centuries, a double danger for the creativity of structural designers. The first danger is the idea that a single, universal material is good for all different kinds of structure, some of which may be supporting loads in compression, some in tension, some withstanding sheer stresses and others torsional stresses. But as Gordon points out, given that the roles which a structure may play can be highly heterogeneous, the repertoire of materials that a designer uses should reflect this complexity. On the other hand, he points out that much as in the case of biological materials like bone, new designs may involve structures with properties that are in continuous variation, with some portions of the structure better able to deal with compression while others deal with tension. Intrinsically heterogeneous materials, such as fiberglass and the newer hi-tech composites, afford designers this possibility. As Gordon says, 'it is scarcely practicable to tabulate elaborate sets of "typical mechanical properties" for the new composites. In theory, the whole point of such materials is that, unlike metals, they do not have "typical properties", because the material is designed to suit not only each individual structure, but each place in that structure.'[14]

This is not to imply that there are no legitimate roles to be played by homogeneous materials with simple and predictable behavior, such as bearing loads in compression. And similarly for the institutional and economic arrangements that were behind the quest for uniformity: the economies of scale achieved by routinizing production and some design tasks were certainly very significant. As with the already-mentioned homogenizations performed by scientists in their conceptions of matter, there were undoubtedly some gains. The question is, what got lost in the process? To give the most obvious example of a hidden cost, the nineteenth-century process of transferring skills from the human worker to the machine, and the task of homogenizing metallic behavior went hand in hand. As Cyril Stanley Smith remarks, 'The craftsman can compensate for differences in the qualities of his material, for he can adjust the precise strength and pattern of application of his tools to the material's local vagaries. Conversely, the constant motion of a machine requires constant materials.'[15] If it is true that much of the knowledge about the complex behavior of materials was developed outside science by empirically oriented individuals, the de-skilling of craftsmen that accompanied mechanization may be seen as involving a loss of at least part of that knowledge, since in many cases empirical know-how is stored in the form of skills.

Additionally, not only the production process was routinized in this way; so, to a lesser extent, was the design process. Many professionals who design load-bearing structures have lost their ability to design with materials that are not isotropic, that is, that do not have identical properties in all directions. But it is precisely the ability to deal with complex, continuously variable behavior that is now needed to design structures with the new composites. Hence, we may need to nurture once again our ability to deal with variation as a creative force, and to think of structures that incorporate heterogeneous elements as a challenge to be met by innovative design.

To conclude, the historical processes of homogenization and routinization have promoted the 'hylomorphic schema' as a paradigm of the genesis of form. Conversely, it is partly thanks to the new theories of self-organization that the potential complexity of behavior of even the humbler forms of matter-energy has been revealed. We may now be in a position to think about the origin of form and structure, not as something imposed from the outside on an inert matter, not as a hierarchical command from above as in an assembly line, but as something that may come from within the materials, a form that we tease out of those materials as we allow them to have their say in the structures we create.

Notes

1 Melvin Kranzberg and Cyril Stanley Smith, 'Materials in History and Society' in *The Materials Revolution*, ed Tom Forrester, (Cambridge, Mass: MIT Press, 1988), p. 93.

2 Cyril Stanley Smith, 'Matter Versus Materials: A Historical View', in *A Search for Structure* (Cambridge, Mass: MIT Press, 1992), p. 115.

3 Ibid, pp. 120–1.

4 Gilles Deleuze and Félix Guattari, *A Thousand Plateaus* (Minneapolis: University of Minnesota Press, 1980) pp. 361–2.

5 Ibid, p. 411.

6 James Edward Gordon, *The Science of Structures and Materials* (Scientific American Library, 1988) New York, p. 18.

7 Ibid, pp. 20–1.

8 Ian Stewart, *Does God Play Dice? The Mathematics of Chaos* (Oxford: Basil Blackwell, 1989), p. 03.

9 James Edward Gordon, *The Science of Structures and Materials*, p. 111.

10 D. Walgraef, 'Pattern Selection and Symmetry Competition in Materials Instabilities' in *New Trends in Nonlinear Dynamics and Pattern-Forming Phenomena*, eds Pierre Coullet and Patrick Huerre (Plenum Press, 1990) New York, p. 26.

11 Gilles Deleuze and Félix Guattari, *A Thousand Plateaus*, p. 408.

12 See Manuel DeLanda, *Intensive Science and Virtual Philosophy* (London: Continuum Press, 2002) for a full discussion of singularities and affects.

13 James Edward Gordon, *The Science of Structures and Materials*, p. 135.

14 Ibid., p. 200.

15 Cyril Stanley Smith, 'Reflections on Technology and the Decorative Arts in the Nineteenth Century' in *A Search for Structure*, cit. p. 313.

Model – Sagrada Familia Church

VIRTUALLY GAUDÍ

Mark Burry

Background

Gaudí's interest in second order geometry – warped surfaces – has only become widely understood since his death in 1926 through the continuing efforts to complete his *magnum opus*, the Sagrada Familia Church in Barcelona. This building was commenced by Francesco del Villar in 1882 but he abandoned it a year later on account of an apparent challenge to his professional opinions. As the architect, he had specified ashlar masonry throughout the construction of the crypt but the client, in order to reduce the costs of this charitably funded project, had insisted on facing masonry around random rubble structural cores. So Antonio Gaudí, 31 years of age and as yet with no significant projects to his name, was made architect Director for this major metropolitan building. His appointment was precipitated by a dispute about the nature of surface and its relationship to the specification of its substrate. More than anything else it was an issue about tectonics that provoked the resignation of his predecessor, resulting in an engagement for Gaudí that lasted until his death years later, spanning almost the whole of his career.

An Enigmatic Architect

We can divide Gaudí's *oeuvre* into approximately three phases. He emerged from an initial historicist and contextual focus to take part in the *Modernisme* movement, Barcelona's Art Nouveau.[1] During his final decade, he almost disappeared from public view altogether by restricting his activities and circle of contacts and collaborators to an inner realm. In this critical third phase, he eschewed all secular projects and dedicated himself to completing the design for the Sagrada Familia Church, a commitment that ultimately led to him living as well as working on site.

Looking at the work emerging today, we can see that there is a consistency to it that may seem quite 'un-Gaudí'. But before forming a judgement that the Sagrada Familia Church is not representative of the creative aspects of Gaudí as we have come to know him through his other completed work and other important works, nevertheless irrecoverably abandoned during his life, it is important to recognise two points. The first is that Gaudí inherited a Gothic Revival church plan from the original architect, who had inalterably committed the project to this schema . At the time of Gaudí's arrival the crypt for the apse was already semicompleted. The second is a remarkable drawing of the whole project, seen side-on, by Gaudí's close associate Rubió in 1906, 20 years before Gaudí's death. All subsequent versions of this drawing that appeared during the remaining years of Gaudí's directorship showed little variation from this first view other than in surface detail. The drawing was possibly the first detailed view of the overall project that Gaudí provided for his client, 23 years after his engagement.

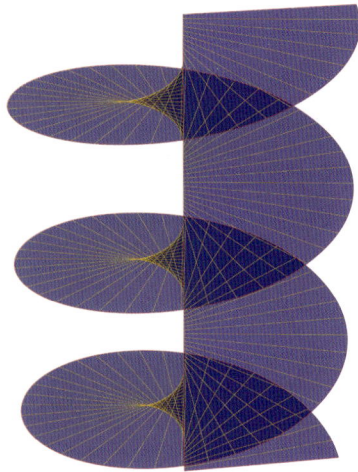

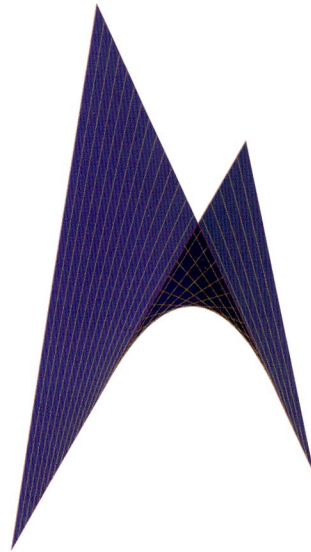

For better or worse, the project can be compared with other great Gothic works. Gaudí apparently set out to complete the unfinished business of his medieval forebears by removing the need for flying buttresses and massive light-occluding piers. In this project he tackled the thorny issue of how to share the design process (as opposed to the ideation) atypically compared with his preceding commissions. He used a necessarily more broad-based and, with an eye to the future, independent team for such a large and demanding project. It is this latter issue rather than any aesthetic prejudgement of the still substantially incomplete building that it is important to focus on.

If Gaudí's entry to the project was the result of an issue of building tectonics, then his point of exit has emerged as an unwittingly prescient establishment of a framework for digital tectonics. This framework has allowed his successors to engage radically with the geometrical codex he developed in this third and final phase of his career. At the beginning of the third millennium, this engagement challenges even the more powerful IT resources. Potentially, it also redefines our thinking about *modus operandi* appropriate to our age of digitally aided design. It is important to highlight this legacy of novel procedures, which can be defined as the architecture of *real absence and virtual presence*. 'Real absence' describes a process where the designer defines not what is materially not present, but what has to be subtracted. 'Virtual absence' describes a process of synthesis of material based on some geometric aspect that is virtually present but elusive in tangible detail. These highly contemporary constructs were core procedures in the description of form by an architect who died more than three-quarters of a century ago. To explain them, we will firstly consider Gaudí's take-up of second order geometry. Secondly we will compare his physical design process through modelling with gypsum plaster with our subsequent interpretation of these models using composite drawings. Finally we will explain the exploitation of these models for the purposes of building using high-end 3-D and time-based computer modelling.[2]

Second Order Geometry: Ruled Surfaces

Before making the distinction between real absence and virtual presence, it is crucial to look at aspects of the design process that Gaudí developed during his final years – ours today through the uninterrupted apprenticeship that provides the continuity between his model-making collaborators and those at work on site. Of course, as such plastic and fondant architecture characterises almost all but Gaudí's earliest work, the model and

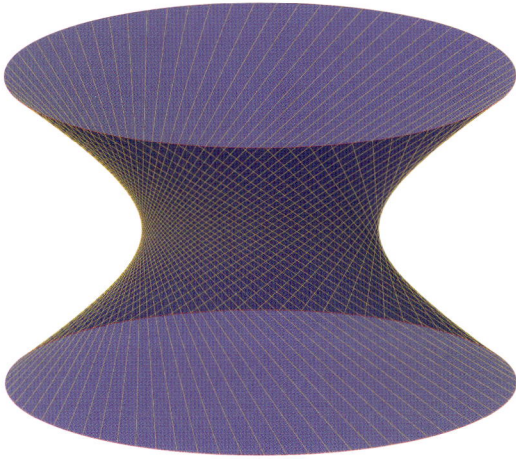

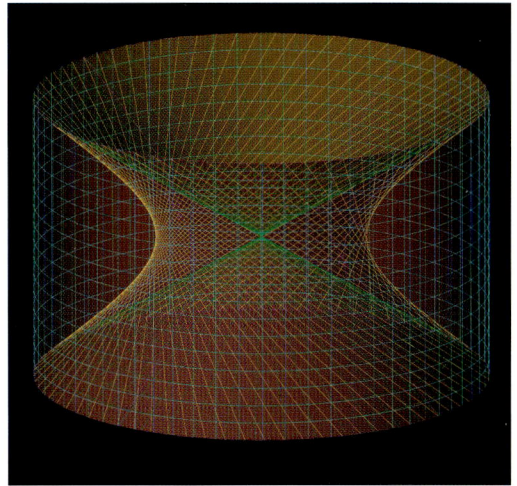

the on-site sketch served him much better than any convention of plans, sections and elevations, which he hardly conformed to other than for the purpose of obtaining both planning and building consents. When we consider the philosophical and practical implications of his introduction of rational geometry in his final design for the church, and compare this with his earlier insistence on the use of free form – notably in La Pedrera (Casa Milá) – we see an elegant compositional and execution strategy appear in his work that is in complete contrast to all that went before. His earlier work was insistently dependent on his masterly eye and his regular presence on site was not far removed from the relationship between a sculptor and the team of masons/founders who actually make the pieces. But we assume that the autonomy his use of geometry provides his successors with was Gaudí's palpable reaction to a growing realisation that the building would not be completed in his lifetime. Presuming this to be the case, we can further assume that his final creative *tour de force* was to establish a means to share his creative workbench with unknown successors who neither robbed him of authorship, nor 'dumbed down' the design to a level that cauterised or trivialised design engagement.

The introduction of rational geometry was no doubt occasioned by many motives: philosophical, mathematical and practical. The surfaces that predominate in the entire composition for the nave, the two facades other than the east (Nativity), the crossing and the sacristy towers are intersected ruled surfaces. He used three in combination: helicoids, hyperbolic paraboloids and hyperboloids of revolution. Many of these forms occur in nature, and although Gaudí may not have been aware of the work of D'Arcy Wentworth Thompson, whose *On Growth and Form* was published around the time he began to deploy this geometry in earnest, he was certainly aware of the developing understanding of the natural connection linking structure and form with geometry.[3] Gaudí is known to have been preoccupied with the apparent models of structural efficiency, aesthetics and composition found in the natural world from the beginning of his career, and latterly this interest, which encompassed both plant and animal life was augmented by a fascination with the inorganic realm of crystallography. Evident in his decorative work from the very beginning, it becomes substantially evident in the fundamental framework and systems behind his composition as opposed to his decoration during this last stage in his work.

At a practical level, his take-up of ruled surfaces is compelling for the facility they offer in first defining the surfaces, the relationships that are formed between them, and

Crypt of the Cólonia Güell

finally the intersection of adjacent surfaces and the paring away of surplus material. This is in marked distinction to attempting such manoeuvres with free-form composition.

Of the three hyperbolic ruled surfaces, the hyperbolic paraboloid is one of the most versatile and expressive in Gaudí's repertoire, and made a timid appearance as a corbel support in a very early work leading to a more robust and significant role for the walls of the Cólonia Güell Church crypt and the ceiling vaults of the exterior porch. Defined as a surface ruled by lines (generatrices) between two non-intersecting lines or 'directrices', its physical properties vary between that of a flat sheet (when the two directrices are coplanar) and a warped surface (when they are not).

In contrast, the hyperboloid of revolution is a more sophisticated cousin of the hyperbolic paraboloid – more versatile in some ways and less in others. In this case the directrices are circles or ellipses, and the generatrices span between them. When the generatrices are at their shortest (that is, connecting points opposite each other on the circles or ellipses) they describe a cylinder. If the ends of the generatrices slide around one of the directrices with respect to the other before ultimately describing two cones that meet at their apices, they form an infinite range of warped cylinders with effects that range from subtle to extreme. Cooling towers are examples of single hyperboloids of revolution in the built environment.

Helicoids have a vertical directrix with the second one spiralling around it. The ruled surface is defined by the generatrices which span between this central spine and the spiral, thus forming a screw. Helical staircases are built examples of helicoids.

What was characteristic of Gaudí's use of these surfaces to compose all the remaining work – the apse was more or less complete and the Nativity facade, whilst not benefiting from the ruled surfaces, was slowly being completed during the 12 years that Gaudí's experiments in these surfaces reached maturity – was not their singularity of use, but the implications of their interaction. There are four methods that we are familiar with for describing this: mathematics, physical modelling, analytical drawing and digital modelling. With the exception of mathematics, the other three techniques have been experimented with as appropriate paths to artistic expression. These are described in brief below.

Physical Modelling

The accompanying series of images shows Gaudí's principal design method using gypsum plaster. Here, half a hyperbolic curve is rotated around a central pivot while a mound of plaster sets during the rotation of the profile – gypsum plaster takes around 20 minutes to set. The outcome is a symmetrical half 'negative' of a hyperboloid of revolution – the master for producing the desired positive forms. There is a relationship based on proportions with regard to the positions of the throats of the hyperboloids of revolution with respect to each other.[4] These shapes are combined by chipping away at their edges while conforming to the underlying composition until they are located in the correct positions, with surplus edges pared to the minimum. The edges between surfaces are 3-D curves of intersection, and the rulings of the surface make it relatively easy to make perfect joints. Where three such lines of intersection themselves intersect, they form 'triple points'. Each hyperboloid has nine variables that govern its relationship to its neighbours: three coordinates that determine the location of the collar; three degrees of rotation, one about each of the three cardinal axes; and three constants that define the elliptical ratio of the collar and the steepness of the asymptote that defines

Gypsum plaster modelling of hyperboloids of revolution with three-dimensional curves of intersection

the surface curvature. Clearly, the designer has infinite choices available that will determine the suitability of any particular combination. It is an extraordinary and sobering thought that Gaudí possessed the conceptual ability to juggle with all nine parameters.

Analytical Drawing

Triple points, by implication, hold the secrets to the underlying geometry as, uniquely, they capture aspects of all the nine parameters governing the nature of the three intersecting surfaces. If the models are damaged, as they were during the occupation of the building, so long as sufficient pieces of model with triple points could be recovered and matched to surviving photographs that show the relative positions of each constituent surface, we could begin the reverse-engineering process in the quest to analyse the total composition.

Clearly the modelling process worked for Gaudí in synthesis but the same process proves to be extremely inefficient if reversed in a process of analysis. Despite the models being created by Gaudí around 1920, it was not until the late 1970s that the project was in the position to consider developing this material for the purposes of building. During the intervening years the team of model-makers (headed for the last 30 by Jordi Cussó) were very successful in restoring the models, interpolating more or less by eye the missing fragments in order to rebuild the whole. The underlying *raison d'être* in the use of the ruled surfaces with regard to their ready description presumes all representations to be accurate, otherwise the advantage of surfaces ruled by straight line geometry is lost. If the models had been accurate it might seem possible perhaps to scale them from their 1:10 and 1:25 scales to full size. 1 millimetre at 1:10 for such complex surfaces would have been nevertheless quite an achievement. In fact the system is so accurate that a millimetre out at 1:10 is a critical 1 centimetre adrift at full scale. On the face of it, this seems a reasonable tolerance whereas in fact it can be quite critical. Triple points grab the eye in these elaborate compositions, and are very demanding in terms of contriving to make three lines of intersection intersect themselves at a given point in space, critical in terms of location in x-y, but also in depth (z). If one line has to migrate through an error as small as 1 centimetre it has to pull the point of intersection, and its companion intersection lines, unacceptably resulting in neighbouring surfaces being considerably out of whack.

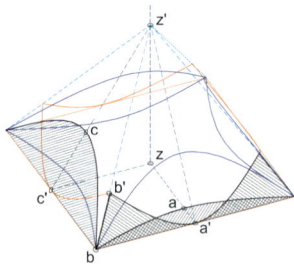

Rather than attempting to extract data from the surviving model fragments and re-interpreting by physical modelling, necessarily involving a time-consuming trial and error approach, a reversion to traditional techniques using descriptive geometry was investigated. Unfortunately Gaudí himself never had to face the task of bringing any of the hyperbolic paraboloids or hyperboloids to full scale in such profusion at the Sagrada Família Church, or indeed anywhere else in his *oeuvre*: the ruled surfaces formed a codex but there was no accompanying description, written or verbal, that provided any clue to their possible use.

Two tasks suggested themselves once the project arrived at the point where the models had to serve a more vigorous purpose, as aids to building rather than merely representing the building in 3-D. The first was to describe the component surfaces, and the second was to plot their intersections. Descriptive geometry lessons formed a significant proportion of the curriculum during Gaudí's years of study. The lessons provided for the formal description of hyperbolic forms, not the means to seek their spatial intersection. Analytically, it was considerably more efficient to reverse-engineer the models through drawing, and in the absence of any precedent in this regard we had to find a

Surviving gypsum plaster model fragment showing clerestory window

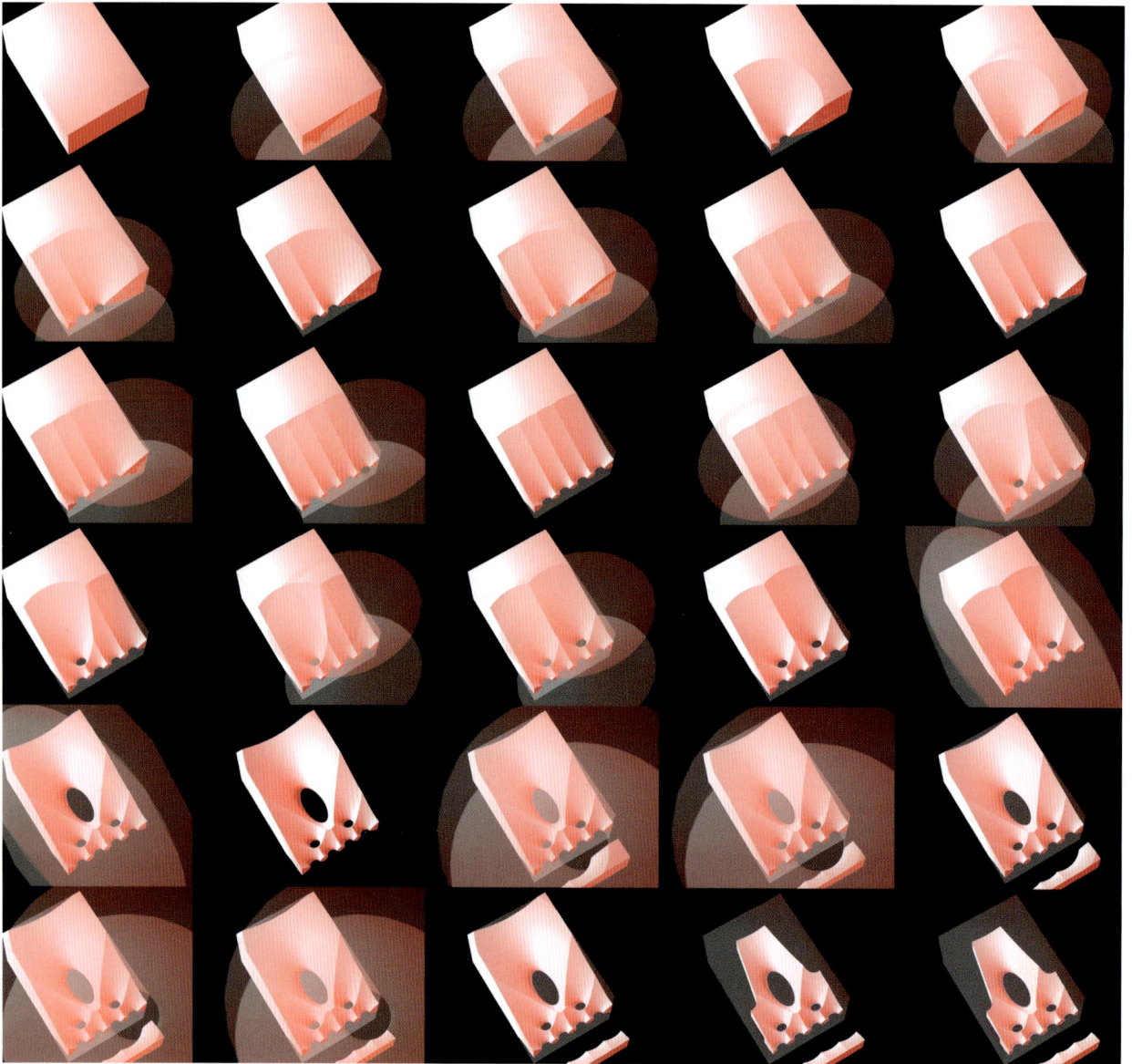

ABOVE **A sequence of subtractions leading to the sculpting of the primary surfaces of the clerestory window**
RIGHT **The architecture of real absence: the Boolean subtraction of designed hyperbolic forms from a notional solid**

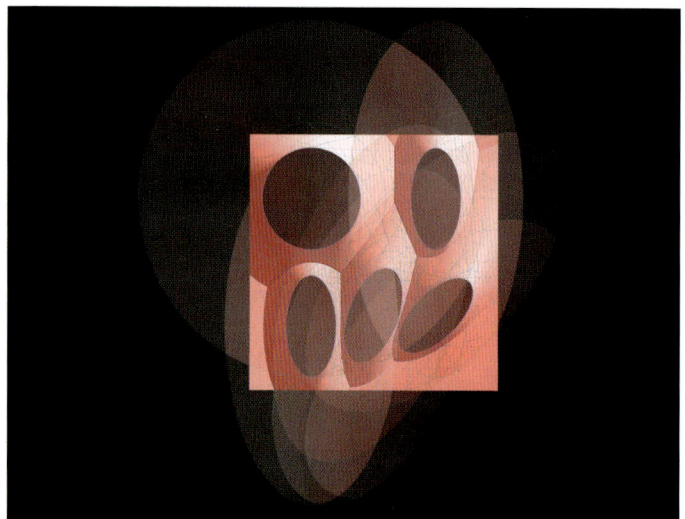

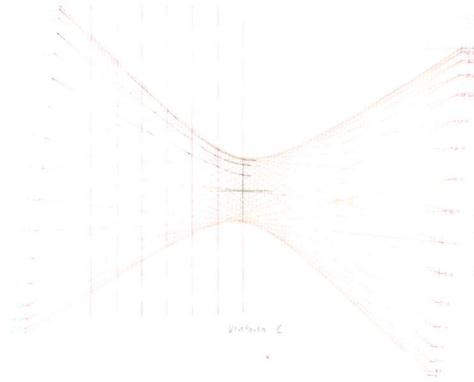

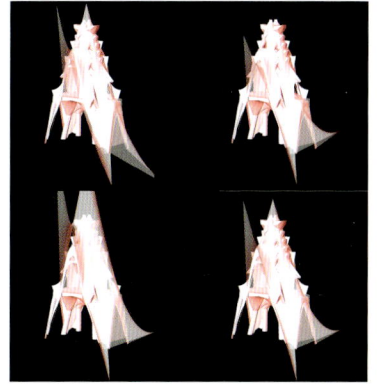

means of our own. The two illustrations above show the basis of the method where first we match a hyperbola extracted from the surface with a descriptive geometry representation of the form as a wire frame. Many of the hyperboloids are elliptical, and therefore especially difficult to produce in gypsum plaster. A single hyperbola cannot be rotated in the method described above: several hyperbolas need to be extracted and tested against a presumed geometrical equivalent. Several hyperboloids are rotated producing further complications.

Once each form has been analysed and reinterpreted as pure geometry with sufficient match, they are then contoured with respect to a notional plane, and in this way intersections between adjacent surfaces can be tested and compared with measurements extracted from the models. In every case, despite having a trio of adjacent surfaces apparently matching their original plaster archetypes, mysteriously the lines of intersection and the associated triple-point would dance elusively distant from where they were required to be. Further patient tweaking of the surfaces, slow when drawing but even slower if a modelling approach had been pursued, while eventually approximating the rogue triple-point would almost certainly corrupt an adjacent triple-point where at least one surface was in common. The entry of the computer might therefore appear to be inevitable.

Digital Modelling

First experiments using CAD took place in 1990 using architectural software which, at the time, seemed to be quite mature. It became apparent almost immediately that none of the software of choice for architects could make a significant impact for this kind of work. Solid geometry software, usually referred to then as 'solid modelling' was making a significant impact in aeronautical and shipping design – creative activities that dealt with similar problems to the ones Gaudí had bequeathed his successors. In the absence of a viable contribution from the architectural arena, it was found that solid geometry software was able to do almost all that was required, stalling only through memory shortfall, a problem that has diminished noticeably in recent years. Today we still rely on the software that has been designed for engineering and vehicle design.

The advantage of the solid geometry software is that the designer uses the software in much the same way as the traditional modellers were using gypsum plaster: we model what is not there. In the *architecture of real absence*, all that is represented is the consequential outcome of the Boolean subtraction of designed hyperbolic forms from another 'notional solid'. This is shown in the accompanying illustrations which show the path to sculpting the primary surfaces for the clerestory window. Moving from left to

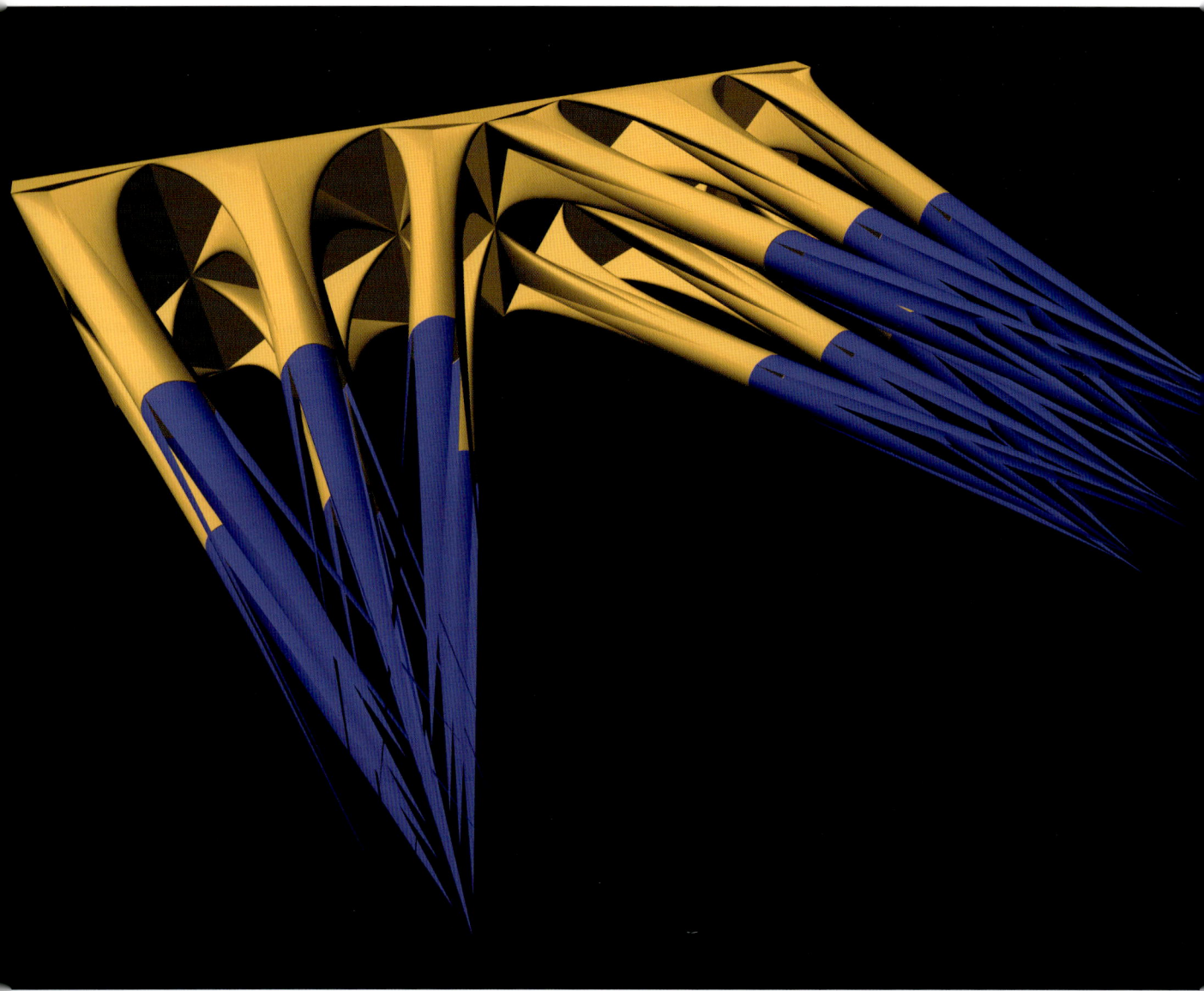

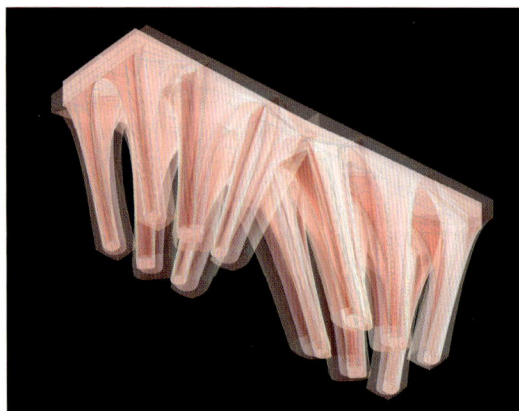

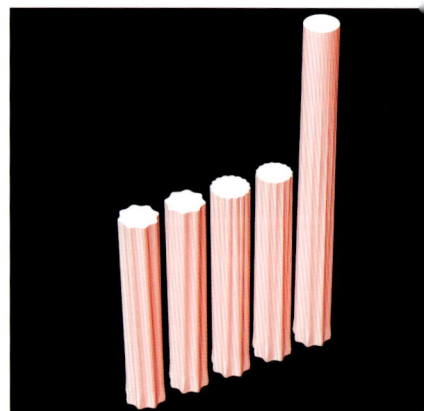

right, top to bottom, the oblong prism is whittled away by a succession of hyperboloids that are born then subtracted in sequence. The resulting articulation of the hyperboloids intersected inter alia is the result of the real absence of the parent forms, whose imprint remains, as the final surface and permanent reminder of the process by which it was formed.

Included with the solid geometry software packages are modules that allow highly sophisticated surface modelling, tools that proved indispensable for the articulation of the second construct, the *architecture of virtual presence*. In this case the parent geometry relates to key parameters, which governed the birth of the compote but only remain as virtual reminders: their presence is virtually explicit but only factually implicit: they are parameters that require to be sought, and are not offered up for ready reckoning. Examples of virtual presence are the crowning hyperbolic paraboloids that combine to form the nave roof envelope, the arrangement of whole and bisected hyperbolic paraboloids that form the triforium, and even the bas relief 'shields' that adorn the perimeter of the major elliptical rose window in the centre of the clerestory.[5]

Concluding Comments

Efforts to continue the building have provoked intense and detailed study of the surviving model fragments, forcing them to give up their secrets for the purposes of building. It is by no means clear that scholarship alone would have revealed the philosophy behind Gaudí's use of ruled surfaces. It has been the need to build from the original material alone that has stimulated the last 20 years' research. What was always tangible within Gaudí's personal conceptual skill base was perfectly realised as tectonic studies undertaken by his immediate model-making colleagues using gypsum plaster. The posthumous task he set his successors was unusually difficult without access to the Master or to any writing by him on his intentions to realise this, the third phase in his creative repertoire. For the last 20 years the team completing the nave has had to work reiteratively, reverse-engineering the decisions leading to their ruled-surface composition. What took months to achieve through physical modelling, and still takes weeks to achieve through analytical drawing, is achieved in minutes using high-end parametric software and powerful computers. It is useless to ponder on what Gaudí might have done given access to digital tools; and more useful to engage in the consequences of his final architectural development, as powerfully stimulating in terms of our contemporary digital tectonics as it was in the tectonic context of his time.

Notes

1 Participation in or coincidence with the *Modernisme* movement (Barcelona's Art Nouveau) – Gaudí's alignment is not as clear as it might first appear, see 'Gaudí', *Sola-Morales:Solà-Morales*, I. (Barcelona: Polígrafa, 1983).

2 The author has been associated with the project since commencing on site as an 'intern' in 1979. He has been responsible for interpreting Gaudí's surviving models first through drawing, and subsequently introducing the technical office on site to new ways of working using innovative IT strategies.

3 D'arcy W Thompson, *On Growth and Form* (Cambridge University Press, 1917).

4 J Bonet, '*L'Ultim Gaudí*', trans MC Burry, *Encyclopaedia Catalana*, (Barcelona), May 2000.

5 MC Burry, 'Teratology and Kinship', 'Hypersurface II' *Architectural Design,* 1998.

Gaudí's Hanging Presence

Mark Goulthorpe (dECOi)

Gaudí's work was sufficiently idiosyncratic for it to be wrong to cite it simply as influential on dECOi's work. The complete nature of the *oeuvre* has become clear, particularly in the Sagrada Familia, which demonstrates a virtuosity in every aspect of architectural endeavour. Gaudí's fervent religiosity never overplays his technical genius, which perhaps is only latterly becoming apparent. The hanging model, for instance, which looks to distribute material in space in a structurally felicitous manner, still taunts the architect to conceive of a more elegant structure/form conceptual tool. Yet it is the parametric studies of Mark Burry that have equally transfixed dECOi's attention, revealing the embedded geometric constraints latent at every scale in every surface, from structural columns to small decorative elements. It is as if Gaudí were able to sweep straight lines in space in his imagination, since every surface is a hyperbolic derivative, a geometric rigour deftly left hanging within the apparently 'organic' forms.

Gaudí recovered efficiency in both the spatial distribution of material, and in the descriptive methodology within a rich and non-standard vocabulary. Far from sanctioning rationalist imperatives, he waltzes in sustained formal virtuosity, culling the effects of a heightened rationalist articulacy.

Burry's parametric modelling has post-rationalizing potential. He uses the 'best-fit' geometric principles inherent in Gaudí's forms, keeping their rationality, and applies them to the actual conditions on site through global distortion. Seeing this, dECOi has thought to use these methods both in post- and pre-rationalizing capacities. In other words, dECOi is embedding geometric constraint into a 'creative' digital parametric model, and then sampling the model for potential derivatives. In setting up such generative models one might wish for Gaudí's geometric prescience, yet this approach marks such a profound détournement of architecural praxis, that dECOi feels it will come only in the wake of sustained experimental deployment.

The *Paramorph* project, undertaken with Mark Burry, is poised between a post- and pre-rationalizing strategy, where an unconstrained formal derivation is closely coupled with a powerful parametric re-editing that allows the form to be best-fit to various geometrical constraints (nurbs, straight-lines, triangulation, etc). A paramorph is a figure that can vary its form whilst maintaining its essential properties. dECOi's *Paramorph* adjusts continually to imbue the spatial flourish with a simple contructive logic: namely the ability to build it with straight-line bars or sheets of aluminium. Here is not the place to talk of the generative impulsion of the form.

One no longer creates an architecture, but the possibility of an architecture . . .

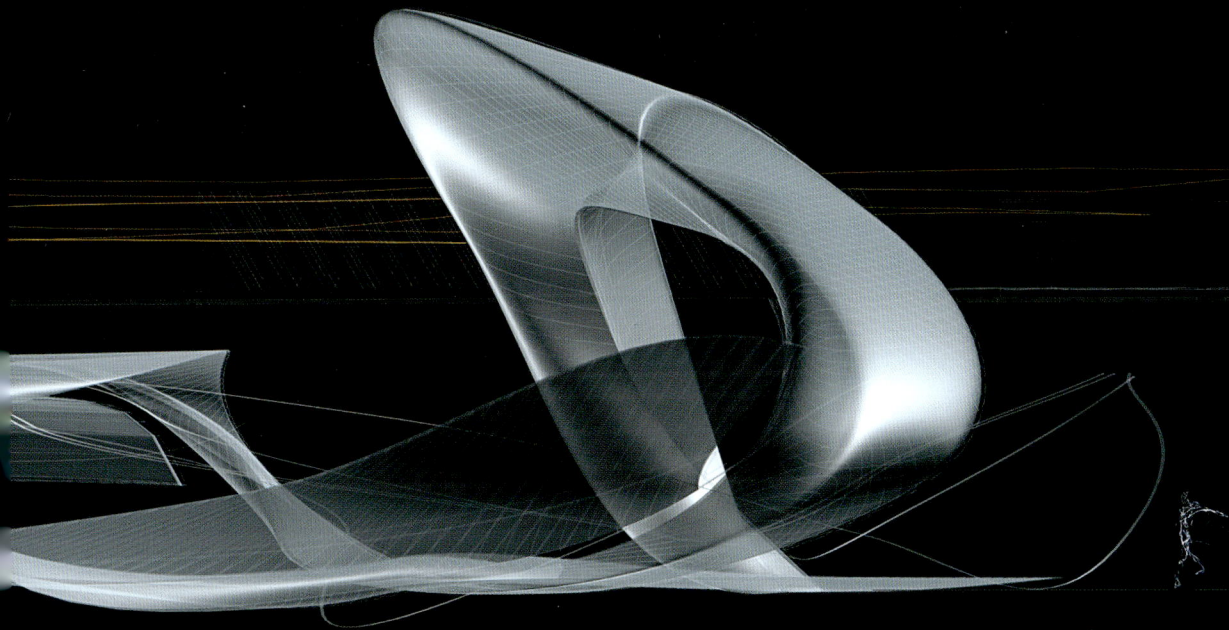

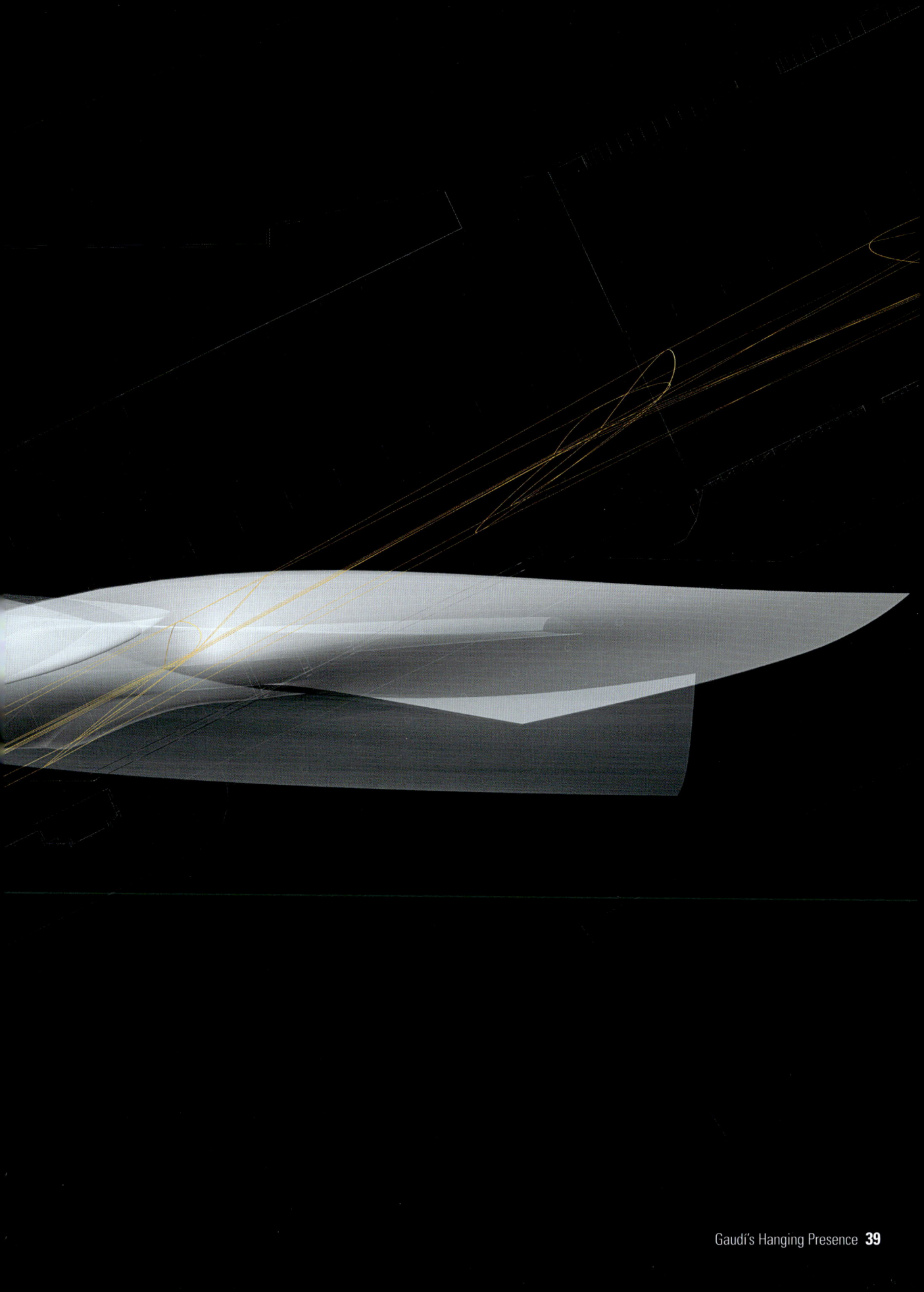

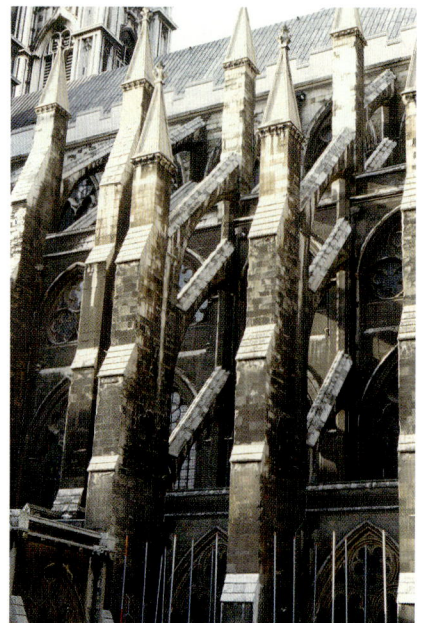

Stone structures – arch and buttress:
Bridge (above) and Westminster
Cathedral (right) (photos: Bill Addis)

Digital Tectonics

Historical Perspective – Future Prospect

Mike Cook

Introduction

The past twenty years has seen a revolution in our understanding of nature and materials. Genetic engineering, and perhaps soon nanotechnology, will give us the ability to make the materials we want rather than accept the constraints of traditional science. And we have seen the digital revolution – computers that can extend the capacity of our imaginations and allow us to communicate as never before.

Behind all this, we have seen how easy it is to harm the planet, abuse its resources and set up our own extinction. We are developing the tools to revolutionise what we build – but we have barely started to use them properly.

Digital tectonics explores the potential of our new-found rapid manipulation of numbers to influence 'design'. But this new apparent freedom from the old constraints could easily lead us down inappropriate paths. Therefore it is worth looking back to appreciate what have been the major factors influencing the form of what man has built.

There have been three key factors:

Material: our ability to use what is around us or to find ways of adapting it.
Ability: our ability to assemble, our ability to come together as a work force and collaborate, and our ability to communicate an idea.
Need: our reason for needing the building, from safe shelter to a symbol of power, something of utility or something of beauty.

These have been the fundamental determinants of what we build and we should look back to appreciate the strength of these influences before we look forward to where we are going and where we might be able to go.

The History

Material

The form that a building can take depends on the laws of physics and the choice of material. Stone, brick, ice are all good in compression and poor in tension. As building materials they have the advantage of being stackable – compression holds them up. Compression structures are straight (columns) or curved (arches or domes). They are well suited to the small-scale construction of the one-man band; as components they can be made small enough to handle. These were the principal compression materials

Iron structure: The Crystal Palace, London

of early man – found material or materials like clay that was easily adapted. They are still important and, with the skill of masons and teams of labourers, great cathedrals and mosques bear witness to the potential of stone in compression. The form of such buildings was determined in part by the capability of the material to hold its shape, creating domes, vaults, soaring columns and flying buttresses. Concrete is a compression material too, but we have found ways to adapt it by adding steel or fibre to carry the tension and this allows it to be used in building frames in ways that stone and pure compression materials cannot.

Timber comes in long, narrow pieces: branches or trunks. It can carry tension as well as compression. It can be used as framing rather than the solid of brick and stone. It is light, too, so it can make useful frames for animal skins, to provide shelter.

Plant fibres or animal hair, bundled or woven, can also become a construction material. This material carries tension and can provide the basis for rope bridges and tents.

Extraction of large quantities of iron from rock gave us a more adaptable material; something that could be cast into shapes and assembled into building frames of great strength and durability. A new scale of building became possible and new form could be achieved. Two noteworthy examples of the new potential have to be the iron bridge at Coalbrookdale, Shropshire, and the Crystal Palace, London. Closer control of the process has given us steel; a relatively cheap and adaptable material that handles tension and compression well. It is an essential part of reinforced concrete and the basis of building frames, and construction over the past a 150 years has relied on steel to form the non-domestic environment that we know. Our recent history has been shaped by steel.

In the past fifty years, plastics and fibres have played a part in construction and have been especially important in the field of long span structures and tension structures, forming weather-tight skins for buildings of exceptional lightness.

The forms we see in the buildings around us have been determined in part by the physical properties of the materials available to us. These properties have been imposed by the laws of physics.

Ability

The second factor determining form is our ability to use the materials available to us.

In the beginning we took for shelter what nature gave us: a cave, a tree. Slowly we gained an ability to adapt nature. Firstly using materials in their raw state and then adapting materials to make bricks, weave cloth, tan hide and so on. Tools helped us shape the raw materials. Fire helped us initiate chemical reactions and find new materials like bronze and iron, but iron was initially too precious to build from.

Drawing as a means of communication allowed us to record ideas and convey them to others. A system of master and apprentice helped transfer experience and perpetuate techniques and understanding; sometimes misunderstanding.

Physical models helped explore ideas and show others how the real thing would look.

Broader education led to broader understanding, not just of techniques that worked but of the underlying principles so that new ideas could be explored and exploited.

Improved methods of making iron made it viable as a structural skeleton – a revolution even when just reproducing old forms. As techniques of manufacture improved, steel came on the scene and revolutionised what was possible in construction and beyond. Developing our abilities to use this material led to cables with great tensile strength, and an ability to span great distances with bridges and roofs.

The ability to use materials has been as essential in shaping our man-made environment as the range of materials available to us.

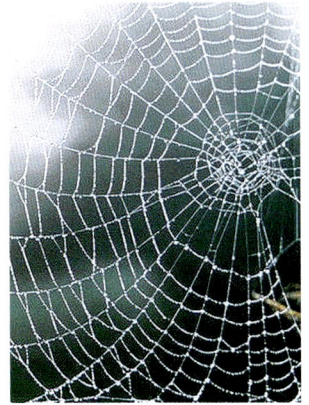

Tension: Spider web (photo: Bill Addis)

Needs

We cannot ignore the importance of changing needs in influencing the decisions we make and hence the forms of buildings we create:

The need for shelter, temporary or permanent, generated small, domestic buildings.

The need for greater security led to us clustering into secure communities and collecting together to build defences.

The need to have a faith in the future with a controlling force to believe in led us to stretch our abilities to the utmost and build giant edifices such as the pyramids, great temples and cathedrals.

The need to harness nature led us to develop dams and spacecraft.

The need to communicate and exchange goods led to the ship, the car and the plane.

There is no change without need, and certainly there will be no revolution in the way we build unless an urgent need for it is perceived.

Jeddah: Cable supported structure (Buro Happold)

The Future

Having considered the way that materials, our ability and our needs have influenced the evolution of our built environment we can look at the influences that are likely to affect the future.

Materials

Genetics has given us a deeper understanding of life's code and an increasing ability to grow things of our choosing. New (organic) materials can be grown to order. This nanotechnology promises us the potential to engineer new materials at a molecular level. Much of this is for the future but it is starting to impact on our everyday world.

Compression: Mannheim – Baumgartenshau grid shell (1974) architect Frei Otto.
TOP **as built, aerial view;** BOTTOM **hanging chain model (photos: Bill Addis)**

Ability

The digital revolution has opened new doors both in our ability to generate descriptions of buildings (virtual buildings) and to communicate this information to other people and machines that will make components. It has also given us the ability to model the physical behaviour of a building – how it stands up. Yet our ability to construct has barely advanced at all. Our building sites would be familiar places to Brunel, Wren and even the early cathedral builders.

Need

The strongest present-day need is to find ways to provide shelter, comfort and even pleasure to the world's population without exhausting its resources or destroying it. The new need is to conserve material and reduce waste. Ultimately there could also be a higher need – one that makes life of greater value once our essential needs are met – but for now our priority has to be environmental survival.

The question should be – how do we harness the new ability of digital creation to use our materials and satisfy the need?

Natural Determinism

We need to take note from nature. Nature has a way of minimising its use of material – material is expensive in nature. It uses valuable resources and energy. Nothing is wasted. This alone is reason to take heed.

In Tension

A spider spins silk of different types, to build a snare for its prey. The silk can be given properties to suit the need. It can have fantastic tensile strength and high stiffness or strength with very low stiffness. The orb spider exploits this by making the radial spokes of the web strong and stiff, thereby holding the web together, but on the other hand circumferential fibres are made stretchy and sticky. With this combination the impact of the prey is absorbed, the web's primary structure is kept intact and the captive insect is glued to the web. When the web needs rebuilding the spider eats it and recycles the material.

Using materials which stretch allows different spiders to lay down webs of different forms to fulfil different functions. The shapes are defined by the forces in the material. Learning from this we can define shapes that are determined by the forces within them.

The soap film is a good example of a material that will stretch to a new form in a strictly controlled manner. The physical laws of surface tension and fluid flow ensure that, whatever the forces acting on the film, it will move to a form where the level of stress in the skin is equal in all directions. Stress concentrations cannot develop. The material is used to its optimum across the whole surface.

Starting in the 1950s, Frei Otto used this as an early means to generate minimal shapes for tension structures so that the material would be used efficiently. Computer modelling has displaced the soap film and broken away from the need to generate surface with uniform stress. The freedom given by the computer has led us to less efficient designs. The constraints of the physical model, one that had to obey the laws of physics, were actually of benefit.

Sage Music Centre, Gateshead (architect: Norman Foster and Partners)

In Compression

The snail generates calcium carbonate to extrude a shell around its body that is extremely thin yet remarkably strong. This is achieved by respecting the material's capabilities in compression and generating a shape that uses these to the full. The forms of man-made shells often take into account the optimum shape that requires the least material.

The cathedral builders sometimes used a hanging chain to define the profile of arches, to ensure that the line of thrust was likely to fall within the stonework of even a relatively shallow arch. Gaudí used a three-dimensional hanging chain model for a similar purpose. And it gave him a way to define, explain and even test a big unified idea in a way that conventional drawings could not. He believed that, as a unified three-dimensional idea it took him 'nearer the angels'. It certainly took him nearer to nature.

Frei Otto used the same technique for compression structures. The timber lattice shell roof for the Bundesgartenschau of 1974 is an excellent example of a building that derived its form from a funicular model and hence achieved direct compression in all members under self-weight. Another interesting thing about Mannheim and this way of building a compression structure is that it is built like a tension structure – assembled flat on the ground and hauled into position in one move.

It is interesting to note that Buckminster Fuller's domes, whilst seeking to achieve efficiency of material, were content to follow a spherical form. Their method of construction was the incremental, traditional compression route of sequential assembly. Simple fabrication and assembly was given precedence over total efficiency.

Efficiency and Buildability

The simultaneous consideration of efficiency of form and reality of construction is the essence of good engineering. Traditionally, the synthesis of form and building method has come from trial and error, and passing down experience through the generations. Physical models that would capture the laws of physics and use them to define form have also played an important part. Such models also helped the builder develop construction methods – the model being the prototype. Now we are free from such constraints it is important to ensure we do not lose our way.

Recent Examples

For the Sage Music Centre, Gateshead (architect Norman Foster), the driving force had

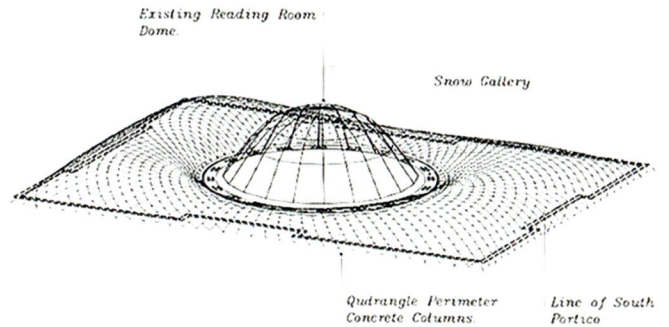

Existing Reading Room Dome.

Snow Gallery

Quadrangle Perimeter Concrete Columns

Line of South Portico

to be economy of materials and ease of construction. This was the only way to meet the building's budget. The concept was to provide three independent halls beneath a single 'free-form' roof. This roof was to be curved like a shell to give it strength as well as creating a stunning image across the river. The waveform is generated using single circular arcs swept through space. This is a 'graphic' method rather than a 'natural' method and did not seek to generate a 'pure' compression form. Rather, the focus was on ease of construction. By exercising this degree of control over the geometry, the pieces that the roof would be made from could be highly repetitive and very easily made on conventional equipment. The form-generation took into account the way the roof would be split into elements and went about generating these elements – it was not a free-form generation but had a grid imposed on it. This means that the roof could be built sequentially in the air over the new hall buildings that would already be in place. There was no flat site such as at Mannheim and no chance of using a lattice approach.

In contrast, the new roof to the Great Court at the British Museum (architect Norman Foster) faced a major constraint in the geometry of the surrounding buildings that the roof had to match – a central circle and an outer rectangle. A second consideration was to make the structure invisible – using as little material as possible so that the sky would be more visible than the roof. A third consideration was to keep the height down to satisfy the planning constraints imposed on the design. A fourth was to ensure that it could be built whilst the museum was working. A fifth was to ensure a pattern of roof elements that would support the glass skin and flow naturally between the circle and the rectangle like a single 'web'.

Finding a form for the roof began with a 'naturally' formed surface. A soap-film stretched between the circle and rectangle inflated into an undulating shell. Ideally, vertical gravity forces would have been used to define the shape rather than pressure, which is normal to the surface, but as the roof was going to be rather flat anyway due to the planning constraint on height it did not make a great deal of difference. Finding this form to be horribly bulbous, Chris Williams (of Bath University), who assisted the form-finding process for Buro Happold, played with the stress levels in the bubble – effectively tightening it in areas intended to be lower and slackening it in areas where it should be higher. In the end this wasn't quite enough and he resorted to describing the form analytically, though with a residual memory of the soap-film form.

For the construction methods, expert fabricators became involved whilst the design was being developed – Wagner Biro, a firm of steel fabricators from Austria. For this site

The British Museum Great Court roof – as built aerial view (photo: Mary Reynolds), and analytical drawing (Buro Happold)

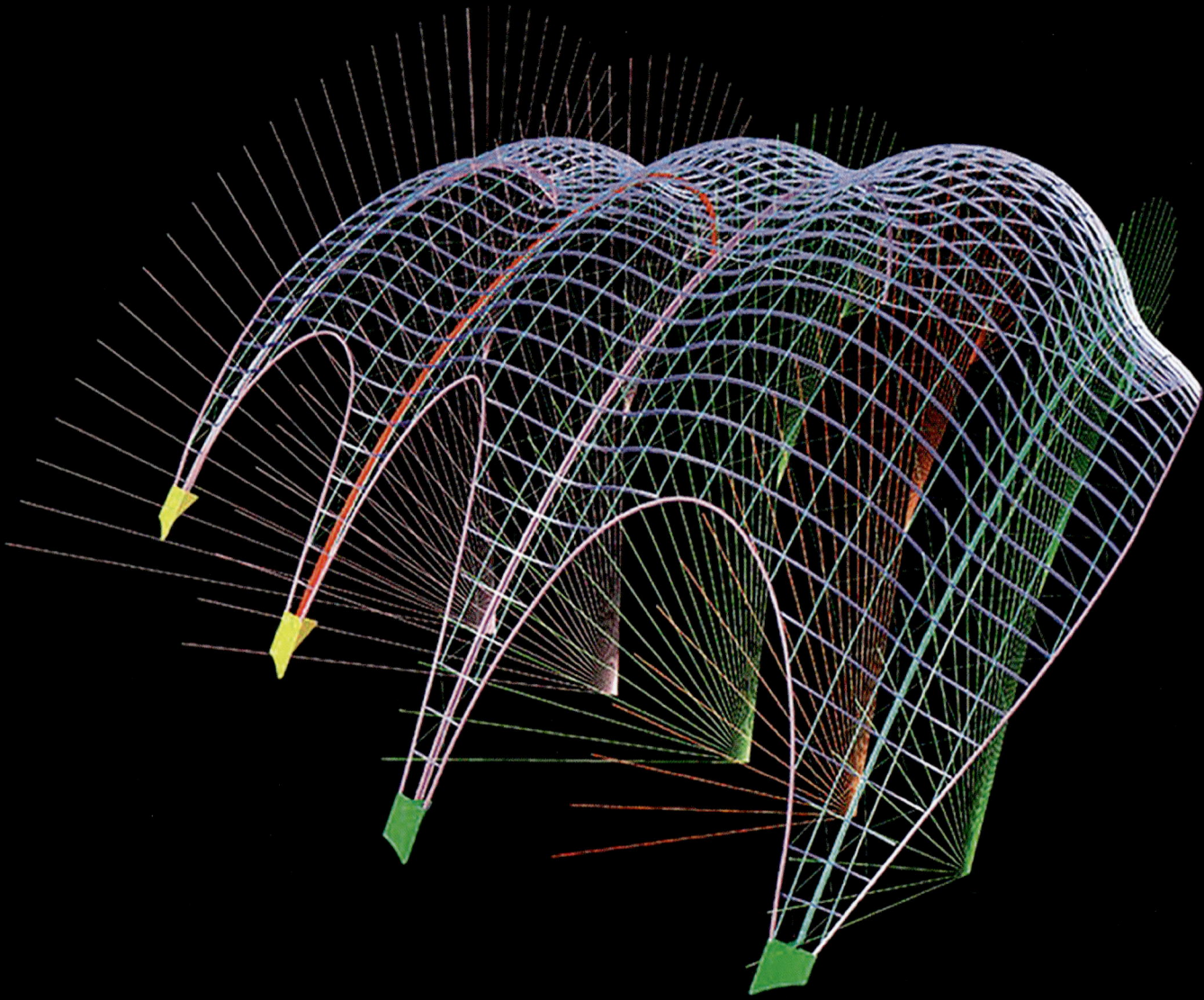

**Sage Music Centre, Gateshead –
Structural Geometry (Buro Happold)**

it was not possible to adopt the Mannheim lattice approach and the geometry was too free-form for the Gateshead approach. So the fabricators developed a way to assemble pieces of roof in multiple triangles, propped off scaffolding and held accurately in final position. Because the geometry was 'natural' – even if it had been tailored to match other constraints – there was no repetition. All steel elements were of different lengths, all nodes had different geometries and all panels of glass were different. This was not a major problem because all the information was available on our computers and this could be transferred to the fabricator's computers. From here it could be fed into the cutting and milling machines that made the pieces and cut the glass. The assembling was just a matter of getting the right pieces, all carefully marked, in the right place.

Conclusion

There is now a greater ability than ever before to create forms that break free from old constraints. Now the challenge is in deciding what form is 'right' – what rules or creative models should be followed?

The future that the digital age will bring is exciting; it will bring new control over our materials. But it is crucial that engineers participate in, and contribute to, the creation of form. Old physical methods of modelling and describing form are still relevant, though they have become overshadowed by digital modelling. Yet what they told us about the efficient use of our materials is still relevant, perhaps even more than ever. We need form-generation models that recognise the laws of physics and are able to create 'minimum' surfaces for compression and bending as well as tension. And we need to extend the virtual building model to virtual construction – not just conception – so that the way a building is fabricated and erected becomes as important a part of design as its efficient use of materials. This will help us create buildings that will conserve material and energy and hence go some way towards meeting today's pressing need – conservation of our global resources.

External views of model

SOFTOFFICE

Lars Spuybroek (NOX)

Introduction

'Muscular movements in general are originated by feelings in general'
Herbert Spencer

SoftOffice is a structure where intensive movement and extensive movement are closely related. We all know, being humans, that our emotions, moods and feelings influence the way we move in space, that our intensive movement is related to our extensive movement. The scheme of this extensive movement always seems skeletal, a mechanical framework of goals and tasks, not just in our lives in general but especially in our work. To be able to control events we often resort to routines and habituation. But if behavior and planning is nothing other than the blind repetition of former actions nothing would ever happen, except maybe on the level of chance; but uncontrolled events make it impossible to organize and manage the work process. Though modern management theory still recognizes there is a necessary rigidity in organizing tasks around set goals, a certain relaxation of their implementation has become vital. While short- and long-term goals are crucial, because they form the hinges of planning strategies, they shouldn't become so fixed that they start becoming unproductive and oppose innovation and creativity. This 'sideways orientation', this flexibility, is not just one of multitasking, but is also a playing with the tasks themselves, a more fundamental way of experimentation. Flexibility is in

General arrangement plan

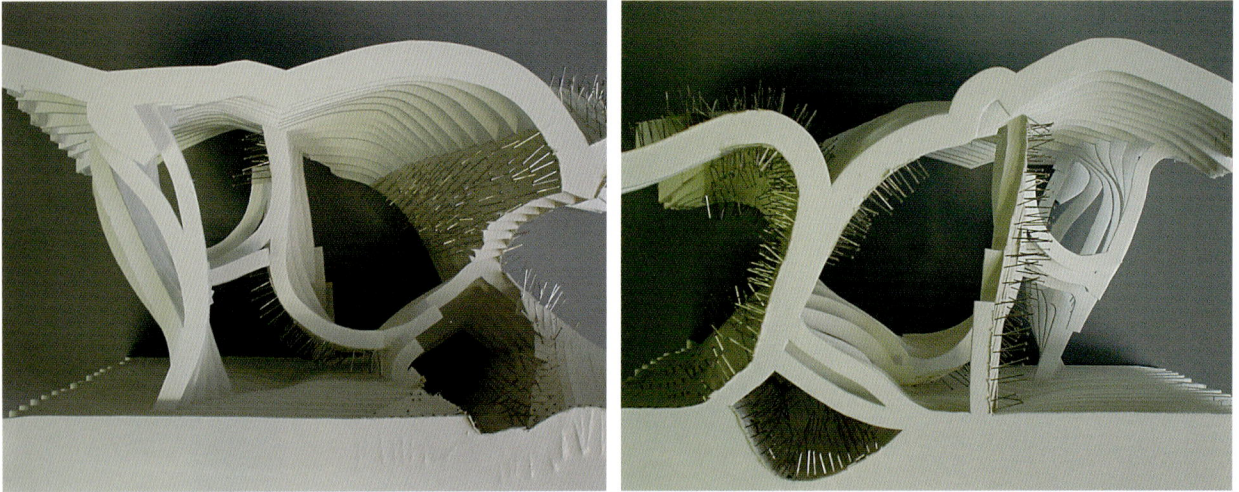

the first place, before anything else, one of the mind, psychological and intensive. Next to time- and people-management the 'loose grip' on events and situations is also one of space and architecture. Because what is on the body's exterior can only happen when we have internalized it first, when we live it, experience it and produce it day in day out in our actions.

In architecture this flexibility has always been associated with a variable usage of space, a multifunctionality that has subsequently resulted in an averaging of program and an equalization, even neutralization of space (either through the hall or the generic office floor). This general openness has always had the effect of generalizing events and being unproductive, because this type of space has not been engaged in the events themselves. In neutral spaces people always enter with either preset notions of space that aren't challenged by the architecture, or a generalized indifference that, as a result, becomes the main target of change for the management. The problem was not 'to open up space to more possibilites', but the concept of the possible itself. The possible as a category is without any internal structure that can define the variations, it doesn't produce variation by itself – it is without any potential. The old choice has always been between either determined functionalism or undetermined multifunctionalism. But potential is something different: 'Potential means indeterminate yet capable of determination . . . The vague always tends to become determinate, simply because its vagueness does not determine it to be vague . . . It is not determinately nothing.' Vagueness comes before the event, neutrality comes afterward. We have replaced the passive flexibility of neutrality with an active flexibility of vagueness. In opposition to neutrality, vagueness works with a differentiated field of vectors, of tendencies, that allow equally for clearly defined goals and habits and as yet undetermined actions. It allows for both formal and informal conduct. This is, however, not a clean and dry co-existence of two behavioral types as a mere addition or alternation, but more a multiplication, as one comes out of the other and shares the same continuum. To be able to switch between one and the other (in time) we need to materialize their in-between in space, clearly opposing Mies's empty openness and replacing it with solid vagueness.

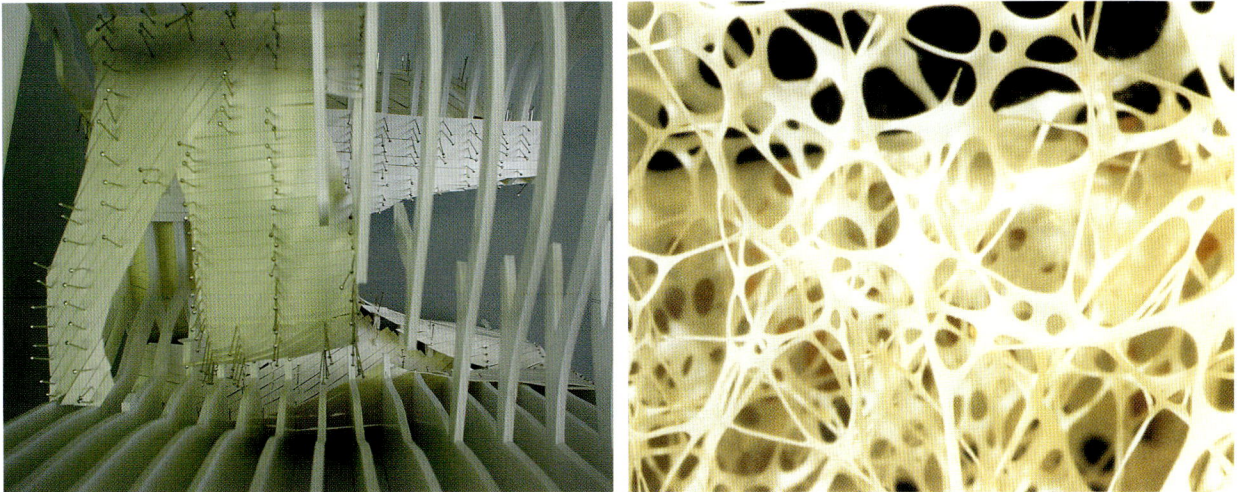

What becomes evident here is that the architecture of group behavior with all its complex dynamics is directly related to the architecture of the building. A behavior of continuous grouping and regrouping, of solidifying into certain configurations then suddenly melting and regrouping into other fixed states. A behavioral vagueness paralleled by an architectural vagueness. If the skeletal structure of actions becomes as soft as cartilage and as complex as cancellous bone structure, so does the architecture of the building. We should find ways where the intensive forces dealing with day-to-day decision-making and coping can actually become the formative forces of the architectural structure.

Intermezzo Flexi-offices

In analyzing flexi-offices it became clear to us that there is a real, daily tension in the effectuation of their usage. This tension between the intended, traditional, static planning philosophies and the viable dynamic structure is actually the force that makes them productive, rather than it being a case of one or the other. In calculating the needed surface area of an office for 60 people performing very different functions (marketing, administration, online production, offline production, management, origination) one would normally end up with at least 1000 m². Yet within the dynamics of an office culture, if one studies the occupancy rate of spaces and incorporates time–space relationships, one would begin to see a very differentiated usage over time. Our research gave us three categories of occupancy rates for SoftOffice: 90%, 75% and 35%. The first group would contain people spending almost all of their time behind their own desk. The second group would contain people who also spend a lot of time at other people's desks and at meetings. The third group travels around a lot more and spends a lot of time in cars, in restaurants, in hotels or at home.

This dynamic structure allowed us to make the office with 675 m². This means 32% of traditional planning has been excessive – a miscalculation of the efficiency duly attributed to static thinking. But it is not just the quantifiable side of an office space that has to change: leaving the structure of the office space the same while reducing its size by a third wouldn't do any good. Leaving a standard double-loaded-corridor type or office landscape

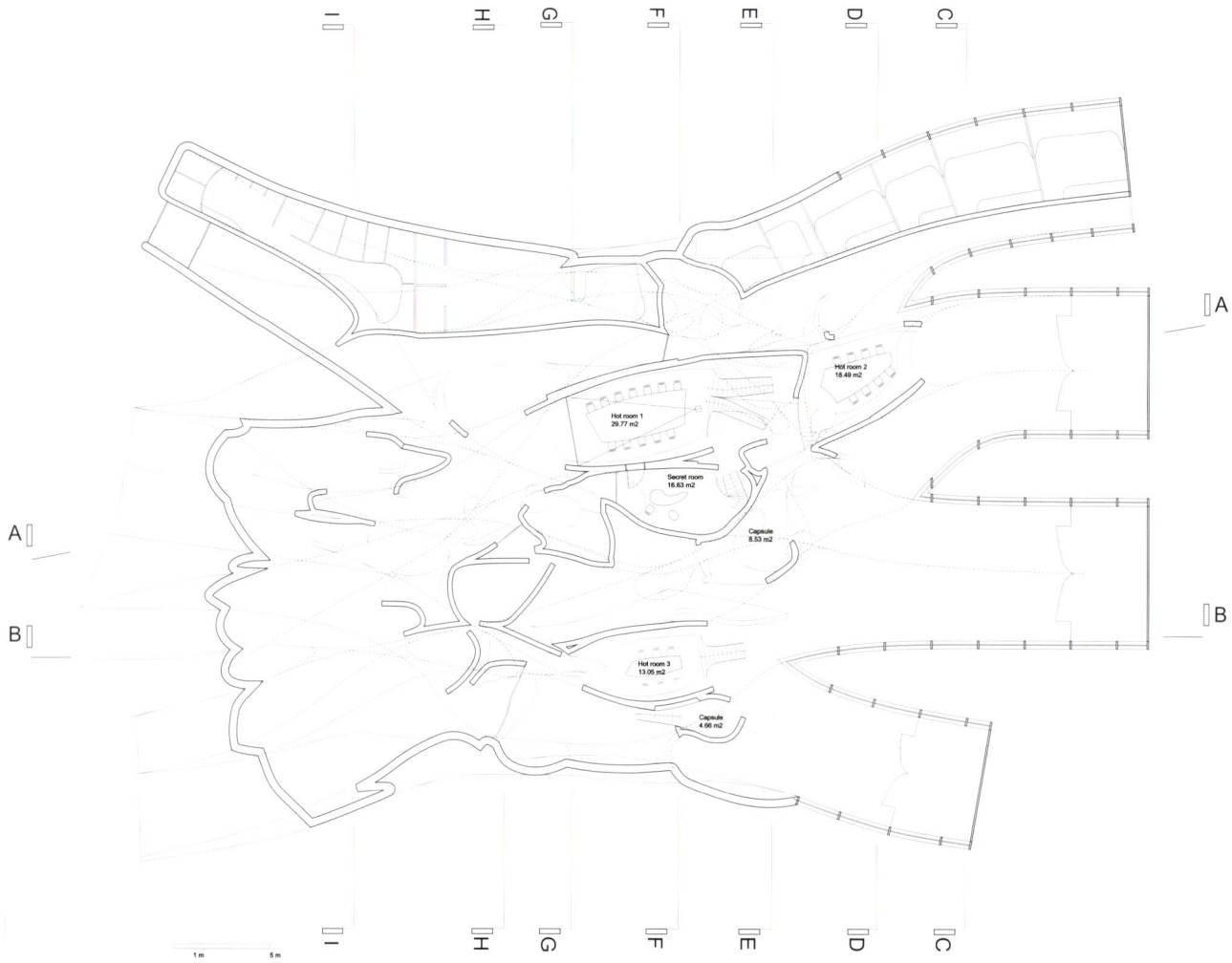

Hot room 2
18.49 m2

Hot room 1
29.77 m2

Secret room
16.63 m2

Capsule
8.53 m2

Hot room 3
13.05 m2

Capsule
4.66 m2

1 m   5 m

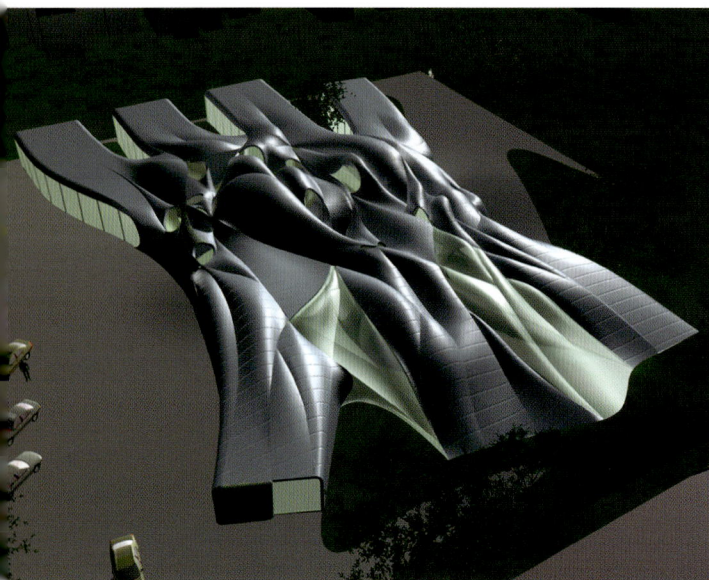

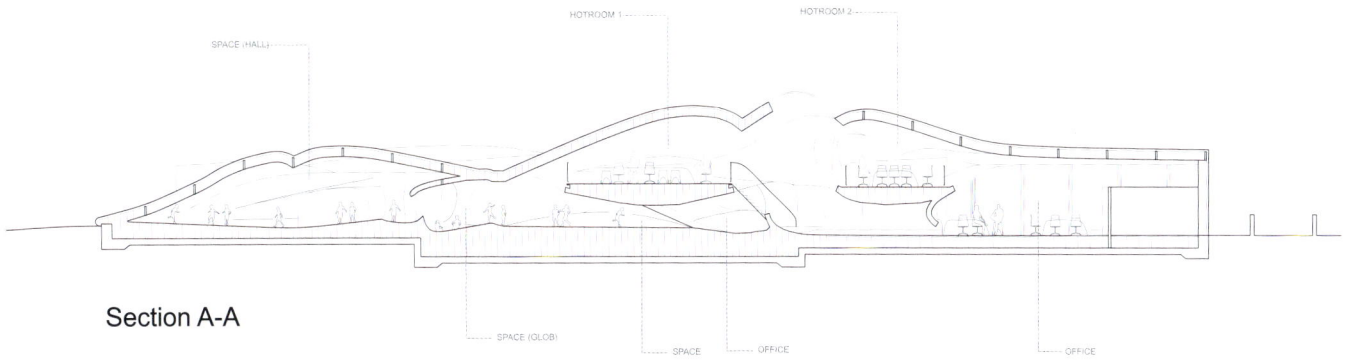

Section A-A

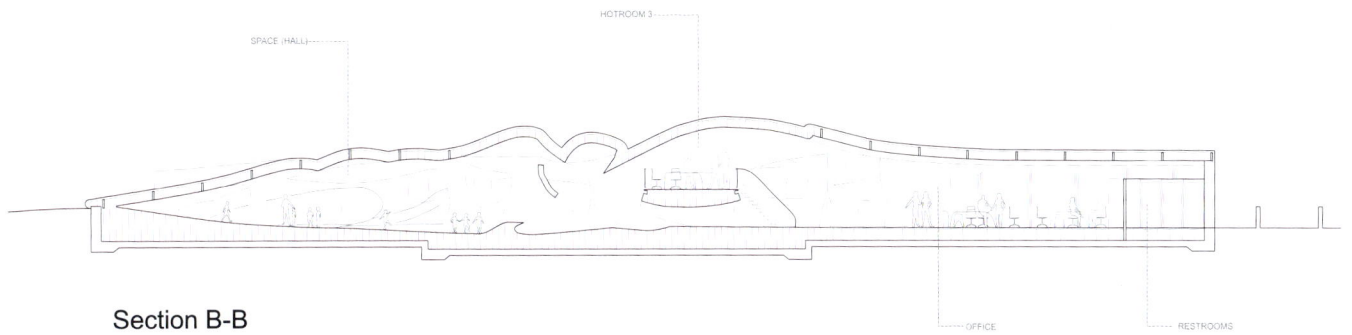

Section B-B

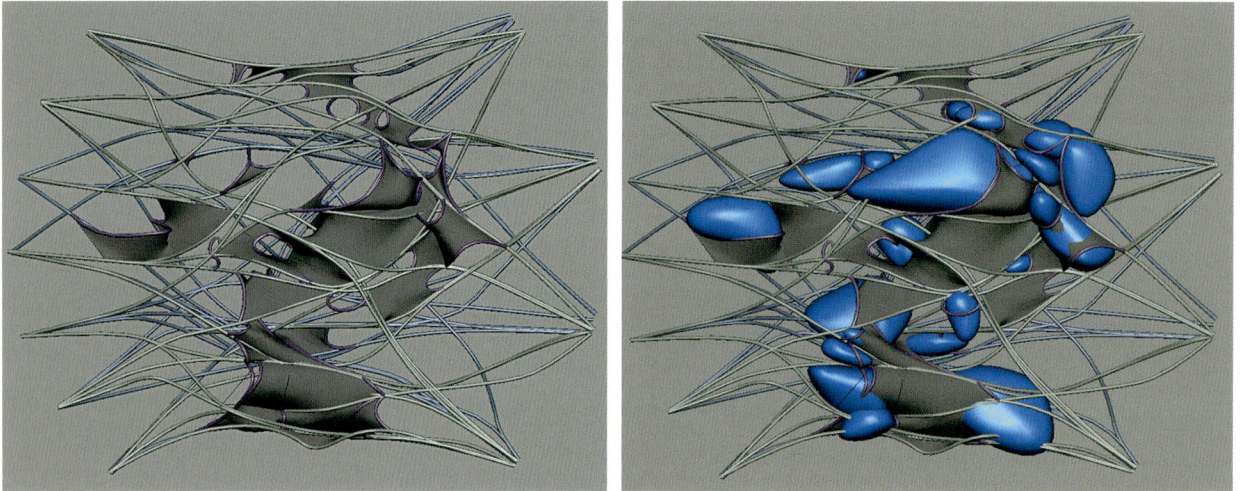

(*bürolandschaft*) doesn't stimulate the desired extra communication and change of behavior. Practically, then, the spaces and furniture of the office do not need to be designated to a particular person, or strictly designed for a type of work; in essence they need to be designed for a state of mind. We set up standard office spaces of general connectivity (flat floor, flat ceiling, general cable access) next to more informal meeting spaces near very small capsules for individual work that desires concentration. The active program is a continuum of both expansion (communicative behavioral types) and contraction (the necessity to shut off, to discuss, meet, write, shout, either in small groups or alone). The passive program, more a sub-program, is one of bathrooms, cleaning rooms, editing suites and the like.

Intermezzo Children's Space

In contrast with the office space the children's space – the scape – is a space of objects, a field or landscape where a substantial part of the movement is propelled by mock-ups from children's television programs. Where the adults in the office find a lateral freedom in a fundamentally longitudinally oriented system, the young children's movement in the scape is gravitational and spiralling. They move 'around 'n' around' the objects. And they move from one thing to another, from one spiral to another spiral, without any overview: all tension is immediately released and rebuilt again. As most of this is brought about by the iconography of mediated images, the architecture absorbs most of the spiralling in and out as an articulation of the floor surface only. This means the architecture doesn't need to follow the full movement of the spiral, especially not its rotational nature, just the fact that it is going inward or outward, which has a slight undulating effect on both floor and roof surface. The rest of the children's movement is produced by a combination of imagery and artificial lighting. Of this there are two categories: objects that are lit and objects that themselves radiate light. The lit objects are less interactive because a pure recognition of the television imagery is sufficient. For other areas a more interactive approach is needed, a zone where the building becomes alive and starts to play with the children. The area is what we have called 'Glob'. Glob is a world designed by

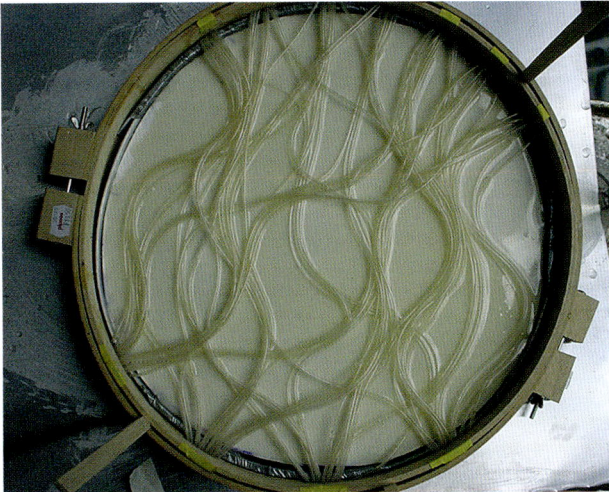

globally networked children. Glob is present both in the building and on a website. Glob is a 'living organism' (some of its responses are calculated with genetic algorithms) that has the special ability to interact with children. Glob will grow, love and of course play. Glob creates an experiential environment for the children that touches upon their senses and humor. Together they will create drawings, music, stories and love.

What is really hilarious is that the adults become the most passive, and in a sense, architectural elements. Like columns, corners or fences they mark the play areas of their children and grandchildren, waiting to be released to buy toys and merchandise for them.

Intensive Design Techniques

To map inward-going and outward-going forces, to map contractive and expansive forces within one continuum, a networked self-organizing technique is required. An intensive technique informs a virtual system that during the processing of that information it will take on an actual structure that is a registering of the information. The process has to take on a highly procedural form, like cooking; the instructions are not applied all at once, but one after the other, where timing becomes crucial. An extensive top-down technique would be satisfied with cutting differently sized holes out of sheet-like surfaces. The closed rooms needed for concentration would be subtracted from the surface of communication. In that case it would hardly be possible to create continuity between both states. And continuity is essential if we want tension between states. We are not using the expansive and contractive as finalized properties, we read them as tendencies, as working forces, as formative, not as forms. In our case we again (as for the OfftheRoad and the wetGRID projects) studied the analogue computers developed by Frei Otto.

Around the beginning of the 1990s, Frei Otto and his team at the Institute for Lightweight Structures studied what they called 'optimized path systems'. Previously, analogous to the chain modelling technique Gaudí used for the Sagrada Familia, they had experimented with material systems for calculating form. Each of these material machines was devised so that, through numerous interactions among its elements over a given time span, the machine restructures, or as Frei Otto says, 'finds (a) form'. Most

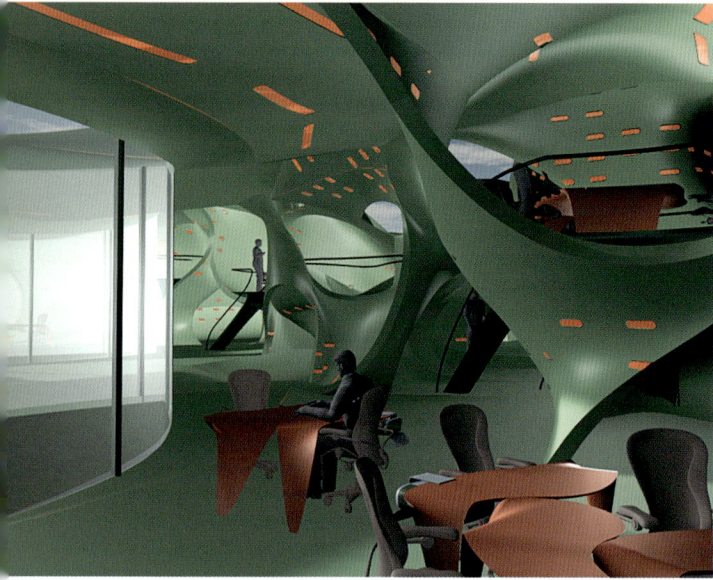

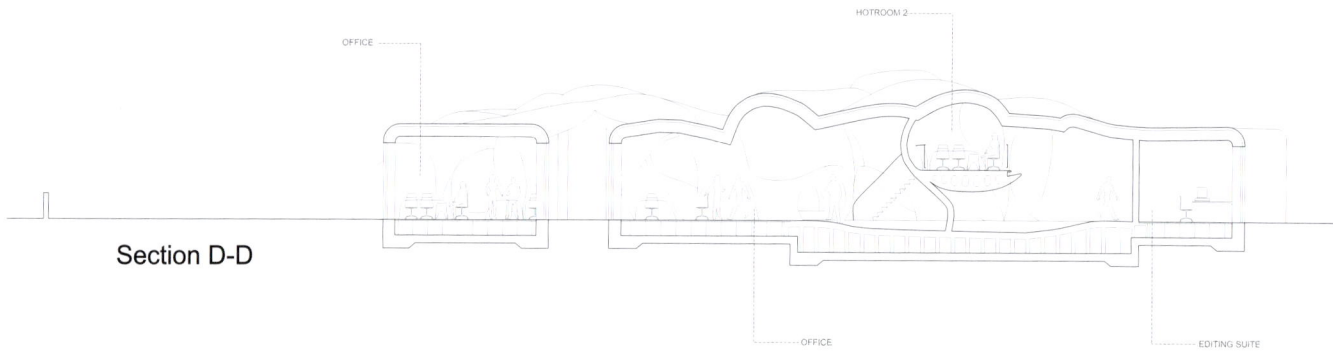

Section D-D

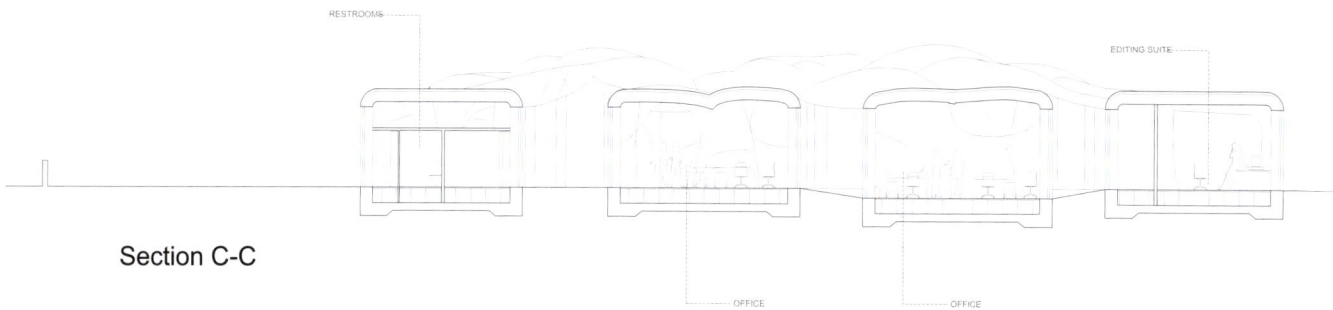

Section C-C

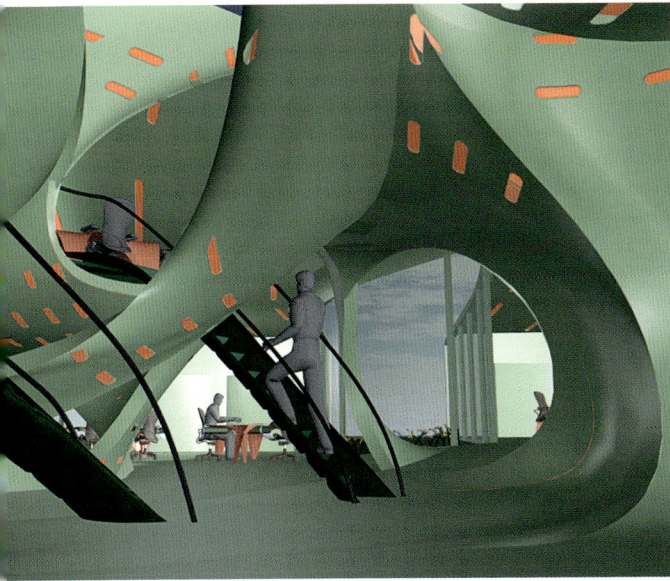

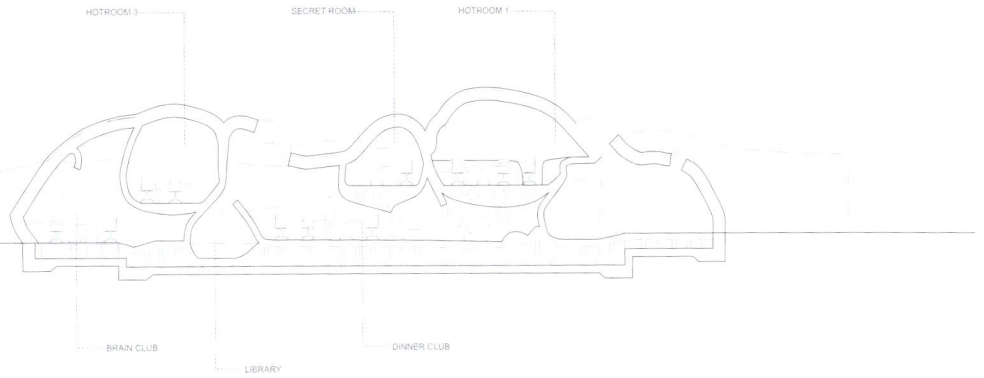

Section F-F

HOTROOM 3 SECRET ROOM HOTROOM 1

BRAIN CLUB DINNER CLUB

LIBRARY

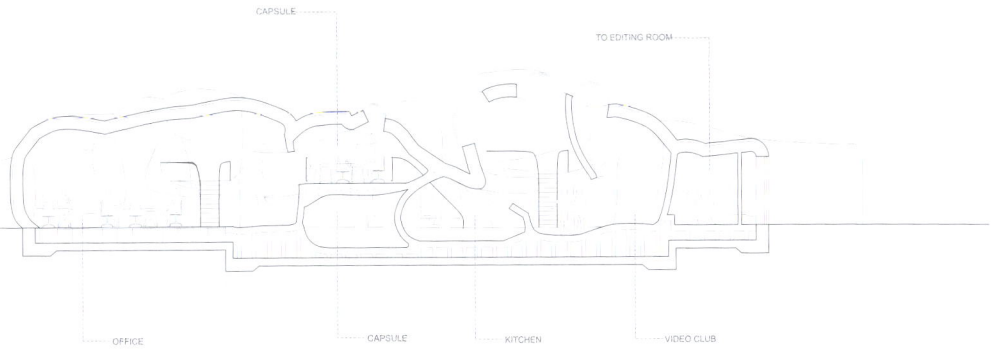

Section E-E

CAPSULE TO EDITING ROOM

OFFICE CAPSULE KITCHEN VIDEO CLUB

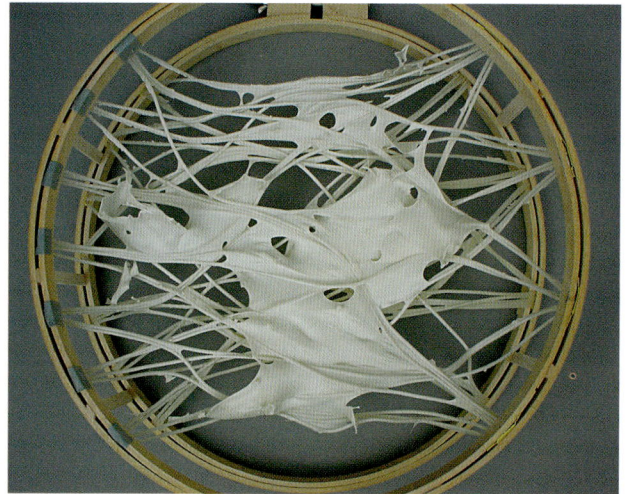

of the machines consist of materials that can process forces by transformation. Since they are 'agents', it is essential that they have a certain flexibility, a certain amount of freedom to act. It is also essential, however, that this freedom is limited to a degree set by the structure of the machine itself. Sand, balloons, paper, soap film (including the famous minimal surfaces for the Munich Olympic Stadium), soap bubbles, glue, varnish and the one we used in the case of the SoftOffice: the wool–thread machines. This last technique was used to calculate the shape of city patterns, of cancellous bone structure but also of branching column systems. These are all similar vectorized systems that economize on the number of paths, meaning they share a geometry of merging and bifurcating.

In our case we combined a varnish technique and the wool–water technique. The varnish technique is a surface-to-line technique. It is based on the effect that varnish, or lacquer, which is highly viscous, can later dry up and store information. For instance one can set up a machine of lacquer surfaces that are being stretched in many directions and break open into holes of various sizes, interconnected by threads of lacquer which is slowly drying up and hardening over a period of three hours.

The wool–water technique is a line-to-surface technique where the lines are given beforehand in the form of wool threads, set up in a pattern where they are fixed to certain points, then given a certain amount of overlength. When the whole system is dipped under water and subsequently taken out, threads start to merge (which is a using-up of the overlength), and holes next to surfaces of crossing threads start to form.

Both techniques are fully systemic: all features are formed simultaneously. The holes are not taken out later, but they are formed together with the various materializations in the system. The system is calculating everything at the same time, solid and void, during the same process, through thousands of minute iterations where each positioning is dependent on the formation of another. Order and form are produced, they come about, they emerge during the process. It is a constructivism, a soft constructivism, not a Russian mechanistic one. The constructive lines are not rigid H-beams but start as flexible rubber lines that meet up and at the end merge into form – bottom-up – into a complex inflexibility. This simply means we use analogue computing techniques to calculate not just structural form, but also – on a higher level – organizational form.

The Rubber-lacquer Machine

We start with a non-volumetric whole where all elements are interconnected: a set of lines made up of rubber tubes (of 2 mm diameter) with an 8% overlength, each attached at certain points on a rigid wooden ring (of 450 mm diameter). Seven points on the side of the children's space and four points on the side of the office space. From each point there is a rubber tube going to each other point at the other side of the ring, which makes a total of 28 lines. We doubled this system: two wooden rings each with 28 tubes that connect not only one side to another, but also one ring to another. This system was dipped into a very liquid lacquer, analogous to the wool–water technique. But while the wool-water model is always flat, the two wooden rings can be separated during the hardening process. Instead of having the holes and mergings in a flat configuration, we can now calculate curvature of the rubber tubes together with the intermediary curvature of the drying-up lacquer in a spatial configuration. The separation of the wooden rings during a three-hour procedure is analogous to the splitting of floor and ceiling. So, while calculating programmatic forces, mental states, we are also calculating structural forces. Complete vagueness: never fully column, never fully wall, never fully floor. The system is negotiating everything with everything without resorting to equalization. Now, what becomes most prominent in this system is that there is both an expression of rigidity and one of flexibility. We found a methodology that allows us to calculate the in-between, to be able to vary between the two states ever though they are on opposite sides. While all flexibility is expressed in the middle of the system, the rigidity is produced close to the wooden rings, at the edge of the system. Type is at the edges, diagram in the middle. Full bottom-up in the middle, full top-down at the edges. Spatially: a spongy porous structure in the middle zone, clean separation of floor and ceiling at the edges (with columns in between). In the scape this clean separation produces the hall-like tendency of the structure, at the office side, four separate 'fingers' with gardens. It is now the in-between that becomes operative: it is not just a Cartesian choice, it is an actual sense of tension, a material state of in-between that is internalized, that becomes effectuated in daily behavior and functioning.

NOX (Lars Spuybroek with Chris Seung-Woo Yoo, Kris Mun, Florent Rougemont and Ludovica Tramontin) 2000–2005 – shop, interactive playground and headquarter office for an anonymous client in Warwickshire, United Kingdom.

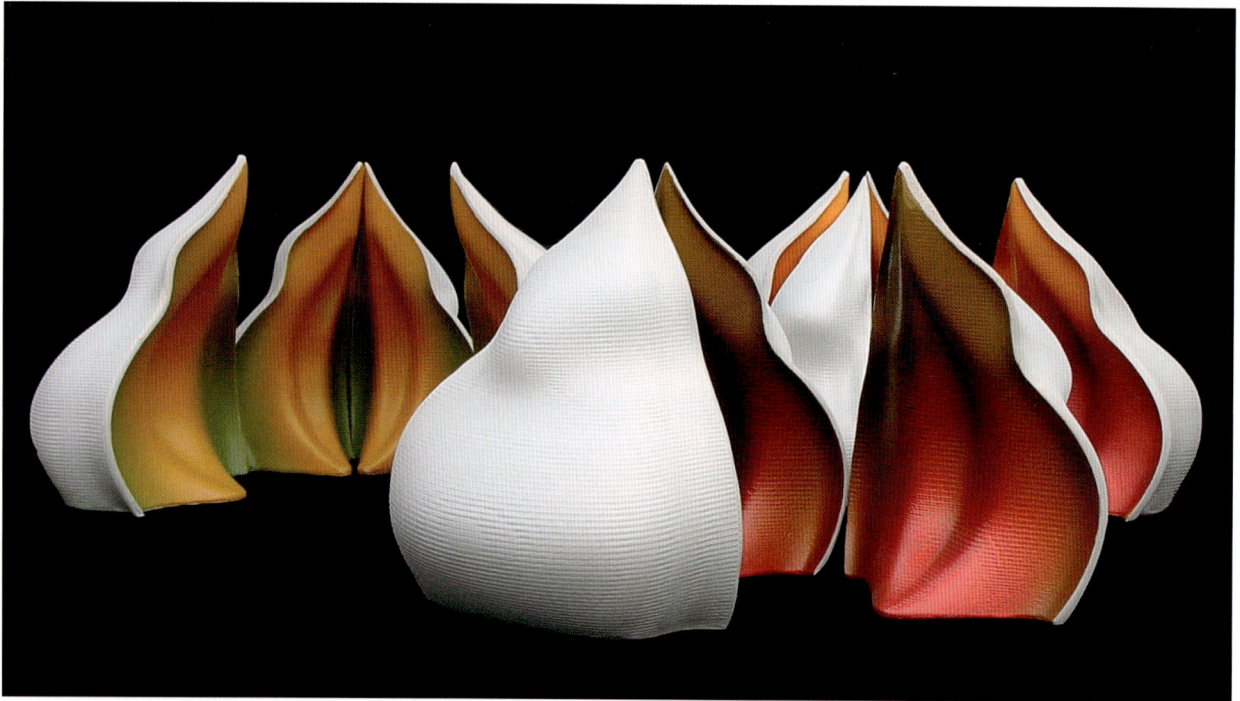

Alessi Project – Tea and Coffee Piazza (2000–3)

Highest grade Aerospace Titanium Alloy (an alloy of Titanium with 6 parts Aluminium and 4 parts Vanadium) – the alloy is super-plastic formed in a process very similar to vacuum forming plastics. First two sheets of titanium are welded together along their edges and a gas valve is attached, forming an inflatable pocket between the two sheets. The sheets are placed in-between a two-part CNC machined tool made from a carbon material that can withstand incredibly high pressure and high temperature. The metal sheets are then heated in an oven in a vacuum comparable to outer space to avoid oxidation and imperfections from airborne molecules. The titanium reaches a plastic state at approximately 900 degrees Fahrenheit. When it reaches this plastic state, argon gas is blown in-between the sheets of metal and ignited. The resulting controlled explosion drives the very strong thin sheets of metal into the carbon moulds. In this way very strong thin sheets can be formed into complex curved shapes while capturing unprecedented detail from the mould. Each part is then robotically cut and welded. The metal is coated with a variable thickness molecular interference film – the depth of the coating changes the refracted colour of the metal creating spectral effects.

THE STRUCTURE OF ORNAMENT

Greg Lynn

Conversation with Neil Leach

NL *Greg, I can sense a new direction in your work, a fascination with the question of ornament. How did this arise?*

GL Since my exposure to post-structuralist analysis of structure and ornament as a graduate student at Princeton University studying with Mark Wigley actually. But in fact, what would even predate that exposure was the summer I first worked for Peter Eisenman on the Frankfurt Biocentrum project. Mark was actually working as a designer for that project along with Thomas Leeser. That was where the Decon show was cooked up and the field was ripe with theories of ornament. Jennifer Bloomer was working at Georgia Tech and later at Iowa State on Sullivan. Catherine Ingraham was doing similar work at the SOM Foundation in Chicago. In fact, ornament was seen as one of the potential sites where Derridian thought would intersect with architectural theory. We can talk about this if it is interesting. I have always been a little tenacious when it comes to theorizing problems that do not reach fruition through textual work, by working them through the theorization of some design technique. Ornament was one of the major issues that I have always thought about.

Even earlier, I would say that the first architectural European tour I took as a freshman undergraduate student was led by Bob Doran who was a Secessionist and Art Nouveau freak. At that time I kept sneaking away to see Corb and Mies but spending three months touring ornamental surfaces at the turn of the century had an impact. The project I did with the painter Fabian Marcaccio at the Secession building also triggered my interest in ornamental surfaces.

Now, the non-autobiographical response . . . I do not want to realize surfaces that are smooth and featureless and so I try to exploit the tooling artifacts that the CNC machines leave on formwork and objects. This gives a highly decorative effect. So there was a forced confluence of the exploitation of a technological feature, the theorization of a design technique and a problem that was speculated on through textual rather than formal means that persisted as an interest.

NL *How would you reconcile this fascination about ornament with the period when you were writing and thinking about Deleuze? Any other architects inspired by Deleuze are concerned with questions of process rather than representation. Indeed discussion about ornament – or indeed beauty – has become somewhat taboo in certain circles.*

GL If one considers ornament as an applied decoration, then it would be thought of in opposition to process or organization. My recent interest in ornament (since we brought

Rendel + Spitz – Expanding the Gap (2002)
A temporary installation for the Cologne Furniture Fair: Large panels of building insulation foam are laminated and formed by a 5 axis router with a large diameter cutting tool. This tool is stepped at broad increments to achieve the rippled pattern of the surface.

a CNC machine into the office) comes primarily from the method of crafting surfaces using CNC technology. The process of converting a spline mesh surface into a tool path can generate a corrugated or corduroy-like pattern of tooling artifacts on surfaces. We are using this patterning technique from the fine scale of $^1/_{32}$-inch lines on the super-formed titanium Alessi coffee and tea sets to 1.5-inch lines for interior wall panels. The decoration emerges from both the design of the spline surfaces and the conversion into a continuous tool path. It is not applied but is intrinsic to the shape and mathematics of the surface, and in this way the ornament accentuates the formal qualities of the surface; like the pattern of an animal that intricately responds to the shape and structure of an animal's form. So, it is just about how the question is formed. If ornament is seen as applied decoration, as it has been seen since the invention of the decorative arts, then it would not be transformed by say, a Deleuzian sensibility. But if it is posed as a question of fused interacting processes (if it is, though intricately) then it is a primary concept for Deleuzian provocation. What is interesting is the attention that decoration received from the Derridians and the neglect it received by the Deleuzians. Ornament is a tar baby for representational analysis by a Derridian and it may be the limited success of these critics that led to the abandonment of the topic by our generation of theorists.

NL *Let's stick with the view of ornament as seen from the perspective of 'fused interacting processes'. Could we surmise that, if ornament can accentuate structural form, structure itself can be seen to contribute to the ornamental? In other words, do we need to allow our understanding of structure also to be 'transformed' by a Deleuzian sensibility?*

GL Yes, in the fusion both terms would be altered. In the Deleuzian sense of 'two-fold deterritorialization' each previously distinct category, in this case 'ornament' and 'structure', would have to open themselves up with some lack or deficiency to then allow the other term to reorganize it internally. So it is not just the expansion of structure into the field of ornament, or of ornament becoming structural, but rather a dependency on collaboration that transforms each category in some unforeseen and unprecedented way. An example would be the skin of the *Predator* project and subsequent interiors where we use the rippling of the tool paths as both ornament and stiffening, yet the logic of both systems is derived from the tooling by which they are each produced.

NL *But the problem must remain the very refusal to discuss aesthetic questions within certain Deleuzian-inspired architectural circles, where most are happy to talk about 'processes' but not 'representation'. It is perhaps easy enough to accept a process-based logic of structuration being introduced into a representation-based logic of ornamentation (even though the very notion of ornamentation has become something of a taboo subject) in order to 'transform' and 'recognize' it internally. But how can we even describe a logic of ornamentation being introduced into a logic of structuration, when the very terms of reference for ornament - 'beauty', 'elegance' etc – have been suppressed?*

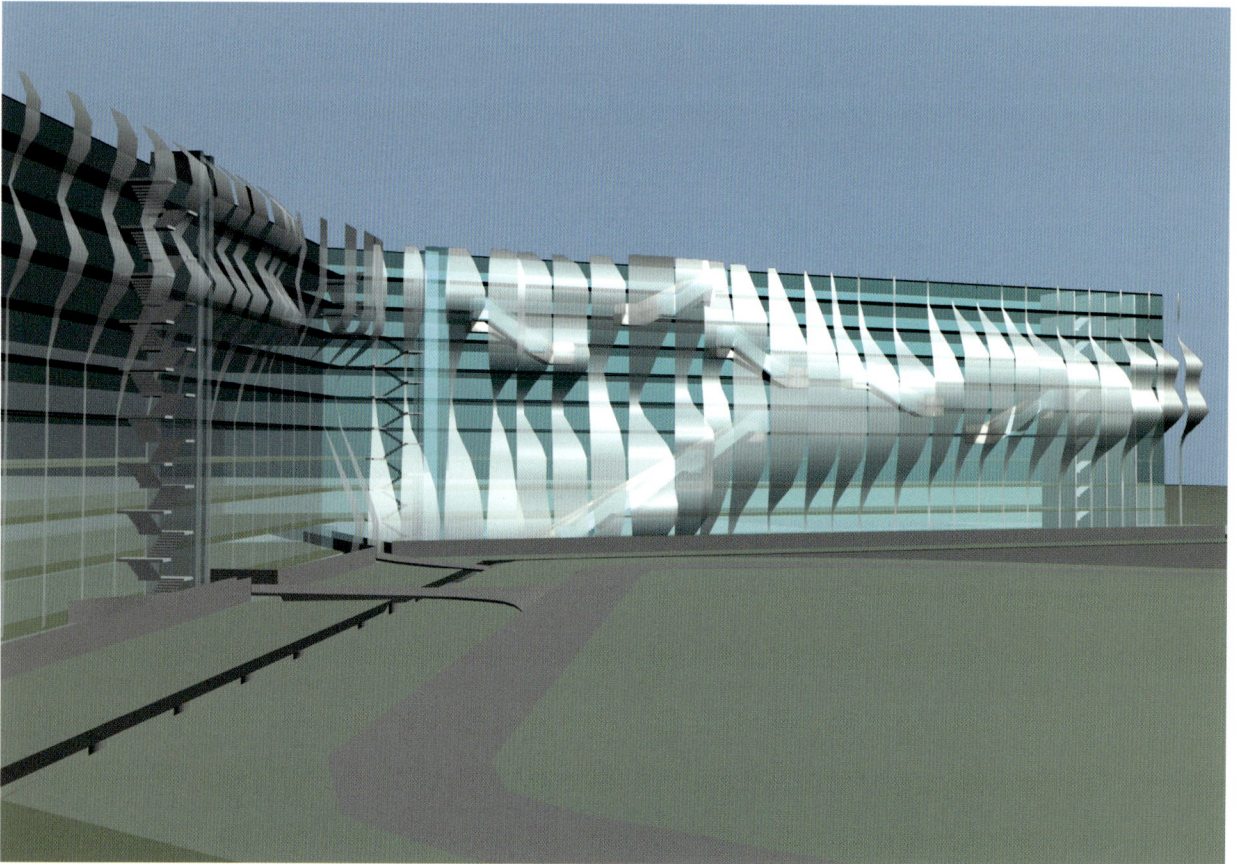

BOTTOM **Kleiburg transformation, Amsterdam (2000-4)**
The scheme is based on transformation rather than demolition and rebuilding. The desiogn achieves diversity in both social and architectural arrangement based on the following assumptions: the reduction of public space; the multiplication of unit types and their grouping into bundles or homogeneous neighbourhoods, the concentration of public access to trunks of circulation and the design of public spaces so that the neighbourhoods have distinct identities. This is achieved through a mixture of elevator and escalator access and circulation paths supported by a series of over 150 uniquely shaped vertical steel trusses clad in a semi transparent steel fabric, hung from the existing concrete structure.

GL What is most interesting is the convergence of Deleuze with the computer. Very much like the discussion that we had in Graz a few days ago, the computer, like any new technology, is at first a de-skilling device and then later an enabling device. The explanation for an inattention to aesthetics, beauty and ornament perhaps, would be that theoretical discourse that thought of the problem of space 'machinically' could be perverted to compensate for a lack of aesthetic skill, given the new tools. I know that the first thing I did when I acquired the expensive hardware and software in the early nineties was that I used a dynamic model of an environment to animate a series of points across the site which were then lofted into surfaces and became the form of the project. This was not Deleuzian machinic design, it was unskilled use of the machine. I would never do something that mechanical now. The difference between the mechanical and the machinic is precisely aesthetics. The machinic implies a creative becoming that is a fusion of the expressive and the mechanical sensibilities. I would use exactly the same tools now but I have an intuition or sensibility for how to use them so that I can now work with, or even better in, the medium rather than at a distance through process. I had an argument with Michael Hensel (at the conference) where I tried to claim that in order to have an experiment or to do research one must have both a sufficiently developed expertise in the techniques and an acute theoretical or speculative model in order to judge the success of the outcome. What we architects have called experiments most other fields would call automatic art. I doubt that any of us could define research in the field of process architecture now, and I know that no one has made a claim at research for the last ten years. Everything was described as a pseudo-scientific experiment or mapping. It is only now, with the expertise in digital technology, that we could have a machinic moment in architecture, because now we have both process and expression. There is only one architect that I know of who is able to work machinically and that would be Karl Chu; his work is also the most jarringly algorhithmic and staggeringly beautiful and decorative.

NL *Certain parallels seem to present themselves. The contemporary 'inattention to aesthetics, beauty and ornament' seems to echo the Modernist opposition to ornament in the writings of someone like Adolf Loos. And the Deleuzian call for a 'creative becoming that is a fusion of the machinic and the expressive' seems to echo Adorno's call (in his critique of Loos) for a more dialectical approach to the relationship between ornament and function. Do you see a connection between these two moments in architectural history, or do you see them as fundamentally different?*

Kleiburg Transformation (2000-4)

GL I think that there is a fundamental difference, that is regarding the notion of Modernity. At the present moment, Modernism is a style promoted by everyone from Rem Koolhaas to Martha Stewart. It has the ability to carry both radical and conservative architectural and cultural messages. Without veering into another discussion entirely, I would say that there does not seem to be a viable Modern project at this time. Loos, Adorno and Corbusier were all working from the assumption that ornament, structure and form were all framed within the horizon of a Modern project that made a strong break from the nineteenth century. Today evolution and mutation are the calls of the day and a strong disjunctive break is not feasible. Radicality and difference have been inscribed within logics of buggery and assemblage by thinkers like Deleuze. History is now much more vulnerable to uses for which it was not intended. This is all courtesy of Postmodernism in its most banal architectural sense. After the decadence and nostalgia of the eighties architectural history has been opened up to unimaginable abuse by theorists and designers. Deleuze is able to make sense out of such a landscape in a way that Adorno cannot.

DIGITAL OPERATIONS

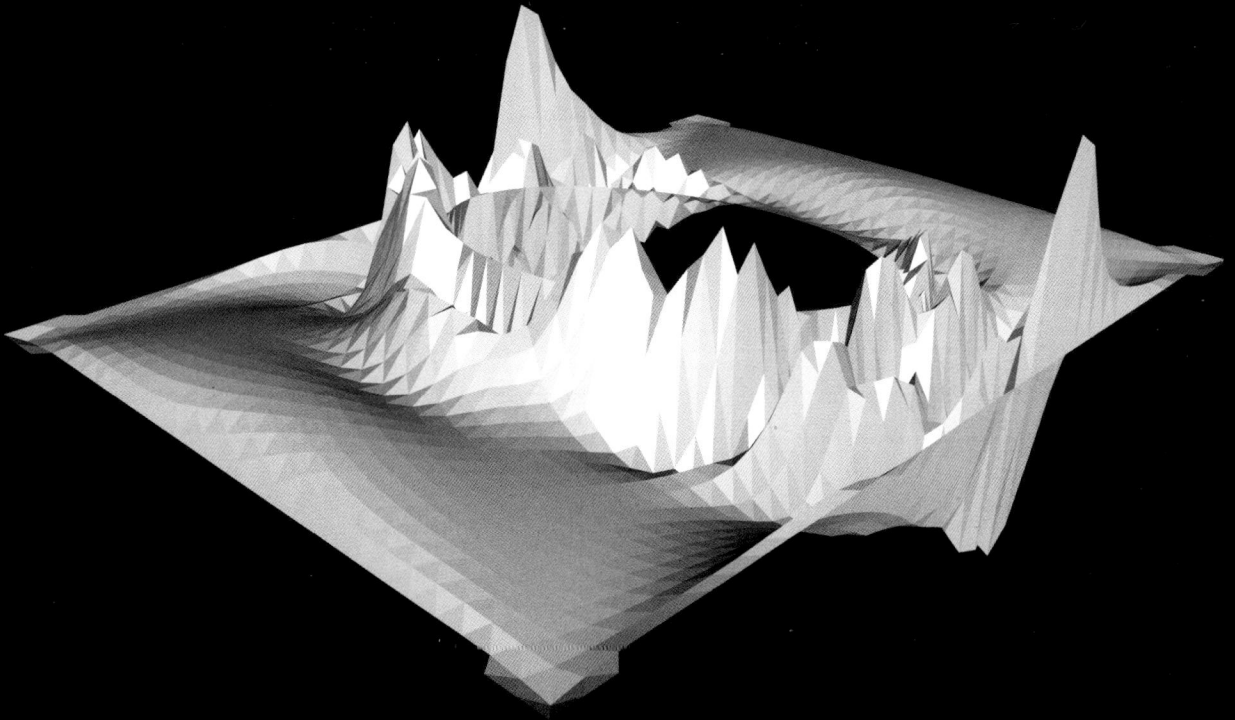

British Museum, Great Court roof – stress function model by Chris Williams for Buro Happold

SWARM TECTONICS

Neil Leach

It can be no coincidence that commentators from a variety of disciplines are now look-ing to biological models to understand structures of behaviour. From hard-line scien-tific research to philosophical enquiry, they are finding that a constructive engagement with biological models is providing new insights into all forms of natural phenomena. It is as though even the structure of the universe itself and its continuous expansion can-not be understood using static theoretical models, but need to be exposed to more dynamic models of behaviour. And it is precisely studies of the 'life-force' within nature – from cellular organizations to swarming and flocking behaviours of insect, plant and animal life – that are opening up understandings of how human beings themselves behave. Just as we have seen biochemistry emerge out of chemistry, biotechnology out of technology, so too we are beginning to see a form of 'biophilosophy' taking hold within philosophical debates.[1]

Broadly put, much recent thinking in science has sought to overcome the traditional conception of nature as governed by closed, static rules, to understand that almost every-thing operates within a dynamic, open system. The Santa Fe Institute in New Mexico has acted as a catalyst for much innovative thinking in this field. Operating within an interdis-ciplinary framework, researchers there have looked to self-organizing systems in nature as models for understanding other structures of behaviour. It is precisely by studying the net-working operations of ant colonies, for example, that the complex interactions in group behaviour, which rely as much on the individual responding to the logics of the mass or the swarm as they do on any single initiative, can begin to be fathomed. And through these the complex nature of any form of cultural life, extending right through to social, political and even economic systems, can be glimpsed, as Kevin Kelly has argued.[2]

Much of the work at Santa Fe has been grounded in the early studies of complexity theory by Mitchell Waldrop and others.[3] Complexity theory strives to understand the processes by which complex patterns of behaviour are generated in nature. Its project is somewhat paradoxical in that, rather than accepting the unfathomable complexity of the universe, it seeks to discover the very structuring principles that have created that apparent complexity. In other words, it attempts to show that complexity is not so com-plex, but born of clear principles.

The urge to symbolize, to order and clarify within conditions of complexity lies at the heart of not just animal behaviour, but all operations. There is a tendency for phenomena in almost every field to self-organize and arrange themselves into some sort of system. This has led researchers at Santa Fe to develop an interest in 'self-organizing systems'. These are systems first developed in the fields of physics and chemistry to describe 'the emergence of macroscopic patterns out of processes and interactions defined at the microscopic level', but which can be extended to social insects to show that 'complex collective behavior may emerge from interactions among individuals that exhibit simple behavior'.[4]

Moreover, the model may also extend to the operations of the computer. Research by Eric Bonabeau, Marco Dorigo, Guy Theraulaz and others has drawn comparisons between ant behaviour and that of computer software programs, and recognizes that both phenomena depend upon interactive vectorial forces that operate within a network and not in isolation.[5] Such thinking looks towards 'swarm intelligence' – 'the emergent collective intelligence of groups of simple agents'.[6] Nor is this limited to insect life. What is remarkable is that within any 'population' – no matter how varied its nature – certain common patterns of operation can be seen to emerge. As DeLanda points out: 'The dynamics of populations of dislocations are very closely related to the population dynamics of very different entities, such as molecules in a rhythmic chemical reaction, termites in a nest-building colony, and perhaps even human agents in a market. In other words, despite the great difference in the nature and behavior of the components, a given population of interacting entities will tend to display similar collective behavior.'[7]

One can see swarm intelligence at work with a flock of birds. The flock veers, dives, soars in a fairly uniform movement – uniform in the sense that each individual bird is more or less conforming to the overall pattern of the group. Conventional thinking might dictate that there would be a leader in the flock – one individual bird taking control of the movements of the others. In fact what is happening is that each bird is responding individually to those around it, obeying simple commands such as 'follow the bird in front' or 'keep a certain distance from the bird to the right', and so on. The net result of these individual responses is a logic of swarm behaviour, which is both the sum of the individual responses, but also – in some senses – greater than it.

These researchers note that in a society of increasing complexity and information overload there is a need to offer 'an alternative way of designing "intelligent" systems, in which autonomy, emergence and distributed functioning replace control, preprogramming, and centralization.'[8] Thus the operations of ants building nests can be recognized as a form of 'stigmergy' – direct or indirect interaction between ants – that lies at the heart of all self-organization. And it is the very effectiveness of ants, creatures with relatively limited cognitive skills, but with a highly advanced capacity for social coordination, that illustrates the extraordinary potential of 'swarm logic' as a means of addressing social problems.

Collectively these ideas come under the heading of 'emergence', a term popularized to describe a development in scientific explanations of the universe, but one which expands to all aspects of social life. It represents a shift in understanding from 'low-level' rules to higher-level sophistication, a kind of bottom-up development of complex adaptive systems that self-regulate, in opposition to top-down overarching principles. It looks to patterns of behaviour, but not those which freeze into one single expression, but rather those which are premised on dynamic adaptation. Constantly mutating, emergent systems are intelligent systems, based on interaction, informational feedback loops, pattern recognition and indirect control. They challenge the traditional concept of systems as predetermined mechanisms of control, and focus instead on their self-regulating adaptive capacity.[10]

Emergent Cities

There is an obvious parallel to be drawn between the self-organizing capacity of ant or termite colonies and the 'natural' patterns of growth of human cities. Indeed some of the early thinking of the Santa Fe Institute was based on the observations of Jane Jacobs in her book, *The Death and Life of the Great American Cities*.[9] Here, in a polemical attack on wholesale urban demolition and rebuilding, Jacobs recognizes the complex choreography of life in the city.[10]

But there has now been a second generation in which these ideas – as filtered through the work of the Santa Fe Institute – have been taken up and developed by figures such as Manuel DeLanda and Steven Johnson, and extended into an analysis of the very structure of our cities.[11] For cities and towns themselves must be understood as amalgams of 'processes', as spaces of vectorial flows that 'adjust' to differing inputs and impulses, like some self-regulating system. John Holland sums them up as follows: 'Cities have no central planning commissions that solve the problem of purchasing and distributing supplies . . . How do these cities avoid devastating swings between shortage and glut, year after year, decade after decade? The mystery deepens when we observe the kaleidoscopic nature of large cities. Buyers, sellers, administrations, streets, bridges, and buildings are always changing, so that a city's coherence is somehow imposed on a perpetual flux of people and structure. Like the standing wave in front of a rock in a fast-moving stream, a city is a pattern in time.'[12]

Cities are physical traces of patterns of social behaviour operating through time. As such, we must always question the need for 'master-plans', or at least recognize the potential of their authority to be determined by 'bottom-up' street level interferences. Moreover, they are governed by principles of self-organization. As Rem Koolhaas has shown in his study of Lagos, the apparent chaos of city life can be understood as an enormously sophisticated self-organizing system that sorts, orders, categorizes and recycles according to quite clear economic principles. Indeed, for the most exacting model of a self-organizing urban system we might perhaps look beyond Lagos and turn towards a city such as Hong Kong, which is thoroughly imbricated within a capitalist framework, and unconstrained by strong historical ties. Hong Kong, with its jungle of social interactions, can be understood not as a chaotic and confused collection of disparate activities, but as a hugely sophisticated connection of interdependent micro-systems that operate within an overall swarm intelligence.

This thinking comes close to the account of the city offered by Deleuze and Guattari. In their terms, the city becomes a complex *machinic phylum* that adjusts, self-regulates, and that becomes the very space of deterritorialization.[13] The city, as a smooth space of networks and flows, can therefore be contrasted to the state, as a striated space of hierarchies and order. The state, in other words, seeks to impose a certain form on everything. The city, on the other hand, is predominantly a result of a process — it is a formation.[14]

Emergent Architecture

DeLanda's book, *A Thousand Years of Nonlinear History*, is effectively a rewriting of the past millennium of urban development according to a broadly Deleuzian framework. It is an approach that focuses on process rather than representation, on formation rather than form. This approach could equally be applied at the level of architecture itself. Indeed one could imagine a volume, parallel to DeLanda's, that attempts to rewrite the history of the last thousand years of architecture on similar principles.

The key to this approach is already to be found in Deleuze and Guattari's own brief references to architecture. It is as though the whole history of architecture can be divided into two contrasting, yet dialectically related, outlooks. One would be a broadly aesthetic outlook that tends to 'impose' form on building materials, according to some pre-ordained 'template'. (And here one immediately thinks of the role of 'proportions' and other systems of visual ordering.) The other would be a broadly structural outlook that tends to allow forms to 'emerge' according to certain programmatic requirements.

The first is described by Deleuze and Guattari as the 'Romanesque'. The term seems somewhat limiting, in that the principle covers a range of approaches which broadly come under the umbrella of the Classical. This would include not only the Classical as such – the Roman and Greek derived style which mutated through successive generation through the Romanesque, and into the Renaissance, Mannerism, Baroque, and neo-Classical – but also any outlook which focuses on appearance over performance. In this sense the neo-Gothic could almost be included in this group, but so too Modern or indeed Postmodern architecture, and even the excessively *formal*, scenographic work of architects such as Frank Gehry.

The second could be broadly defined as the Gothic, which is configured not as a style, as it was in the nineteenth century, but as a method. It is a way of designing that privileges 'process' over appearance. Architecture becomes the result of competing forces. It is a programmatic architecture that registers the impulses of human habitation, and adapts to those impulses. Deleuze and Guattari analyse the distinction between the Gothic spirit and the Romanesque as a 'qualitative' distinction, between a static and a dynamic model of understanding architecture.[15]

Emergent form 'evolves' over time, much as the Gothic vault 'evolved', becoming ever more refined in its structural efficiency, until it reached its glorious culmination in the fan vaulting of the English Perpendicular style. The task for designers, then, would be to 'fast forward' this process, and to imagine how forms would have evolved so as to be totally adapted to their patterns of colonization. It is an architecture, then, of the 'future perfect' tense, trying to predict through exhaustive analyses the activities that will have happened, so as to facilitate those processes, by enabling connectivity and so on. In its most advanced form it would be an architecture that is open to those processes themselves, an adaptive, responsive environment, that does not crystallize into a single, inflexible form, but is able to reconfigure itself over time, and adjust to the multiple permutations of programmatic use that might be expected of it.

Rather than describing these two different outlooks in terms of style, Deleuze and Guattari refer to them in terms of different 'sciences'. One is a science of intensive thinking that understands the world in terms of forces, flows and process.[16] The other is a science of extensive thinking, that seeks to understand the world in terms of laws, fixity and representation. In other words, the one is a smooth science, and the other striated. Deleuze and Guattari also describe this opposition as being between a nomad, war machine science and a royal, state science. The latter is a science of fixed rules and given forms, a hierarchical system imposed from above.[17] By contrast, the nomad war machine science is a bottom-up model that responds in each individual instance to the particularities of the moment.[18]

There is a genealogy to this Gothic outlook. It is articulated clearly within the Gothic tradition, but so too within a certain approach to structures, such as bridges.[19] Yet, the principle of designing according to efficiency and minimal use of materials lies behind all good engineering practice. More recently, one might find certain incarnations of this Gothic science in the work of Antonio Gaudí at the beginning of the twentieth century, and Frei Otto towards the end. At the beginning of the twenty-first century, one might recognize within the work of Foreign Office Architects, Reiser and Umemoto, Mark Burry, Mark Goulthorpe, Lars Spuybroek and U N Studio, traces of a re-articulation of this spirit. The work of this group shares a common goal, a sympathetic engagement with the principles of structural engineering, that embraces structural concerns not as some practical afterthought, but as a vital component folded into the whole conceptual process of designing. This work has been described as 'post-Gaudian praxis'. Importantly, it relies heavily upon computational methodology.

Digital Tectonics

But how might these operations be facilitated by the digital domain? At first sight there is little to suggest that the question of structure and structuration has much to do with operations of the computer, in that one remains a decidedly material domain, and the other an immaterial one. Yet, once we reinterpret the computer, not as a nomadic machine, but as a 'population' of smaller, nomadic components operating within the logic of swarm intelligence, the possibility becomes more evident. Here we might recognize that structures themselves operate in a highly complex manner. Never as discrete and self-contained as they first appear, structures operate parametrically as 'self-organizing systems'. It would be better to think of their operations in terms of networks or even meshworks.

Research has already demonstrated the theoretical links between ant behaviour, computer networks and structural forms, and this principle has been further corroborated by programs being devised to understand structural behaviour.[20] For some time architects and engineers have used computer programs to test the structural stability of their designs. But programs are now being developed for actually generating novel structural forms. These go beyond the already very sophisticated use of genetic algorithms championed by Karl Chu and others, to produce forms which have their own structural integrity.

One such example is the eifForm program, devised by Kristina Shea, that generates forms in a stochastic, non-monotonic method using a process of structural shape annealing.[21] The 'designer' merely establishes certain defining coordinates, and then unleashes the program which eventually 'crystallizes' and resolves itself into a certain configuration. Each configuration is a structural form which will support itself against gravity and other prescribed loadings, and yet each configuration thrown up by the program is different. Such is the logic of a bottom-up, stochastic method.

It is through programs such as eifForm, that we recognize the potential for the computer to simulate structural operations, precisely because it is based on populational behaviour. But the possibilities go further. What we encounter with such programs is the potential to view the whole design operation as a process. What applies to structure, could equally well apply to other aspects of the building process – to acoustic or environmental concerns, to constructional or programmatic issues. The computer provides an efficient search-engine that is premised on the notion of efficiency. Hence the real potential of such operations does not lie as an indulgent designer toy of the affluent West, but also as a social tool optimizing resources within less privileged regions of the world.

But this also has a significant impact on the very nature of design. The computer is being used not as a tool of representation, but as a generative instrument that is part of the design process itself. In other words, at a most radical level, the computer has redefined the role of the architect. No longer is the architect the demiurgic form-maker of the past. The architect has been recast as the controller of processes, who oversees the 'formation' of architecture. With the development of new computational techniques, we find ourselves on the threshold of a new paradigm for architecture – a paradigm in which 'swarm tectonics' plays a crucial role.

Notes

1 Keith Ansell Pearson, *Germinal Life*, (London: Routledge, 1997).

2 Kevin Kelly, *Out of Control* (Cambridge, Mass: Perseus Books, 1994); *New Rules for the New Economy* (London: Fourth Estate, 1998).

3 Mitchell Waldrop, *Complexity: The Emerging Science at the Edge of Order and Chaos* (New York and London: Simon and Schuster, 1992); John Holland, *Emergence: From Chaos to Order* (Oxford University Press, 1998).

4 Eric Bonabeau, Marco Dorigo and Guy Theraulaz, *Swarm Intelligence: From Natural to Artificial Systems* (New York and Oxford: Oxford University Press, 1999), p. 6.

5 Bonabeau, Dorigo and Theraulaz, *Swarm Intelligence*. See also James Kennedy, *Swarm Intelligence* (New York: Morgan Kaufmann, 2001); Mitchel Resnick, *Turtles, Termites, and Traffic Jams* (Cambridge, Mass: MIT Press, 1994).

6 Bonabeau, Dorigo and Theraulaz, *Swarm Intelligence*, p. xi.

7 Manuel DeLanda, 'Material Complexity', unpublished manuscript, delivered at Digital Tectonics conference, University of Bath, March 2002.

8 Bonabeau, Dorigo and Theraulaz, *Swarm Intelligence*, p. xi.

9 Jane Jacobs, *The Death and Life of the Great American Cities* (New York: Vintage, 1961).

10 'Under the seeming disorder of the old city, where the old city is working successfully, is a marvellous order for maintaining the safety with the streets and the freedom of the city. It is a complex order. Its essence is intimacy of sidewalk use, bringing with it a constant succession of eyes. This order is all composed of movement and change, and although it is life, not art, we may fancifully call it the art form of the city and liken it to the dance – not to a simple-minded precision dance with everyone kicking up at the same time, twirling in unison and bowing off en masse, but to an intricate ballet in which the individual dancers and ensembles all have distinctive parts which miraculously reinforce each other and compose an orderly whole.' Jacobs, *The Death and Life of the Great American Cities*, as quoted in Steven Johnson, *Emergence: The Connected Lives of Ants, Brains, Cities and Software* (London: Penguin, 2001).

11 Manuel DeLanda, *A Thousand Years of Nonlinear History* (New York: Zone Books, Swerve Editions, 1997); Steven Johnson, *Emergence: The Connected Lives of Ants, Brains, Cities and Software* (London: Penguin, 2001).

12 John Holland, as quoted in Johnson, *Emergence*, p. 27.

13 'The town exists only as a function of circulation and of circuits; it is a singular point on the circuits which create it and which it creates. It is defined by entries and exits: something must enter it and exit from it. It imposes a frequency. It effects a polarization of matter, inert, living or human; it causes the phylum, the flow, to pass through specific places, along horizontal lines. It is a phenomenon of transconsistency, a network, because it is fundamentally in contact with other towns. It represents a threshold of deterritorialization because whatever the material involved, it must be deterritorialized enough to enter the network, to submit to the polaralization, to follow the circuit of urban and road recoding.' Deleuze and Guattari, 'City/State' in Neil Leach (ed), *Rethinking Architecture* (London: Routledge, 1997), p. 313.

14 The city is therefore contrasted to the state, as the space of deterritorialization. And yet, as with deterritorialization itself, which will always be prone to fold into its opposite – territorialization – so too the city threatens to become stratified and to fold into the condition of the state. It is not that we can ever

avoid such processes of reciprocal presupposition – they remain an inherent part of the model that Deleuze and Guattari offer – and yet, crucially, they would always wish to commend one over the other. These should not be seen as 'opposites' within a condition of binary opposition, for Deleuze and Guattari seek to overcome such polarization, seeking to invest their attention in the notion of process – the oscillation or movement between two extreme conditions, rather than the conditions themselves. The 'tendency' towards multiplicity, fluidity and process that the city embodies would therefore be preferable to the 'tendency' towards unicity, stasis and representation, that the state embodies.

15 'Gothic architecture is indeed inseparable from a will to build churches longer and taller than the Romanesque churches. Ever further, ever higher . . But this difference is not simply quantitative; it marks a qualitative change: the static relation, form-matter, tends to fade into the background in favor of a dynamic relation, material-forces. It is the cutting of stone that turns it into material capable of holding and coordinating forces of thrust, and of constructing ever higher and longer vaults. The vault is no longer a form but the line of continuous variation of the stones. It is as if Gothic conquered a smooth space, while Romanesque remained partially within a striated space (in which the vault depends on the juxtaposition of parallel pillars).' Gilles Deleuze and Félix Guattari, *A Thousand Plateaus: Capitalism and Schizophrenia*, trans Brian Massumi (Minneapolis: University of Minnesota Press, 1987), p. 364.

16 'One does not represent, one engenders and traverses. This science is characterized less by the absence of equations than by the very different role they play: instead of being good forms absolutely that organize matter, they are "generated" as "forces of thrust" (*poussées*) by the material, in a qualitative calculus of the optimum.' Deleuze and Guattari, *A Thousand Plateaus*, p. 364.

17 'Royal, or State, science only tolerates and appropriates stone cutting by means of *templates* (the opposite of squaring), under conditions that restore the primacy of the fixed model of form, mathematical figures, and measurement.' Deleuze and Guattari, *A Thousand Plateaus*, p. 365.

18 A further way to distinguish these two models of operation is the distinction Deleuze and Guattari make between 'minor' and 'major' sciences: 'the tendency of the broken line to become a curve, a whole operative geometry of the trait and movement, as pragmatic science of placings-in-variation that operates in a different manner than the royal or major science of Euclid's invariants and travels a long history of suspicion and even repression.' Deleuze and Guattari, *A Thousand Plateaus*, p. 109.

19 Deleuze and Guattari cite the example of the 18th-century bridge designer, Perronet, who attempted to reduce the mass of a bridge and to design it to perform as efficiently as possible: 'To the heaviness of the bridge, to the striated space of thick and regular piles, he opposed a thinning and discontinuity of the piles, surbase, and vault, a lightness and continuous variation of the whole.' Deleuze and Guattari, *A Thousand Plateaus*, p. 365. Bridges are not always designed this way, and, as Deleuze and Guattari observe, Perronet himself soon found his experimentation obstructed by the state.

20 See Bonabeau, Dorigo and Theraulaz, *Swarm Intelligence*, especially Chapter 6, 'Nest Building and Self-Assembling', pp. 205–51.

21 Annealing refers to the method of heating and cooling metals. The eifForm program simulates this process, so that the eventual form 'crystallizes'. The process is stochastic because it contains a random element to the search process, which is controlled to allow for exploration of concepts that are initially worse than the current design. It is therefore also non-monotonic, in that it is constantly under revision, often negating previous developments. For a discussion of the eifForm program see Kristina Shea, 'Creating Synthesis Partners' in *Architectural Design*, no 72, pp. 42–5.

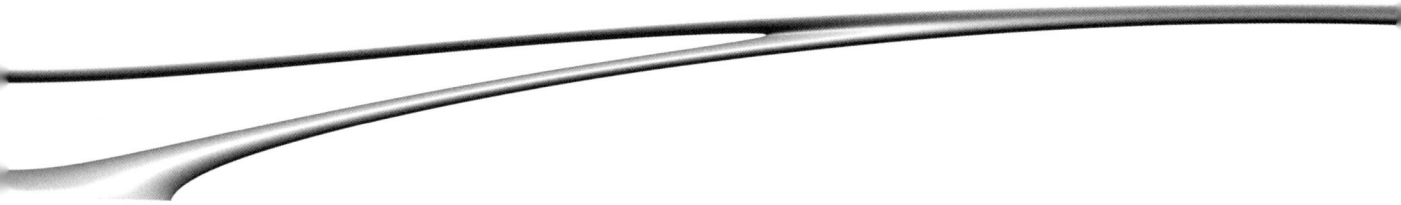

Study for bridge

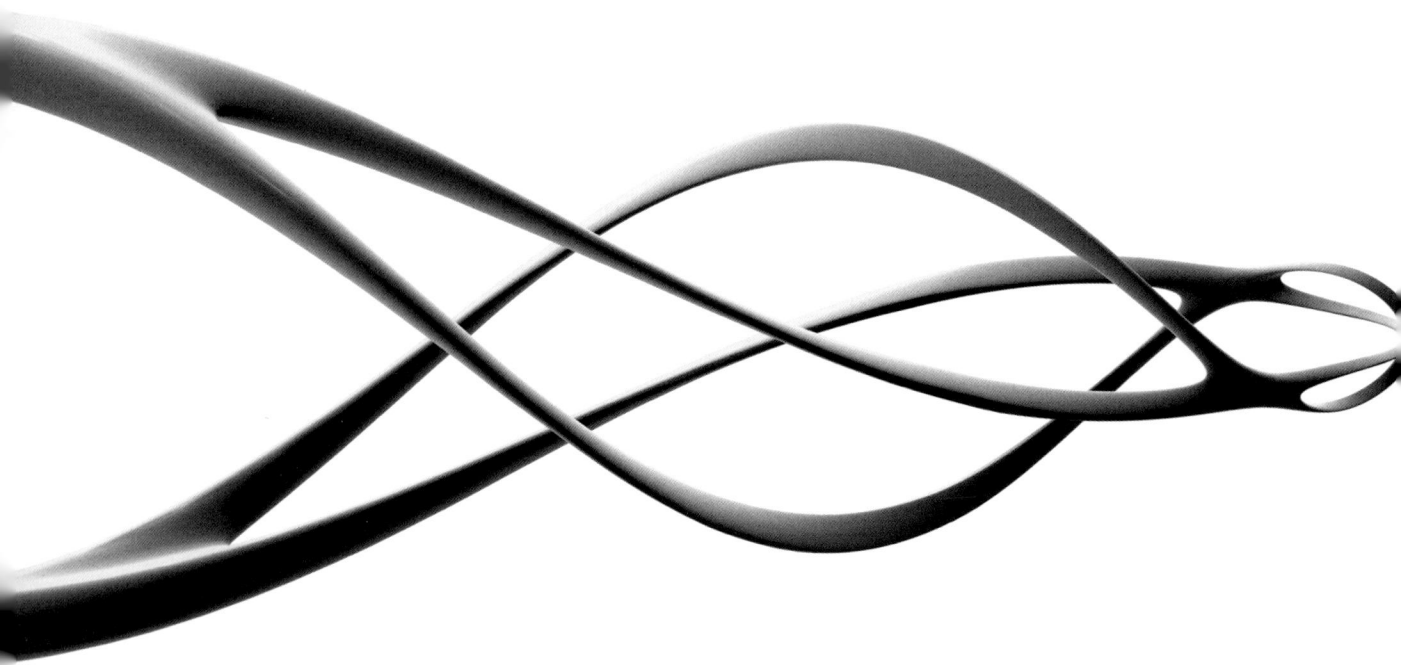

Study for sculpture

DESIGN BY ALGORITHM

Chris Williams

Introduction

The importance of the use of computers in design cannot be overstated. The development of these methods of design has been mainly in the aerospace and automobile industries. Yet the Boeing 707 and Citroën ID19 were designed 50 years ago, without computers, and are not that dissimilar to their modern equivalents. The advances in aircraft and cars in the first half of the 20th century were far greater than in the second.

Computers are used in many ways in design. Usually the designer wants to have full control over what the computer is doing, so that the computer takes over the role of the drawing board, clay model or slide rule. However, the computer can be used to generate geometric forms that are not directly controlled by the designer.

Computers have no intelligence but enormous calculating power. Humans, and other animals, have enormous intelligence, but limited calculating power in terms of arithmetic. But just walking about requires the analysis of all sorts of data from the senses and the control of innumerable muscles. This is way beyond the most powerful computers with the most sophisticated software. All that computers can do is to follow simple rules quickly and reliably. A piece of software may contain thousands of rules and this gives an illusion of intelligence.

Boeing 707

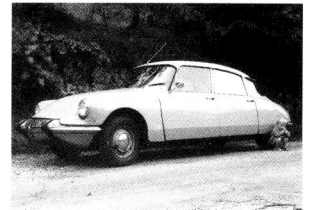

Citroën ID19

Algorithms

The Oxford English Dictionary[1] defines an algorithm as, 'A process, or set of rules, usually one expressed in algebraic notation, now used especially in computing, machine translation and linguistics.' Each rule of an algorithm must be open to only one possible interpretation, which means that no intelligence is required in using the rule.

When a person designs an object they will consciously or unconsciously adopt a set of rules. These may be some rules of proportion or the principles of structures or fluid mechanics, or a limitation on cost or the materials available. The rules are extremely unlikely to be in the form of an algorithm; they will be vague, incomplete, contradictory, open to dispute and require a great deal of intelligence to interpret. One of the main functions of the professions is to make sure that their rules are so complicated that only their members and their expensive software can interpret them.

Running the same program will always produce the same result, even if it contains a random number generator, unless the program is 'seeded' by some number that is never repeated, like the date and time. However, the first time a program is run the result may not be predictable, because a change to one rule out of thousands may have far-reaching effects.

An algorithm is only complete when every rule it contains is fully described. Thus to

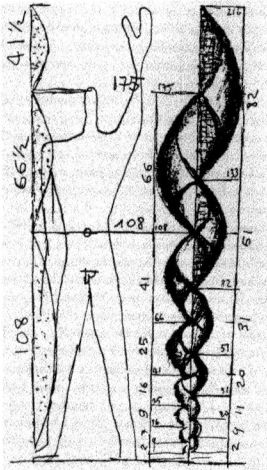
Le Corbusier's Modulor

Hanging chain model

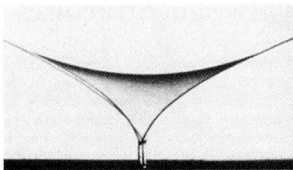
Soap film

Mannheim grid shells

Munich aviary

say that the algorithm for Le Corbusier's modulor[2] is that dimensions should lie in the ratio $\left(\dfrac{1+\sqrt{5}}{2}\right)^{n}$ where n is an integer, positive, zero or negative is almost meaningless since there must be many other rules before a design of a complete building is determined. This suggests that one should only expect algorithms to be used for parts of the design of objects, like the profile of a wing or the exact shape of a shell structure or the proportions of a window, rather than the whole aeroplane or building. To expect computer programs that analyse fluid flow and prepare accounts to communicate is even more fanciful than to imagine people who do those jobs doing so.

Physical Analogies

So, given that one can only expect an algorithm to produce a design for one aspect of a complex object, how can one proceed to construct an algorithm? One possibility is to mimic some rule of nature as pioneered by Gaudí in his hanging tension models that were inverted for his compression vault structures. Frei Otto continued this work in his experiments on hanging chains and soap films. These techniques led to the design of the Mannheim grid shells and the Munich aviary. Even though physical modelling was used for these projects, in the end their geometry and structural action was determined by computer analysis. This took place in the 1970s and there was a fierce debate, particularly in Germany, between the more freethinking model-makers and the computer programmers. This debate is now over and sketch models are used for initial design, but all final fabrication information is computerised.

A similar debate is now taking place over the use of wind tunnels or of computational fluid dynamics in the analysis of wind loads on structures. In the end the computational approach is bound to win.

Returning to soap films: they are minimal surfaces, that is surfaces that minimise the surface area for given boundary conditions. One might have thought that the people who write computer programs that produce such surfaces all speak the same language. However, there are many different approaches. Generally brute force and ignorance, and number crunching methods are best for the design of fabric structures because they can include cable boundaries, cutting patterns etc. However, those more mathematically inclined would instead search for analytic solutions, such as the Costa surface.[3,4] This surface is described by

$$x = \frac{1}{2}\Re\left\{-\zeta(w)+\pi w+\frac{\pi^2}{4e_1}+\frac{\pi}{2e_1}\left[\zeta\left(w-\frac{1}{2}\right)-\zeta\left(w-\frac{i}{2}\right)\right]\right\},$$

$$y = \frac{1}{2}\Re\left\{-i\zeta(w)-i\pi w+\frac{\pi^2}{4e_1}-\frac{\pi}{2e_1}\left[i\zeta\left(w-\frac{1}{2}\right)-i\zeta\left(w-\frac{i}{2}\right)\right]\right\} \text{ and}$$

$$z = \frac{1}{4}\sqrt{2\pi}\log\left|\frac{\wp(w)-e_1}{\wp(w)+e_1}\right| \text{ where } w=u+iv, \ \wp \text{ is the Weierstrass elliptic function}[5] \text{ and}$$

$$\frac{d\zeta(w)}{dw}=-\wp(w) \ \ i=\sqrt{-1} \quad \text{ which, in this instance, has no connection with the Lacanian}$$

metaphor of the erect male organ. The lines on the surface are in the directions of the principal curvatures if lines of constant α and β are plotted where.

$$\alpha + i\beta = \int \sqrt{\frac{1}{2} + \frac{\wp^2(w)}{\wp^2(w) - e_1^2}} \, dw$$

Conformal Mapping

A feature of the maps from complex analysis, that is analysis involving the $\sqrt{-1}$ is that they are made up of curvilinear squares. Such maps are said to be conformal because they preserve the angles between lines. D'Arcy Thompson[6] used conformal mapping in his study of the geometry of living forms. Such mapping techniques can be used to generate two- and three-dimensional forms. However the derivation of the function, or algorithm, to produce the desired shape is not always easy.

Differential Equations

Differential equations can be used to generate geometric forms that have a certain uniformity. Readers may have noted that hosepipes are reinforced by a helical winding of yarns. This is so they can be bent. This raises the question, what are the possible shapes of a pressurised equal mesh net surface of revolution? This leads to the differential equations $\dfrac{dr}{du} = \sqrt{c^2 - r^2}\sqrt{1 - \dfrac{\left(a^2 - r^2\right)^2\left(c^2 - r^2\right)}{b^6}}$ and $\dfrac{dz}{du} = \dfrac{\left(a^2 - r^2\right)\left(c^2 - r^2\right)}{b^3}$

where cylindrical polar coordinates, a, b and c are constants and u is a parameter. The resulting sections have a certain complexity.

Fractals and Nature

Mandelbrot[7] describes the application of fractals to the derivation of form. The fractal image was produced by the successive refinement of a square grid of points on plan in which the height of each new point is the weighted average of the surrounding existing points plus a random number times the current grid spacing.

Costa minimal surface

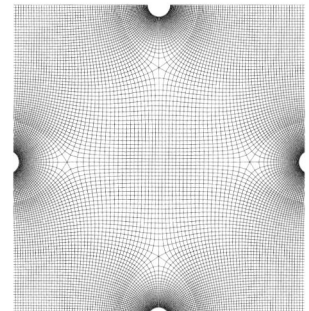

Map for principal curvatures on Costa minimal surface

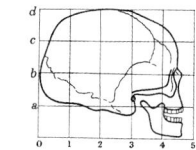

Fig. 177. Human skull.

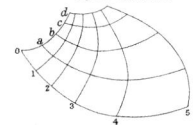

Fig. 178. Co-ordinates of chimpanzee's skull, as a projection of the Cartesian co-ordinates of Fig. 177.

Fig. 179. Skull of chimpanzee.

D'Arcy Thompson's conformal mapping

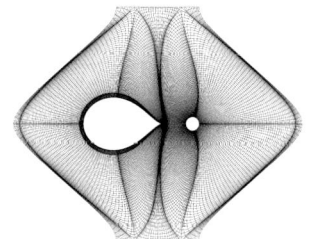

Study for shell structure

Fractal mountains

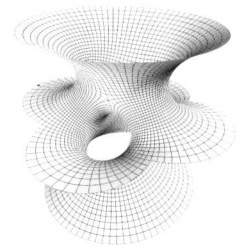

axis of rotation

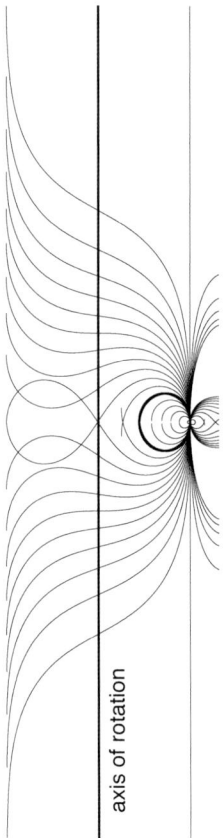

Hose sections

Getting Started

It is not possible to know all there is to know about mathematics, computer programming, architecture, structures, etc etc and therefore one just has to launch into creating something as best one can. The following c++ program, which should run on any computer, produces a dxf file, which can be rendered to produce an image of a continuous deformation of a surface from a catenoid to a helicoid. All the surfaces are minimal surfaces and the deformation only requires bending of the surface, not stretching.

```cpp
#include <fstream.h>
#include <iostream.h>
#include <math.h>
#define    Maxmplus1 101
#define    Maxnplus1 51
int    i,j,k,m,n,numsurf;
float PI,a,u,v,lambda,
x[Maxmplus1][Maxnplus1],y[Maxmplus1][Maxnplus1],z[Maxmplus1][Maxnplus1];
ofstream Maud("Surfaces.dxf");
int main(void)
{
PI=4.0*atan(1.0);m=Maxmplus1-1;n=Maxnplus1-1;a=10000.0;numsurf=5;
for(k=0;k<=numsurf;k++)
{
lambda=(PI*k)/(2.0*numsurf);
for(i=0;i<=m;i+=1)
{
u=((2*i-m)*PI)/(1.0*m);
for(j=0;j<=n;j+=1)
{
```

Bending from catenoid to helicoid

```
v=((2*j-n)*PI)/(1.0*m);
x[i][j]=a*(cos(lambda)*cosh(v)*cos(u)+sin(lambda)*sinh(v)*sin(u));
y[i][j]=a*(cos(lambda)*cosh(v)*sin(u)-sin(lambda)*sinh(v)*cos(u))-2.5*a*(2*k-numsurf);
z[i][j]=a*(cos(lambda)*v-sin(lambda)*u);
}
}
Maud<<"0\nSECTION\n2\nENTITIES\n";
for(i=0;i<=m-1;i+=1)
{
for(j=0;j<=n-1;j+=1)
{
Maud<<"0\n3DFACE\n8\n0\n";
Maud<<"10\n"<<x[i+0][j+0]<<"\n20\n"<<y[i+0][j+0]<<"\n30\n"<<z[i+0][j+0]<<"\n";
Maud<<"11\n"<<x[i+0][j+1]<<"\n21\n"<<y[i+0][j+1]<<"\n31\n"<<z[i+0][j+1]<<"\n";
Maud<<"12\n"<<x[i+1][j+1]<<"\n22\n"<<y[i+1][j+1]<<"\n32\n"<<z[i+1][j+1]<<"\n";
Maud<<"13\n"<<x[i+1][j+0]<<"\n23\n"<<y[i+1][j+0]<<"\n33\n"<<z[i+1][j+0]<<"\n";
}
}
}
Maud<<"0\nENDSEC\n0\nEOF\n";Maud.close();
cout<<"DXF file written, end of program\n";
return 0;
}
```

Only three of the program lines are used to define the surface, and modifying these lines
can produce any number of different shapes.

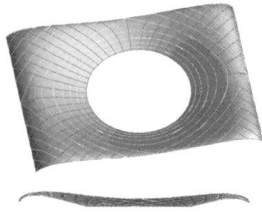

Structural form

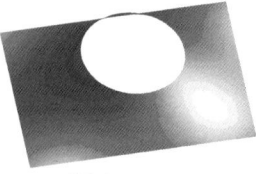

Stress function

Initial study

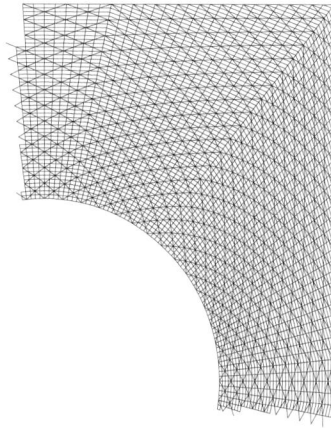

Grid before relaxation

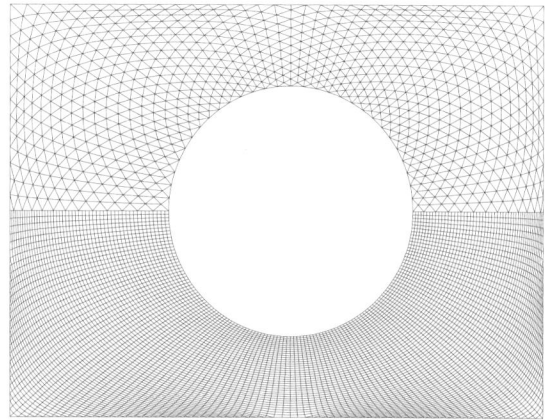

Grid after relaxation

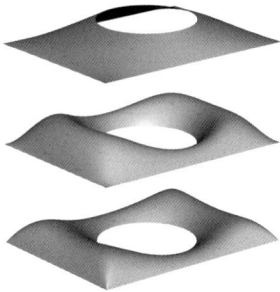

Surface functions

British Museum Great Court roof
Architect: Foster and Partners;
Consulting engineers: Buro
Happold; Steel and glass contrac-
tors: Wagner Biro

The British Museum Great Court Roof

The algorithm used for the geometric design of the British Museum Great Court roof used a number of different types of rule. Initial studies used the relationship,[8] between the load, w, the stress function, $w = \varepsilon^{\alpha\beta}\varepsilon^{\lambda\mu} z_{:\alpha\lambda}\phi_{:\beta\mu}$, and the vertical coordinate, ϕ, to derive an 'optimum' structural form. However, this approach was abandoned because other constraints could not be accommodated.

The final form is described by the three functions,

$$z = \frac{h\left(1-\dfrac{x}{b}\right)\left(1+\dfrac{x}{b}\right)\left(1-\dfrac{y}{c}\right)\left(1+\dfrac{y}{d}\right)}{\left(1-\dfrac{ax}{rb}\right)\left(1+\dfrac{ax}{rb}\right)\left(1-\dfrac{ay}{rc}\right)\left(1+\dfrac{ay}{rd}\right)}$$

$$z = H\left(1-\frac{x}{b}\right)\left(1+\frac{x}{b}\right)\left(1-\frac{y}{c}\right)\left(1+\frac{y}{d}\right)\left(\frac{r}{a}-1\right) \quad \text{and}$$

$$z = \frac{\eta\left(\dfrac{r}{a}-1\right)}{\left(\dfrac{\sqrt{(b-x)^2+(c-y)^2}}{(b-x)(c-y)}+\dfrac{\sqrt{(b+x)^2+(c-y)^2}}{(b+x)(c-y)}+\dfrac{\sqrt{(b-x)^2+(d+y)^2}}{(b-x)(d+y)}+\dfrac{\sqrt{(b+x)^2+(d+y)^2}}{(b+x)(d+y)}\right)}$$

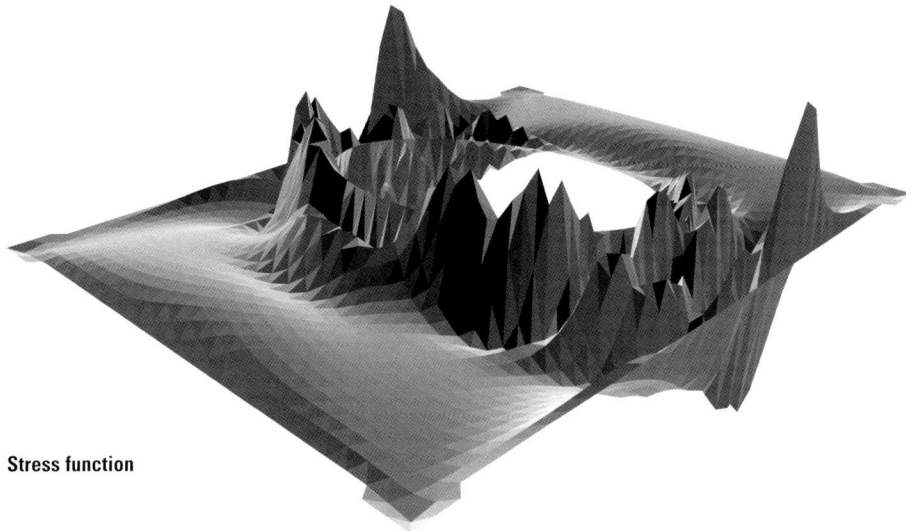

Stress function

weighted and added together, and are the Cartesian axes, and all other quantities are constants. The weighting functions also vary with position in plan. The first function gives the change in level between the circular Reading Room boundary and the outer rectangular boundary. The second two functions differ mainly in their behaviour at the corners. One is smooth and the other gives a concentration of curvature. This was important for the structural action – the roof is supported on sliding bearings and exerts no horizontal thrust on the existing building.

The position of the nodes of the steelwork grid upon this surface was determined by a relaxation process applied to a 'numerical grid'. The coarser structural grid is obtained by joining diagonal nodes of the numerical grid. The relaxation process involved moving each of the nodes on the numerical grid until it was the weighted average of the surrounding nodes. This process was repeated for the whole grid a large number of times, until the grid stopped moving. The weighting functions varied with position, mainly to try and limit the maximum size of glass panel.

Once this process was complete the structure was analysed in a number of ways – including the application of a stress function corresponding to the roof trying to work in compression and tension only. However sharp folds indicated that this is not possible and therefore significant bending and torsional moments are to be expected in the structure – as confirmed by more conventional analysis methods.

Notes
1 *The Oxford English Dictionary* (Oxford: Clarendon Press, 1989).
2 Le Corbusier, *The Modulor*, trans Peter de Francia and Anna Bostock (London: Faber and Faber, 1963).
3 A Costa, 'Examples of a Complete Minimal Immersion in of Genus One and Three Embedded Ends', Bil. Soc. Bras. Mat. 15, 1984, pp. 47–54.
4 H Ferguson, A Gray and S Markvorsen, 'Costa's Minimal Surface via Mathematica', *Mathematica in Educ. Res.* 5, 1996, pp. 5–10.
5 E T Wittaker and G N Watson, *Modern Analysis*, 4th edn. (London: Cambridge University Press, 1935).
6 D'Arcy W Thompson, *On Growth and Form* (abridged edn) (Cambridge University Press, 1962).
7 B B Mandelbrot, *The Fractal Geometry of Nature*, (New York: W H Freeman, 1983).
8 A E Green and W Zerna, *Theoretical Elasticity*, 2nd edn (Oxford University Press, 1968).

_____ biot(h)ing _____ a syn(es)))thetic poem _____

by alisa andrasek

_____ the eerie :nature of material reality as prophesized in both sci-fi and horror genres is being
re-disc:::overed by con((temporary science _____ the physical world is in:::corporeal _____
_____ as we approach what computer scientists have called the age of calm intelligence
when technology recedes into the background of our lives and be)comes almost like a form of artificial weather _
design disciplines have become similarly dematerialized _ a new form of in::::corporeality which embeds programmatic
behaviors with its physical systems _____

'… Reality therefore has become a form of machinic alchemy…"
_____ Karl Chu _ The unconscious destiny of capital _ Designing for a digital world _____

_____ this e:::merging dimensional shift is opening sources for new realities beyond our imagination and questioning
the 'hardware' of the ones we know - rendering them as soft::::::::ware and subject to change _____ design is expanding its
per((formance as an ecology of linkages and relationships _____ soft:::::wa::re be::::comes a hard::::::ware _____ architecture
becomes software _X = G >>>++&&&>> A _____

D = F >>>++&&& D_____ biot(h)ings _____   "...A city is a kind of pattern-amplifying machine…"
_____ Steven Johnson _ Emergence _____

point cloud _____ borrowed from a 3d scanning technology _____ point cloud is a raw data output of a 3d scan _ points are generated
by projecting a laser line onto the object and captured by high-res cameras _ the point registers the intersection

point _ c::loud _____ data _ weather _____ meta _ tectonics
point of the laser line and the object _____ 3d reality indexed as a form of artificial weather _ point cloud _____ 3d data can be sampled and remixed _____

the axiomatic infrastructure of multiple L systems activates through a set of mapping rules that breed a
– – –––Aristid Lindenmeyer developed the L-system to simulate biological growth in 1968. He based it on a recursive replacement of characters according to a set of rules called the grammar. The
specific formation of generative cells _____ emergent formal and temporal events include aggregation_
recursive replacement is limited by the number of generations specified for a run
multiplication_ repetition _ array_ a capturing of time-based flows _____ an intermediate stage
between the incorporeal and the actual comprises a set of mapping rules _____ these rules
function as a mechanism for translating abstract branching structures into architectural morphologies _____

```
axiom _ 07 _
_ 35 _ 1 _
G _ G=EEEEEEE
E = I C\ I C I C\ I C I C\ I C I C \
C = c < [ $B ] fffff AA - (170) A
A = FA + < F
B = FB + < (90) Fd
@
```

```
axiom _ 03 _
7 _ 67 _ 15 _
[ P ]  fffff [ P ] fff P
P = [ X ] [ cD ]
X = GA
D = UD
#              "...All possible branches are real…" ____#____ Borges _ Garden of Forking Paths
G = EEEEEEE
E = I CC I CC I CC
C = c < [ A ] fffff A - (170) A
A = FA + < F
#
c = < (240) c + < (1) F·········immaterial matrix is an expression of the universe of branching
@                    systems forming into various constellations… …………………………
```

```
axiom _ 04 _
7 _ 53 _ 15 _
P  fff P fff P
P = [ X ] [ cD ]
X = G >>>++&&&>> A
D = F >>>++&&& D
#
G = EEEEEEE
E = I CC I CC I CC I CC
C = c < [ A ] fffff A - (170) A
A = FA + < F
@
```

"…Just as the body lives between dimensions, designing for it requires operating
between logics. To be sufficiently abstract, topological architecture needs to welcome translogical…"
_____ Brian Massumi _ Parables for the virtual_ p.207

via topologics immersed into translogics
_____Brian Massumi is suggesting that the space of the body and "concrete" experience is
inseparable from dimensions of lived abstractness _ ones that can only be conceptualized in topological terms _____ via a notion of
the biogram _ a lived topological event perceived through a cross-sense referencing of two body systems of perception
_ experiences unfold through a synesthetic system that operates in between exoreferential visual sense and self-referential proprioceptive _____

_____ a wide range of vivid behaviors may be educed from the noise of wild complexity _____
_____ the first generation of transformations is compressed into super codes and processed
through a second one _which affects the extensive properties of its cells 1_2_3_5_7_11_13_17_19_23_29_31
_____ at critical points transpositional movement of magnitude and direction between cells
triggers the system to bifurcate from one stage to another _____ meta tectonics undergo
continuous and multiple transformations _ running through an infinity of transformations_____
"… He believed in an infinite series of times, in a dizzily growing, ever spreading network of diverging, converging and parallel times. This web of time
- the strands of which approach one another, bifurcate, intersect or ignore each other through the centuries - embraces every possibility…"
_____ Borges _ Garden of Forking Paths

_____ out of an infinite number of possible formations specific
atmospheres crystallize through an aggregation of an axioms' phenotypes
_____ different stages of fluctuating meta tectonics occur and dematerialize through
this process of differential participation generating instances of
emergent _ unforeseen design _____ an ephemeral _ ever changing _
_ fantasy-expanding environment
_ an atmospheric system constantly in flux and in_formation
alchemy of nature and a vast new artificial nature
emergent _ never static _____
_____ in a perpetual state of becoming_____

_____cellular membranes are re-::programming the landscape and natural fluid dynamics_ simultaneously mapping current processes of cultures
in_formation _____
they are receptacles for multiple fantasies and in:::dividual and collective forms of power_ upgrading the existing environments into increasingly
larger_and_faster_than_human environments _____ complex syn(es)))thetic resonance between cultures _____

scripting syn(es)))thesia
_____ biot(h)ings are explored through :::behavioral patterns ____ ::::a multitude of interlinked transformational filters
that code and decode ____ :::::creative potential of time processes such as delays _ phasing _
_ transitory in::habitations _ pulsating patterns _____ this self-organizing creature is augmenting its environment
by making it highly responsive _____ $N = R^* x fs x fp x ne x fl x fi x fc x L$ _____ a vaporous
dreamscape_____ emanating from immaterial source of computation and actualizing as
ex::perience patches that up:grade ex::::::::ternal spatial sensations into multisensorial im:mersive ………….
bio:::t(h)ing:s are com:patible to bio:::::::::grams of the body events of per:ceptions …………_____
"… Synesthetic forms are dynamic. They are not mirrored in thought; they are literal perceptions. They are not reflected upon; they are
experienced as events…"
_____ Brian Massumi _____ Parables for the virtual _ p.186 _____

_____ transformation of material reality as prophesized in both sci-fi and horror genres is being
re-disc:::overed by contemporary science _ zooming into the scale of the quantum particle's _ it's continuous
field of probabilities _____ the physical world is in:::corporeal _____ life is in_formation
_____ we are approaching what computer scientists would call the age of calm intelligence
axiom_t07 _____ a major dimensional shift is opening sources for new realities beyond our imagination and questioning
the 'hardware' _____ running in the background of our lives and be[comes almost like a form of artificial weather
per((formance a_____ contaminating relationships _____ soft:::wa::re be:::comes a hard:::::ware _____ architecture

G_ G=EEEEEEE
E = lemergent c never static
C = c < [$B] fffff AA - (170) A
DA = FA + × F + &&& D
B = FB + < (90) Fd
@

emergent _ never static
in a perpetual state of becoming_____
biot(h)ings
becomes software X = G >>>+&&&>> A

Fig 1. Anish Kapoor's installation Marsys in the turbine hall of the Tate Modern in collaboration with Arup (London, UK)

DIRECTED RANDOMNESS

Kristina Shea

The convergence of the geometric freedom offered by CAD tools and new manufacturing capabilities provide great opportunities for moving away from traditional compositions based on symmetry and repetition to explore new forms. The use of digital design tools has now moved way beyond early use for the production of final drawings. An integrated design process involving CAD, solid modelling, a range of analysis tools, and rapid prototyping is forming and has been essential in the design of today's most unique structures. Lately, through the development of parametric and associative geometry, CAD tools are able to parametrically vary design concepts keeping in step with design intent. However, the fundamental geometric constructions remain static. The next step in digital design lies in considering the computer as a *collaborative partner* in the design process capable of generating ideas and solutions in response to robust and rigorous models of design conditions and performance. A new way of designing structure and architectural form in parallel is emerging.

Computational Creativity and Generative Design

The potential for computational creativity has been debated in circles of artificial intelligence and computer science for several decades now. Recent applications of genetic algorithms and genetic programming in architecture to generate new funky forms shows promise for the computer as an active creative partner in design.[1] Generating new forms while also having instantaneous feedback on their performance from different perspectives (space usage, structural, thermal, lighting, fabrication, etc) would not only spark the imagination in terms of deriving new forms, but guide it towards forms that reflect rather than contradict real design constraints. However, the software can be developed in a way that means it is not over-constrained by reality. Digital design tools will then be used to not only generate new funky forms but direct this generation towards efficient forms that can be built effectively. The aim is to use generative design tools to aid in achieving a balance between aesthetic intrigue, innovation and efficiency in new structural forms.

Generative computational representations and processes have been under development mainly in computer science and linguistics research areas since the arrival of the computer. The theoretical foundation behind generative design methods generally stems from two triggers: natural analogy and logical basis.[2] Nature has been widely used as a source of inspiration both for creating and optimising generative computational processes including well-known work in neural networks, cellular automata, genetic algorithms, genetic programming, artificial life and more recently particle swarm optimisation and self-organising systems. The particular analogy used influences both the computer representation and the generative process, which are often highly inter-twined. For example, the representation of the generated object must be encoded into a string of bits and then decoded in order to understand the object. Taking a logical basis requires a study of the underlying logic of objects and systems of objects to form rules that generate a language of valid objects. Post developed the first generative system for producing well-formed strings of parentheses and it was later expanded into generative grammars by Chomsky. These are now integral to computer languages and compilers.[3] In architecture and design it would be more natural to compute with shape directly rather than symbols. This idea prompted the creation of shape grammars[4] and have been applied in architecture to produce languages of architectural form often to re-create and extend the style of a particular architect. Recently, Duarte[5] has been developing a performance-driven implementation of his grammar for the design of customised mass housing designed by the architect Álvaro Siza at Malagueira, Portugal.

Similarly, but from a performance perspective, engineers and mathematicians have been exploring how the computer can be used to generate lightweight structures, both discrete and monolithic forms. While some methods are now embodied in commercial tools and used today in aerospace and automotive design, these techniques have been used relatively little in the realm of generating architectural form due to their emphasis on engineering performance alone. As noted by Mike Cook from Buro Happold in this volume, engineers need tools to keep up with the creative processes of architects. Form-finding techniques used in the design of tensile membrane structures are the nearest example of performance-driven architectural form generation. Changing and adding forces within the technique pulls around the form of the membrane. This often requires a collaboration between architect, engineer and software to manipulate the design and agree on a suitable and viable shape. Form-finding techniques have managed to produce some amazing designs (Fig 1) but these are generally limited to either pure tensile or pure compression structures. Tools are still needed for generating mixed-mode structural forms.

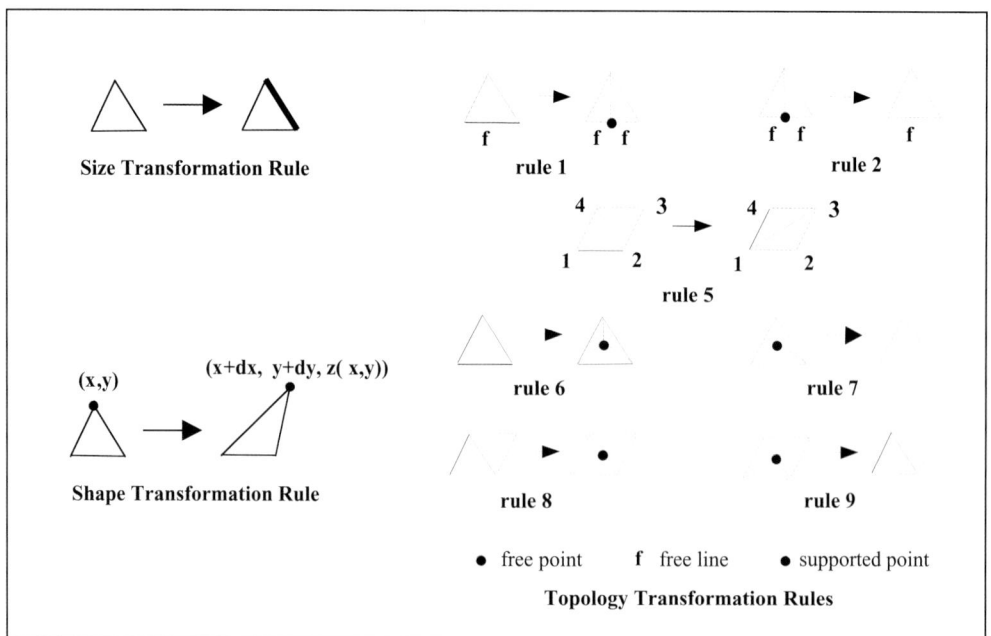

Fig 2a. Single-layer space truss grammar derived from geodesic dome patterns

Generating Performance-driven Structural Topology and Form

To take a generative approach to structural design requires a design representation that moves beyond static and even parametric geometry towards a representation that encodes design topology using, for example, the connectivity of primitives. Equally, a computer representation is needed not only of form but of structure. Now, rather than manipulate form separately and then solve the structural sub-problem, well-formulated logical relations between form and structure are created using a structural shape grammar. A structural shape grammar can then be used to generate design topology and geometry, so that they can add, remove and modify primitives and their connectivity, while maintaining structural meaning. These relations or 'rules' are developed by studying existing classes of designs. For example, it is possible to write a grammar for constructing traditional geodesic patterns focusing on how the connectivity of lines within patterns are developed, irrespective of the exact geometry (Fig 2a).[6] The rules can be applied both backwards and forwards adding and removing structural members to the design to create a non-monotonic generative process. The power of the grammar is in the topologic and parametric properties that can be instantiated into exact geometry. Given the desire to reproduce a Fuller dome the precise geometric parameters to the rules are supplied and applied to a determined sequence while maintaining symmetry (Fig 2b).

However, when transformations are applied iteratively in random order and at random locations in the design, the grammar defines an infinite language of structural shapes for single-layer space trusses (Fig 3). The language of designs defined by the grammar includes conventional dome designs, both in layout and geometry, designs with standard layouts but new geometry and new layouts that simply cover an arbitrary polygon. Iterative random application of structural shape rules to a design is analogous to monkeys typing random letters; eventually the monkeys will produce Shakespeare and eventually Fuller domes will be generated. Somewhere in the language a set of designs exist between exact Fuller replicas and completely random triangulation. Adding restrictions on computational precision, not to mention building precision, and restricting the number of structural members generated makes the language of designs finite, yet enormous, and would

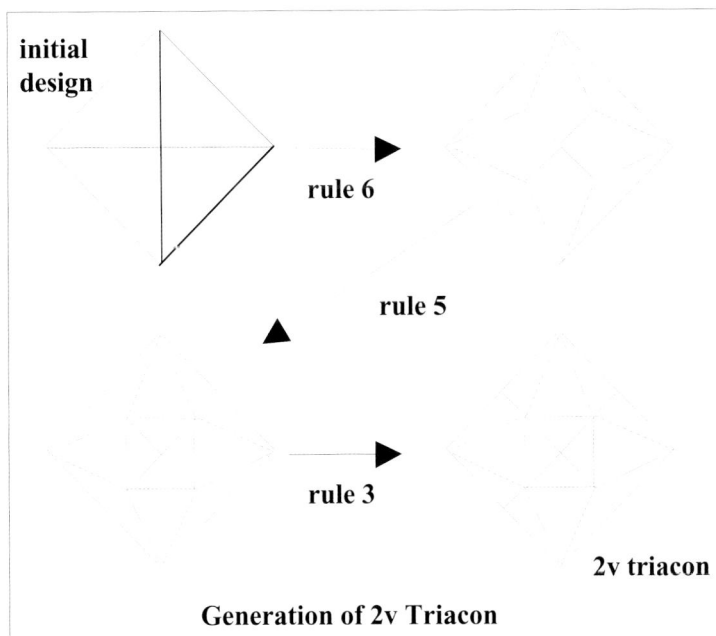

initial design

rule 6

rule 5

rule 3

2v triacon

Generation of 2v Triacon

Fig 2b. Sample design generation sequence of Fuller's 2V triacon breakdown (top view).

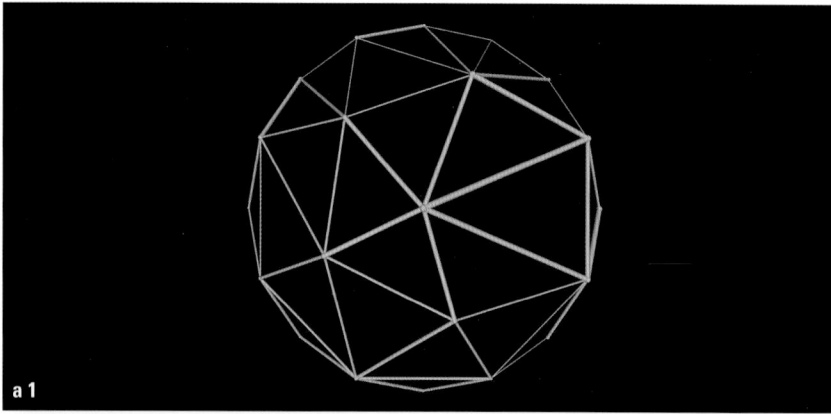

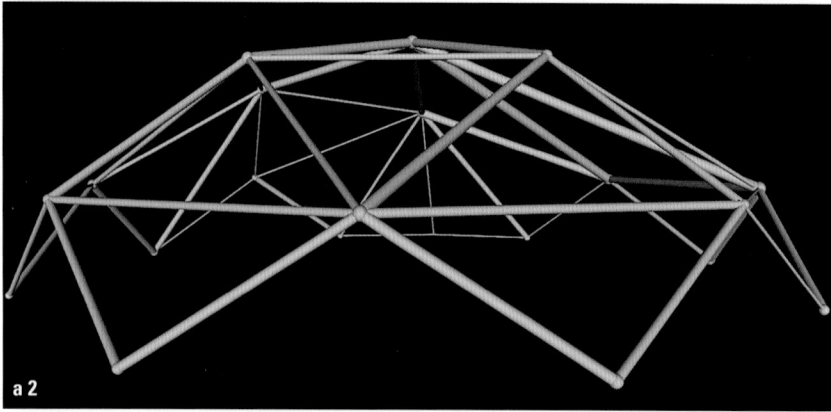

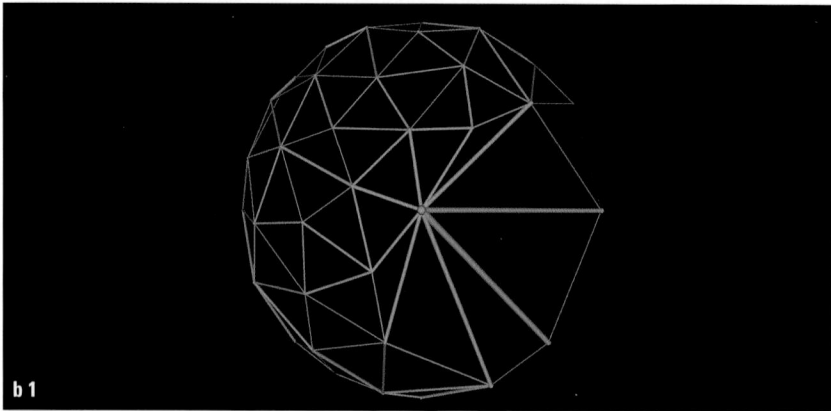

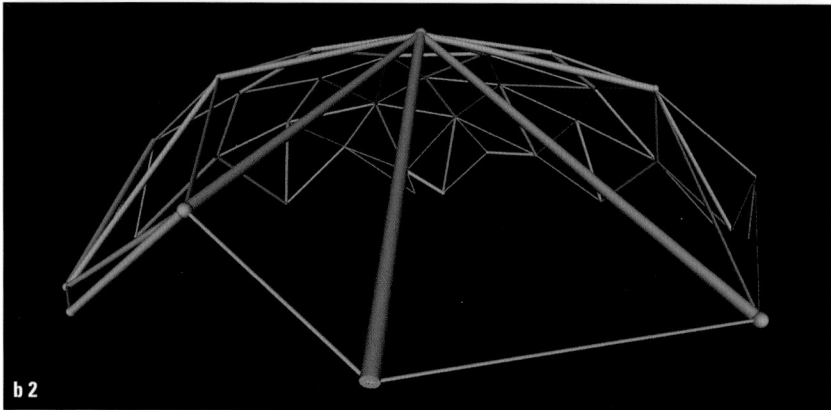

Fig 3. Dome designs generated
using eifForm
a a maximum of 50 structural
   members and
b a maximum of 100 structural
   members, illustrating the
   extent of the design language
   and a new performance trade-
   off between mass, member
   length uniformity, surface area
   and enclosure space

require exponential time (possibly years) to search completely. To direct the randomness of design generation, a search algorithm from artificial intelligence is applied, as well as rigorous performance models providing quality feedback on the designs within the language. Keeping in mind that a potentially creative method is desirable, the search process should be non-deterministic, including a random element, and should allow weaker designs to be explored. These aims fit nicely with the type of search algorithm that can be used to search the massive design language in a reasonable amount of time. The actual procedure used for search is an optimisation technique called simulated annealing[7] based on an analogy to crystallisation processes in the treatment of metals. This is a stochastic optimisation technique that tests a batch of semi-random changes generated by the structural shape grammar, measures their performance and then chooses one that is near the best. The amount of deviation from the best is gradually reduced throughout the process, but not necessarily from one design to the next. The process is non-monotonic. The combination of a structural shape grammar and simulated annealing optimisation[8] creates an interesting generative design process. It combines the logical basis and explicit design representation of a grammatical method, meaning there is no encoding and decoding necessary, with enticing properties for design creativity usually found in natural analogy processes.

This method is called structural shape annealing and has been developed into research software called eifForm.[9] It is quite comprehensive in its action, in that it develops the overall form of a structure, together with its triangulated breakdown into structural elements and joints, and finally sizes the individual members (Figs 2a and b). It works by repeatedly modifying an initial design with the aim of improving a predefined measure of performance, which can take into account many different factors, such as structural efficiency, economy of materials, member uniformity and even aesthetics, while at the same time attempting to satisfy structural feasibility constraints.[10] For example, eifForm might be asked to design a squashed dome which carries a certain set of loads to defined supports, by minimising weight and surface area, maximising enclosure space and uniformity of member lengths while avoiding tensile or buckling failure (Fig 3a). With this process, highly unconventional designs that are perfectly rational can be produced, and in difficult scenarios often better adapted to their purpose than the conventional solution. For example, if eifForm is asked to produce another squashed dome with the same overall dimensions but is allowed to search a language that includes designs with twice as many members, a different trade-off of performance objectives can result (Fig 3b).

The fundamental algorithm is very flexible both in terms of the kinds of structures that could be considered, and in the formulation of the performance measure, and so particularly well suited for the exploration of structures which are free form, but far from arbitrary. Due to the stochastic nature of the process, any one initial design and set of design conditions can produce multiple, often equal quality designs. Since the rules implemented apply to any single-layer truss structure eifForm can also be applied to create a conoidal roof for an octagonal aeroplane hangar (Fig 4) and a free-form landscape/canopy structure.

Designing with eifForm

The design and construction of a canopy and landscape for a small courtyard can be used to illustrate both the potential and challenges of using a performance-based

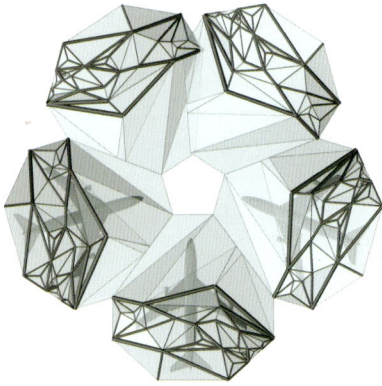

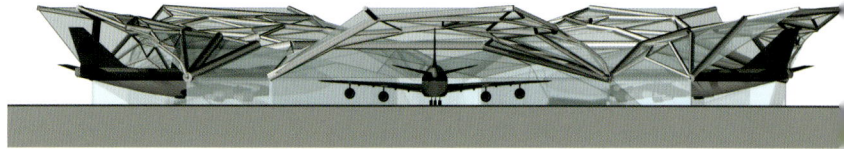

Fig 4. Conoidal roof for an octagonal aeroplane hangar

generative design tool like eifForm in design. The installation was constructed in a student workshop for the end-of-year party in June 2002 at the Academie van Bouwkunst in Amsterdam (Fig 5). The courtyard occupies a central space in the school adjacent to the main lecture hall and contains a historic cobblestone court. This was the first 1:1 prototype of a design produced using eifForm and, almost certainly, the first architectural structure built where both the form and related structure were generated by a computer via design parameters and conditions rather than explicitly described geometry. The budget was small, the amount of construction time short and it could not be assumed that any of the students had experience in construction beyond basic skills.

The project was a remote collaboration involving three architects, Neil Leach, Professor of Architectural Theory at the University of Bath, Spela Videcnik from OFIS architects in Ljubljana, Slovenia, and Jeroen van Mechelen of the academie, myself as an engineer, and eifForm. Jeroen was on site providing essential information while Neil was the only other member of the design team to have visited the site during the design process. Collaboration within the design team was primarily via the internet. All other information and impressions were gained from email conversations and the exchange of digital images and design models.

Fig 5. Transformed courtyard at the Academie van Bouwkunst in Amsterdam (looking north).

The installation was intended to be a space in which to explore, relax, drink, talk and gather. The courtyard is an irregular polygon roughly 13.9 m by 24.4 m along the longest lengths. The aim was to design a canopy that would become landscape in portions through varying the heights of the surfaces throughout the structure and interpreting portions of the generated design as landscape. One could walk under the landscape canopy and there would be areas for viewing or possibly walking above. Wood sections, a local material that could be easily ordered from nearby warehouses and is easy to build with even for a novice, were used. The structure was covered using sheets of pearl corrugated plastic, which alluded to Dutch greenhouses, donated by Rodeca and illuminated so that the canopy appeared like shards of coloured light floating over the courtyard.

Using eifForm for design generation requires creating a starting point that reflects intent through a model of the design conditions. The initial design stemmed from drawings developed by Neil and Spela illustrating the desired flow of people through the installation during the party, along with design conditions indicating the desired heights of the canopy in certain locations (Fig 6). One would enter the canopy from one of the two south entrances, wander through the canopy, possibly looking out of it from time to time, and emerge above it near the tree and the east entrance. The main feature of the courtyard is a large tree towards the northwest corner. It was difficult to decide whether to incorporate the tree into the canopy or to avoid it entirely. Designing remotely from the site, it was decided to avoid the tree since it seemed to be a potential source of difficulty.

The flow design conditions were used to formulate a more accurate initial design using measurements from the courtyard drawings. Most notably, the height at the south entrance was raised to accommodate the door that opened into the courtyard. Areas near the entrances had to be kept free of structure so that people could enter initially at an acceptable height for even the tallest person. From the initial design and parameters, the investigation started with triangulating the entire courtyard in an attempt to cover maximum space, and initially ignored the tree (Fig 7a). These designs were generated for minimum mass and maximum uniformity of member length while adhering to stress, buckling and displacement constraints. The design of the canopy involved a series of generation processes each using an incremental modification of the previous initial design and generation parameters. Based on the first iteration, a notch around the tree was added at ground level to wrap the canopy around the tree.

In the design of the canopy, the architect generally took a new role of interpreting and analysing forms rather than explicitly creating and manipulating geometry. Several designs from the first iteration were emailed back to Spela (Figs 7b, c) who then added annotations to the drawings, noting aspects of the design she liked and areas requiring improvement (Fig 7d). Design intent needed to be described in terms of parameters that could be fed into eifForm. The main requests for the next design iteration were to create a more sweeping curve around the tree, to eliminate the few, very long member lengths and distribute the triangulation more evenly.

One of the designs was then modified by cutting off some of the structure, 30 members, near the tree, dropping the joints that were previously interior joints to the ground and allowing these joints to only move along the ground but avoid the previously defined region around the tree (Fig 8a). This modified design was used as the next initial design. This appeared to be about the maximum number of structural members that should be included in the design, 129 members, due to construction time and budget limitations.

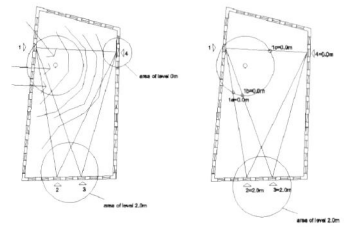

Fig 6. Courtyard schematic annotated with flow and design conditions forming the starting point for design generation using eifForm

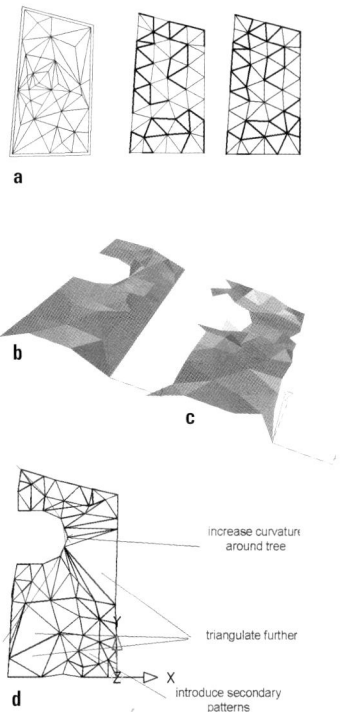

Fig 7. Preliminary designs (top to bottom)

a Uniform triangulation
b Coarse notch around the tree
   Maintaining a fixed design boundary
c Allowing the canopy boundary to change during design generation
d Annotated version of (b) returned by the architect

a

b

c

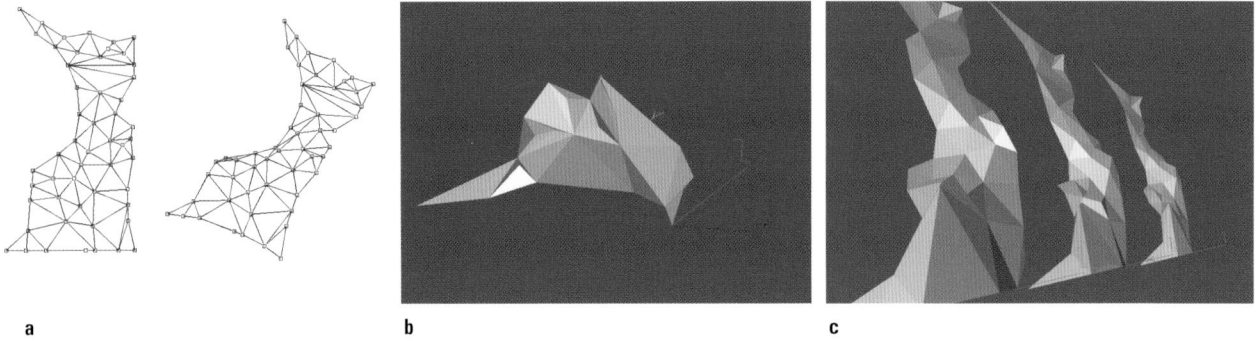

Fig 8. Design development (left to right)

a New starting point for design generation developed from 7c

b Computational study of possible secondary patterns in the canopy paneling

c Three eroded canopy variations generated from (a) that push themselves away from the tree

So, during the next generative process only changes to the joint locations and section sizes were allowed. No further structure was introduced using triangulation rules, and the topology of the structure was now fixed. However, one study was carried out to generate different topologies for the canopy with the same number of members by just shuffling around the connectivity of structural members rather than adding or removing elements. The design was allowed to erode along the west and north edges during this design generation, pushing the canopy in towards the south and east walls. Lengths were coerced in the generation process to a maximum length, shorter than what could be purchased, but this was not a hard constraint.

In the final design iteration, it was decided that the south and east edges of the canopy should follow the walls. So these joints were dragged to the wall and then in the subsequent generation were allowed to move along their respective wall. It was also discovered that maintaining the height of the structure along the south entrance at 2.5 m and sloping the canopy to ground level near the tree created a large region of central space under the canopy at an awkward height of approximately 1–1.5m. Rather than manipulate the geometry by hand, one lower central point was raised to a height of 2.6 m, was fixed that height during the subsequent design generation and allowed the rest of the canopy to fall out from there. This created an open space just on entering the canopy. A possibility of incorporating sub-patterns in the panelling was experimented with computationally but time did not permit construction (Fig 8b).

Since eifForm uses a non-deterministic design process, several design variants are always generated for each initial design and set of design conditions (Fig 8c). The design selected in the end of the process was a simply supported canopy connecting the four corners of the courtyard and spanning a maximum space of 12.85 m by 23.3 m while pushing away from the tree (Fig 9). While the design is not a dome structure, a relation between the structural patterns produced and geodesic patterns is evident. The canopy design lies somewhere between a Fuller replica and a pure random triangulation. The canopy was 2.5 m high at the south entrance, had a maximum height in the interior of 2.6 m, and reached ground level near the east wall and around the tree. It consisted of 132 unique length members, only two unique section sizes, 56 different joints and 74 unique panels. Although at first appearance the structural form may appear somewhat random the progression from the near uniform triangulation of the courtyard can be seen (Fig 7a), as well as the design conditions that moulded the design to its final form. The randomness in the design is a product of the type of directed search method used to explore the enormous design language, and the design team directing the series of generation processes through adding and removing design conditions. The series of

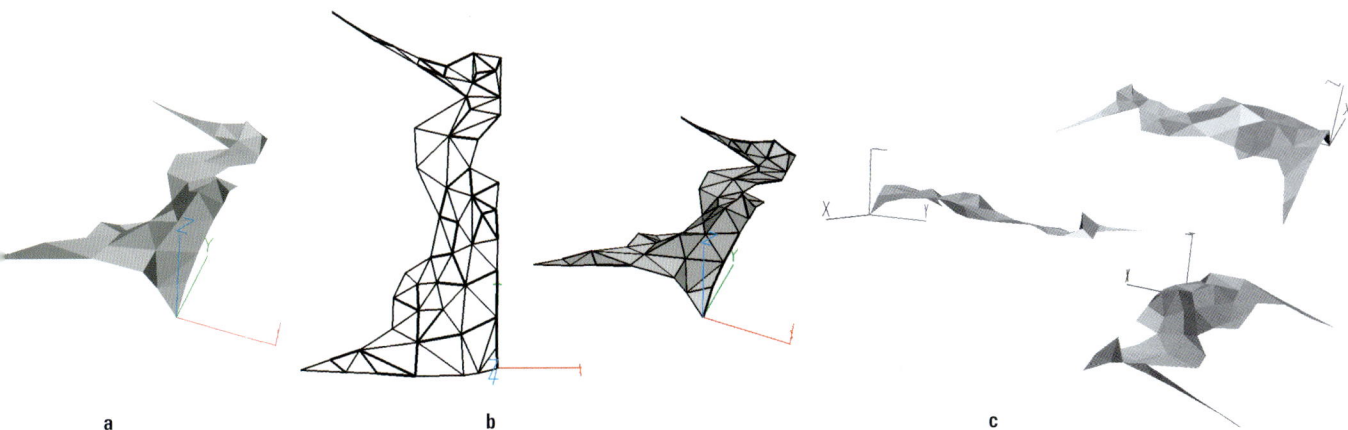

a   b   c

initial designs and design condition models becomes a documented description of the design process, illustrating influences and decisions en route to the final form.

Construction of the structure using low-tech techniques resembled putting an intricate structural puzzle together, each piece fitting just into place (Fig 10). Due to the source of the design, the design team and students participating in the workshop had an inclination to take a 'rule-based' approach to the detailing and panelling of the structure. There was an inherent understanding that every small bit in the design was 'calculated' and there for a purpose, aside from just aesthetics. Due to an initially proposed idea of creating a forest of supports underneath the canopy structure, all interior joints assumed a support in the vertical direction during design generation. In the constructed design, this requirement could be reduced but not eliminated. So, in keeping with the language of the design, triangulation schemes were used to create the interior supports by connecting three canopy joints to the ground to form a tetrahedron beneath the triangular surface. In one case an angled triangle was used to support only two joints. In future versions, eifForm should generate supports in parallel with the overall structural form.

Similarly, to avoid the complexity of the joint region when panelling, the panels were cut short of the joint where the length of the gap was proportional to the length of the panel side, approximately 1:9. A longer panel side creates a larger gap (Fig 11a). Each bolt to support the panel was also placed in relation to the length of the member,

Fig 9. The final canopy design (left to right)
a **3-D model of proposed final canopy design**
b **Structure schematic**
c **Different views**

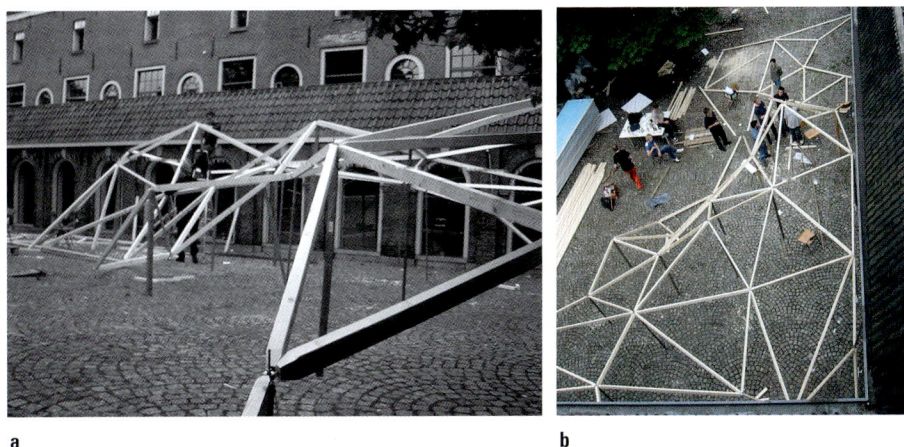

a   b

Fig 10. Constructing the canopy (left to right)
a **Side view showing the temporary props**
b **Top view showing part built and new members laid on ground ready for erection**

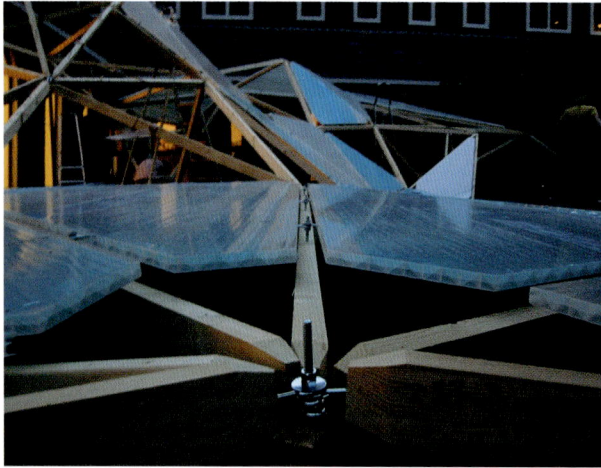

a

b

a

b

approximately 1:5 (Fig 11b). This approach resulted in clean lines between panels, members and joints, striking interior reflections from panel-shortening patterns (Fig 11c) and rather elegant detailing for low-tech construction (Fig 12).[11]

Interpretation, Ambiguity and Creativity

The Amsterdam canopy illustrates a structural form that is highly irregular and novel leaving some scope for interpretation. Ambiguity in shape grammars is a key element to their use as creative computational partners.[12] Spiller discusses ambiguity in design computation in relation to Paul Klee (Fig 13): 'If we take into consideration the complementary relationship between two views, this figure may be interpreted as linear or planar. From a linear point of view, it is a square with two diagonals; from a planar point of view, it is a square divided into four triangles.'[13] Considering one joint connecting four structural members, eifForm has interpreted the structural components taking only a linear viewpoint, although both linear and planar viewpoints are used to calculate the loading. While there may seem to be many ambiguities in the resulting design, the performance model, specifically the underlying structural analysis, reduces these ambiguities. The structural form cannot be as freely interpreted as Klee's image but must be interpreted with respect to at least the physical aspects of the performance model

c

Fig 11. Proportional detailing (left to right)
a The length of the gap is related to the length of the panel
b Proportional connection detail
c Interior reflections from open triangular patches and panel shortening patterns

c

it is responding to. In comparison, generative systems that are purely spatial play on these ambiguities to provide inspirational sources for designers' imaginations. With performance-driven forms, ambiguities may be reduced, but hopefully not the potential for providing novel and creative designs. Taking designs out of the context in which they are generated changes the emphasis of the software to form generation, but may be useful to spark ideas and in some cases extrapolate performance indicators. Enabling eifForm to act on ambiguities, spatial or functional, as noted by Mitchell,[14] is the primary route to creating a tool with enhanced creative possibilities.

Taking a planar viewpoint of the canopy, as a triangulated 3-D truss structure with non-structural surfaces, there were several possibilities for panelling it to create closed and open space, landscape and canopy. One option was to panel each triangular patch exactly as shown in the computer model (Fig 9a), but the canopy did not need to be watertight and the panel material was light, making their position not critical to the loading. So the space could be interpreted to create openings for people to poke their heads out or gather in as they moved through the structure. How the space under the canopy would be used was then largely determined by the location of the interior supports turned into features, and the panelling arrangement which could only be considered once the frame work had been built. Although the canopy is small, within a design team

Fig 12. The completed canopy (left to right)
a Night view
b Students relaxing after the workshop
c Panorama

Fig 13.
a Linear vs. planar viewpoints
b structure vs. surface viewpoints in the canopy

of four each possible pair walked through the structural form deciding different places for panelling on top and side, leaving openings relating to how the space would be used and the effects of lighting at night. Rules and rationale were even formulated to describe and reason about why one triangular patch would be covered and another left open (Fig 14). The structural frame was fairly unambiguous due to the underlying structural model but the potential surface was full of ambiguity, creating an inside-out design process. Including the surfaces as structural material within the design generation process is desirable but at the same time removes this ambiguity.

Physicality

The Amsterdam canopy is the first 1:1 prototype of a structure generated by eifForm. The project illustrates a novel combination of computation and experimentation mixing digital design with low-tech construction techniques. It was very exciting to build a design generated by eifForm on this scale and be able to walk through it, as the structures generated by eifForm are often very different to those that have conventionally been thought possible and are often difficult to interpret. The use of 3-D digital models that one can examine and 'fly through' is not comparable with the impression and understanding of a new geometry and structural form when walking through it and shaking it! For example, during the design phase, it was difficult to determine where people would make the transition from walking under the canopy to emerging above the landscape. A few good ideas emerged from looking at the digital models but the final design did not crystallise until the structure was built, but not covered, and one could actually walk through it. One joint was then moved along the east wall to create an exit, with the structural analysis rechecked on a laptop on site. Even with the best advances in digital modelling and visualisation, physical prototypes remain irreplaceable.

Impacting Architectural Design

There are challenges left in developing performance-based generative systems before they are ready to be used widely by architectural designers. The software evolves partly by theoretical advance and partly by designing with it. Further structural classes need to be developed, such as frames and structural surfaces, and their requisite performance models. To engage architects it is important to create interactive, dynamic and qualitative tools. Currently, effective use of eifForm can require some internal hacking, programming on the fly new design conditions and performance requirements particular to projects. It is not anticipated that architects will become experts in programming. However, for designers to use the software to its full potential it cannot be just a black box, rather a certain, even high, level of understanding of how the generative process works must be developed to drive it. Equally, in order to interpret the resulting designs and understand their potential ambiguities, contextual visualisation must be used to

Fig 14. Interior view illustrating panelling

highlight the relation between generated designs and the performance model that shaped them. Lastly, the generative process needs to be extended to take into more explicit consideration fabrication constraints, so that generated designs are suitable to available materials and processes. The impact on architectural design of performance-based generative design tools will be a new way of designing structure and form in parallel, involving a collaboration among architects, engineers and generative software to produce unimaginable forms that are efficient and buildable.

eifForm is currently research software under development by the author and her research team in the Engineering Design Centre at Cambridge. The software is based on the structural shape annealing method developed during her PhD thesis, 'Essays of Discrete Structures: Purposeful Design of Grammatical Structures by Directed Stochastic Search' at Carnegie Mellon University (USA) with Jon Cagan. This paper is an extended version of a talk given at the Digital Tectonics Conference at the University of Bath in March 2002. For further information about eifForm and using eifForm please contact the author.

Notes

1. P Testa, 'Emergent Design: a crosscutting research program and design curriculum integrating architecture and artificial intelligence', *Environment and Planning B*, 28 (4) 2001, pp. 481–98.
2. T Knight, personal communication 2002.
3. G Stiny, and J Gips, 'Production Systems and Grammars: A Uniform Characterization', *Environment and Planning B*, vol (5), 1980, pp. 5–18.
4. G Stiny, 'Introduction to Shape and Shape Grammars', *Environment and Planning B*, vol (7), pp. 343–51.
5. J P Duarte, 'Customizing Mass Housing: The Grammar of Siza's Houses at Malagueira', *Environment and Planning B: Planning and Design*, 2002, forthcoming.
6. K Shea and J Cagan, (1997), 'Innovative Dome Design: Applying Geodesic Patterns with Shape Annealing', *Artificial Intelligence for Engineering Design, Analysis and Manufacturing*, vol (11), 1997, pp. 379–94.
7. S Kirkpatrick, C D Gelatt Jr, and M P Vecchi, 'Optimization by Simulated Annealing', *Science*, 220:4598, 1983, pp. 671–9.
8. J Cagan and W J Mitchell, 'Optimally Directed Shape Generation by Shape Annealing', *Environment and Planning B*, 20: (issue no), pp. 5–12.
9. K Shea, 'Creating Synthesis Partners', Contemporary Techniques in Architecture, issue of *Architectural Design*, Ali Rahim (ed) March 2002, ppXXX.
10. K Shea and J Cagan, 'Languages and Semantics of Grammatical Discrete Structures', *Artificial Intelligence for Engineering Design, Analysis and Manufacturing*, 'Generative Systems' issue of *Design*, 13 (4) 1999, pp. 241–251.
11. K Shea, 'Digital canopy: high-end computation/low-tech construction', *Architectural Research Quarterly*, 2003, forthcoming.
12. Knight, op cit.
13. J Spiller, *Paul Klee: The Thinking Eye*, (New York, George Wittenborn, 1961).
14. W J Mitchell, 'Vitruvius Redux' in *Formal Engineering Design Synthesis*, E K Antonsson and J Cagan (eds) (Cambridge University Press, 2001), pp. 93–125.

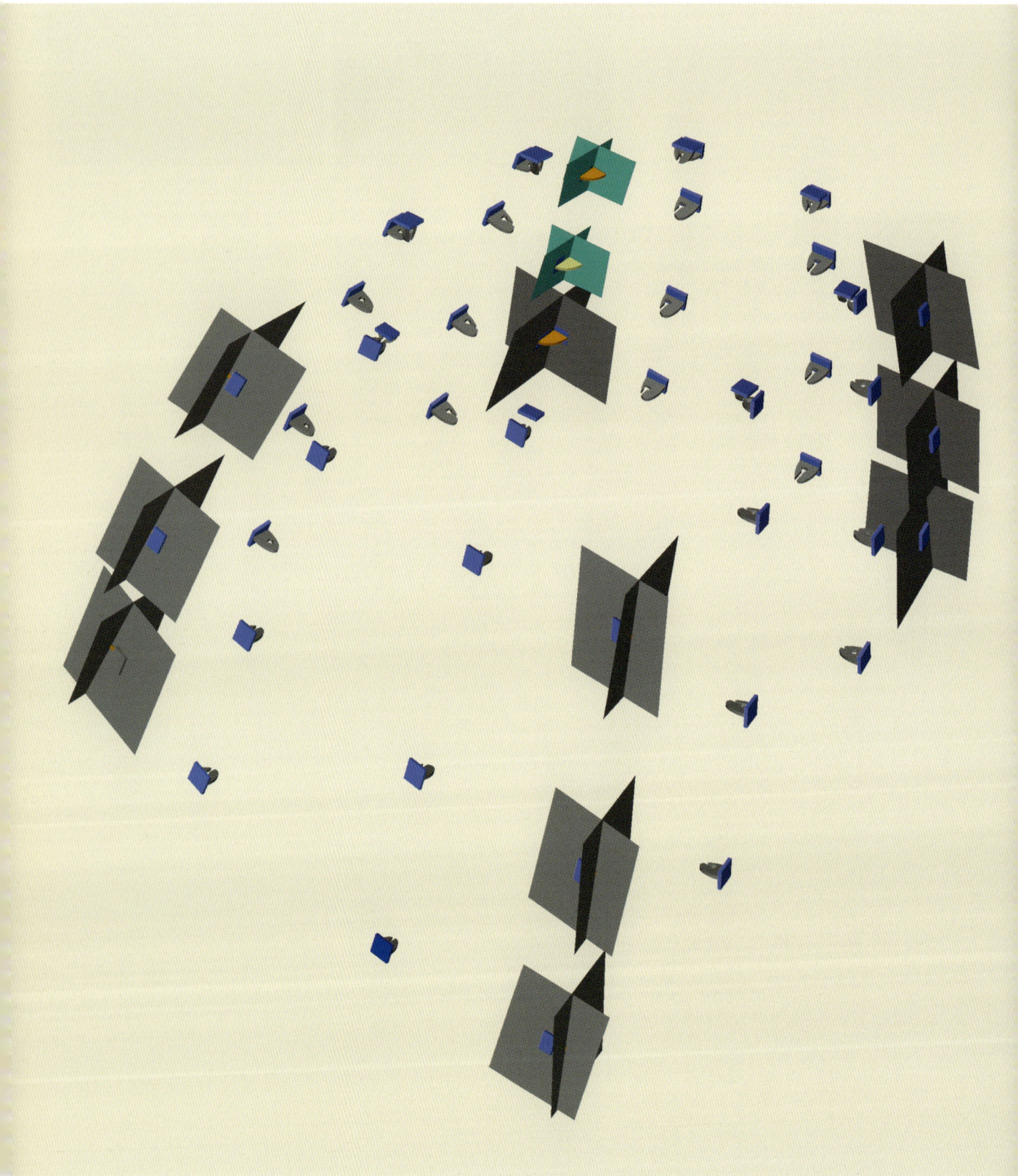

TOWARDS AN ASSOCIATIVE ARCHITECTURE

Bernard Cache

It is Objectile's aim to develop all procedures, both software and hardware, that will make digital architecture a reality at an affordable cost for small architecture practices and average customers. After a series of experiments at the scale of objects, furniture and sculpture, Objectile developed a series of wooden decorative panels as basic building components. Objectile now focuses on small-scale architecture where the current state of the art in software is just starting to make it possible to contemplate a fully digital architecture.

The Semper Pavilion presented in Archilab (1999) was one of the very first pieces of digital architecture where everything from design procedures up to the manufacturing process was generated on the same software platform. Complex interlacings and undulated surfaces were algorithmically generated and then manufactured on a numerical command router down to the very last detail: ie, the control of the tool path which creates the texture on the surfaces. But such a small a piece of architecture required two months' work from the office. Furthermore, it was unclear whether the design of the pavilion would need to be changed, and whether most of the tasks would have to be duplicated, and if so how it could be done without a significant loss of time.

Hence the move towards fully associative design and manufacture, which appears to be the key issue of digital architecture. In an associative architecture, design procedures rely on a limited number of geometrical and numerical parents which can be easily modified and then regenerate the whole design of the building as well as its manufacturing programs. On a limited scale architecture like the Philibert de L'Orme pavilion (presented in Batimat 2001), associativity means to establish a seamless set of relations between a few control points and the 765 machining programs needed to manufacture it on a numerical command router.

Due to the double curvature cladding of a non-orthogonal structure, every single piece is different: the 12 structural elements, the 45 curved panels machined on both sides, as well as the 180 connecting pieces. Already, the automatic naming of the pieces has become an issue. So let us check what was the state of the art at the time of the manufacture of this second pavilion and examine why Objectile keeps on focusing on software development.

Projective Architectural Skeleton

The general architecture of the pavilion is a projective cube whose three sets of ridges are made to converge in the finite space. By moving those three vanishing points, the whole of the pavilion is to be reconfigured down to the very last technical detail. Very much in the same way as Philibert de L'Orme conceived of his famous 'trompes' as a

OPPOSITE **All connecting pieces of the Philibert de L'Orme Pavilion**

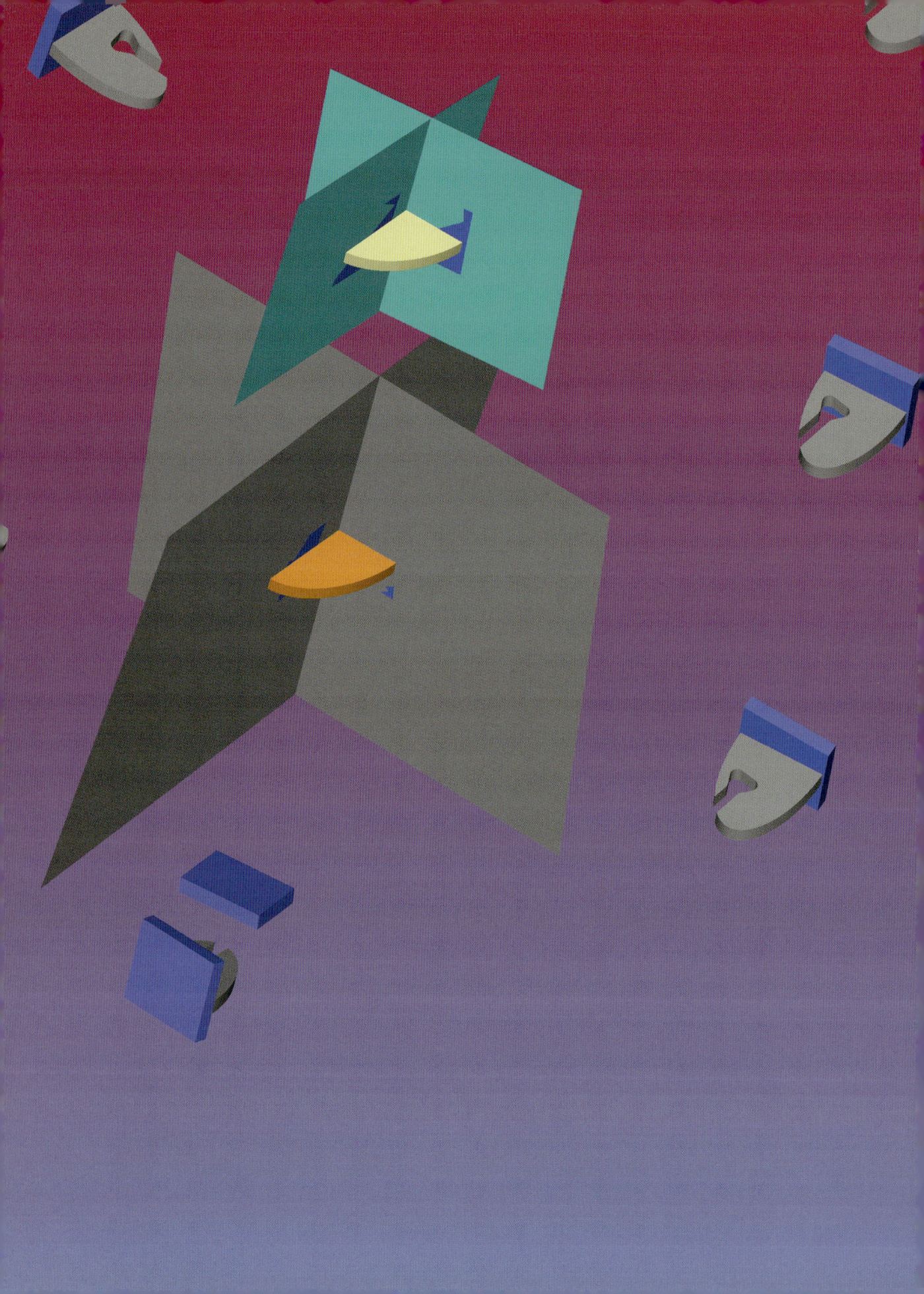

Series of connecting pieces

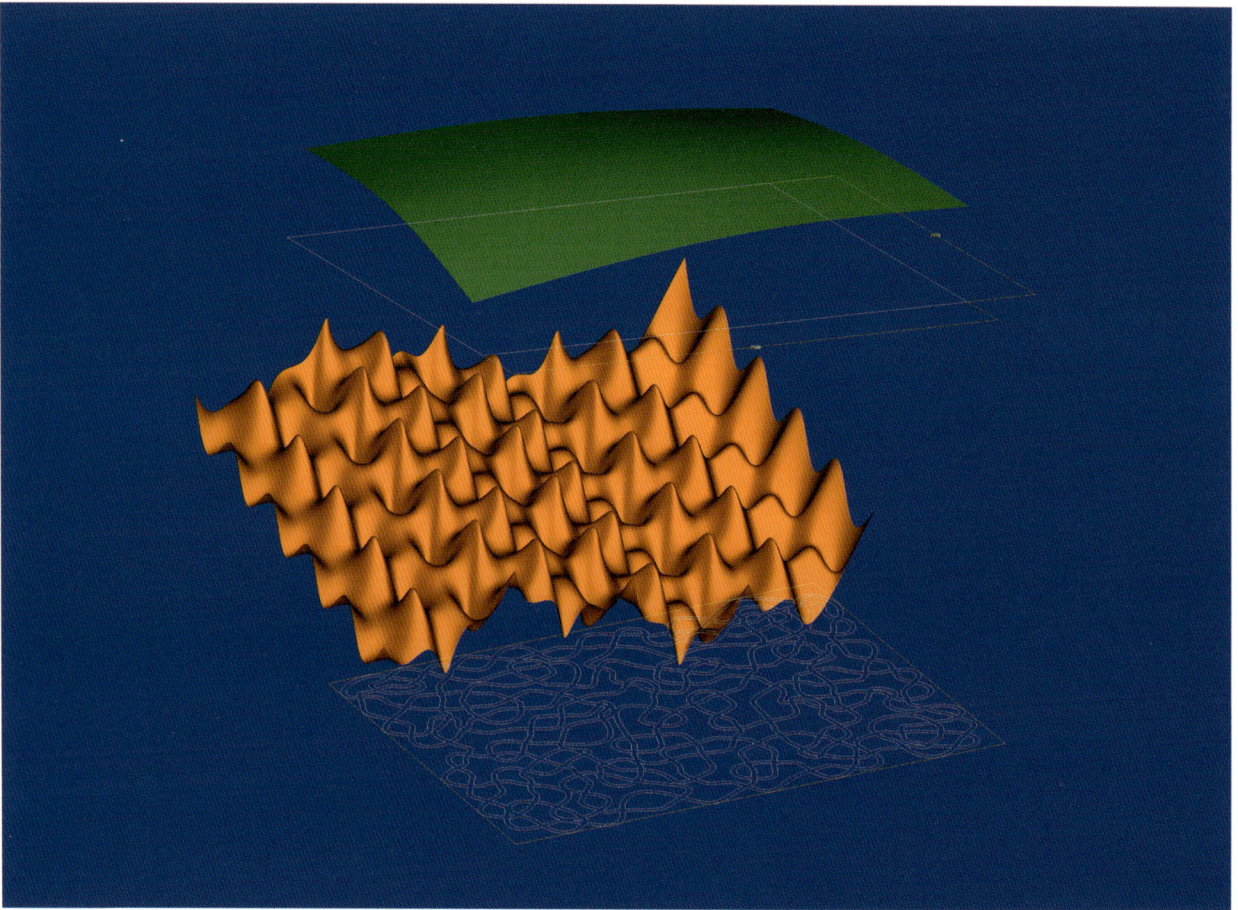

Mapping the interlacing of the Philibert de L'Orme Pavilion

general system of two intersecting conical shapes,[1] this pavilion was designed as a homage to the inventor of stereotomy which would, later on, be systematized by another French architect: Girad Desargues. It is very important to remember that projective geometry has implications much deeper than the Brunelleschian representation, and that its fundamental concepts have yet to be integrated into CAD systems. As a result, the future of the next CAD software generation lies somewhere between 1550 and 1872.

Curvature

Just as a set of parallels is to be considered as a cone whose vertex is a vanishing point, each wall of the pavilion was considered as a plane to be deformed into an ellipsoid tangent to the corresponding plane of the projective cube, defined by its two vanishing points and centred on the third vanishing point. Due to the lack of projective geometry in current CAD software, such a procedure has yet to be implemented. When we designed the pavilion, we just drew an intuitive curvature. We are now close to a mathematical solution based on the principal sections of the ellipsoid. This involves intermediary constructions based on intersecting circles. Whereas two circles might not always intersect as figures in the real plane, they always have two intersection points in the complex space. Unfortunately, current CAD software is not able to take advantage of Poncelet's principle of continuity (1822, Traité des Figures Projectives). Otherwise we would easily deform a standard cube with planar faces into a projective cube with curvy faces. This is only one example of what we can expect from future projective CAD software.

Panelling

Each curved wall is divided into nine panels according to a 3 x 3 grid. Our software enables us to deal with dividing lines which could be of any type. In this pavilion, they were curves resulting from the intersection of the curved surface of the walls with the four structural planes. Given the dividing lines and a series of 23 parameters such as the width of the joints between panels or the diameter of the ball nose toll, the abstract surface of the wall with no thickness is converted into a series of 9 panels, each filed into a directory with a proper name, and automatically oriented the way it has to be positioned on the table of the machine.

One strong hypothesis of the Philibert de L'Orme Pavilion was that each wall was referred to the plane given by the corresponding face of the projective cube. This plane was intended to make things easier by providing a common reference to:

- the table of the machine
- the MDF boards
- the assembly of the rough shape and its two countershapes
- the supports at each of the corners by which the 9 panels were to be connected to the structure
- and, last but not least, the orthogonal plane to the vertical tool of a three-axis router.

This software application has rendered the reference plane unnecessary. Of course everything continues to become more complex, but it is now possible to automatically determine, for each of the panels, the plane which minimizes the initial enclosing block of matter from which the machining operation starts. Not only is the matter required minimized, but all the manual operations required to prepare the rough shape are simplified. This is the way digital architecture should be conceived: concentrate all the complexity in the software and the machining operations, in order to make the manual operations continually fewer and more intuitive. It is important that those two options of a common reference plane or a specific plane that minimizes the enclosing block corresponds to the two traditional techniques of stereotomy: '*la taille par équarissement*' and '*la taille par panneaux*'.

Interlacings

Another strong de L'Ormian feature of the pavilion consists in the interlacings carved into the panels of three of the walls and the roof. One only needs to pay a visit to the church of Saint-Etienne du Mont, 100 metres behind the Pantheon in Paris, to be convinced that Philibert de L'Orme actually built there the most Semperian piece of architecture. Knots and interlacings have been a constant leitmotiv of the French Renaissance architect. Furthermore, if we consider the vocabulary of Desargues's Brouillon project (1638), we are surprised by the continuity between the French order of Philibert de L'Orme – a ringed tree trunk with knots and cut branches – and the basic concepts of the author of the mathematical treatise: trunks, knots, branches, foldings. Everything appears as one: the most contemporary domain of topology, ie knots, coiled into the very origin of projective geometry, anticipating the architecture of geometry that would be clarified by Felix Klein in his Erlangen's Program (1872).

A general knot theory is still lacking that would explain the mathematical entity left invariant throughout the various configurations assumed by the same knot when submitted to deformations. Nevertheless there exists a palette of techniques to generate knots on the basis of graphs. Objectile's application transforms these mathematical techniques into design tools which, for instance, enable the threads' thickness to be varied. Interlacing screens introduce an intermediary state between transparency and opacity and create shallow depth spaces that were already experimented on in many traditions, originally in Islamic architecture, and keep on being worked out by contemporary artists such as Brice Marden. If one is to give faith to the historians arguing that the Modern Movement takes roots in Laugier's writings, the birth of Modern Architecture can be dated from a gesture of demolition: the destruction of the rood-screen within the whitewashed Cathedral of Amiens, recommended by no other than the same Laugier. Transparency is an old and essential myth of modern society which has only taken new forms with information technology.

Panel Machining Programs

Objectile's application is written in order to cope with surfaces of any type of curvature, without any process of standardization, be they spherical, torical or ruled surfaces, swept, etc, not to mention triangulation. As a result, every single panel is to be machined with specific programs for a whole series of 8 operations:

- contour elements in boards
- drill the elements in order to establish a precise positioning of one element on top of the other with dowels
- engrave them in order not to prevent any assembly mistake
- surface the inner face of the panel
- contour the support at each corner of the panel
- surface the outer face of the panel after turning it upside down
- contour the panel
- contour the interlacings.

Since the manufacturing programs (G-code) go directly from the computers in the office to the machine, without additional control by any third party, they must be absolutely error-free. As such, they must be automatically generated. We are currently in the process of rewriting this piece of software in order to refer each panel to the plane that will minimize its enclosing block. The series of operations will then be much more complex because we will have to take into account undercutting situations.

Structure and Connecting Pieces

Because the curvature of the panels is a general architectural problem that leads to a complex manufacturing process, it is obvious that there is no other way to solve it than writing software. Meanwhile, the time needed to draw and generate the programs of the 12 structural elements and the 180 parts needed to connect the panels between themselves and with the structure was largely underestimated. Because of the projective geometry of the pavilion, each of these pieces is different, and their geometry, although planar, has to be built between planes which make constantly varying angles.

Certainly, once each of these pieces was drawn, they were caught within the associative network of relations which, in the last instance, made them dependent on the position of the three vanishing points. To adjust one of those three points would affect the whole geometry of the pavilion down to these very last elements, as well as their machining programs. Some progress has been made in regard to the Semper Pavilion, which achieves a first level associativity. Once the project was finished it could be changed to, and produce, a series of varying pavilions.

But it took us two months to design those 192 pieces. And the whole drawing

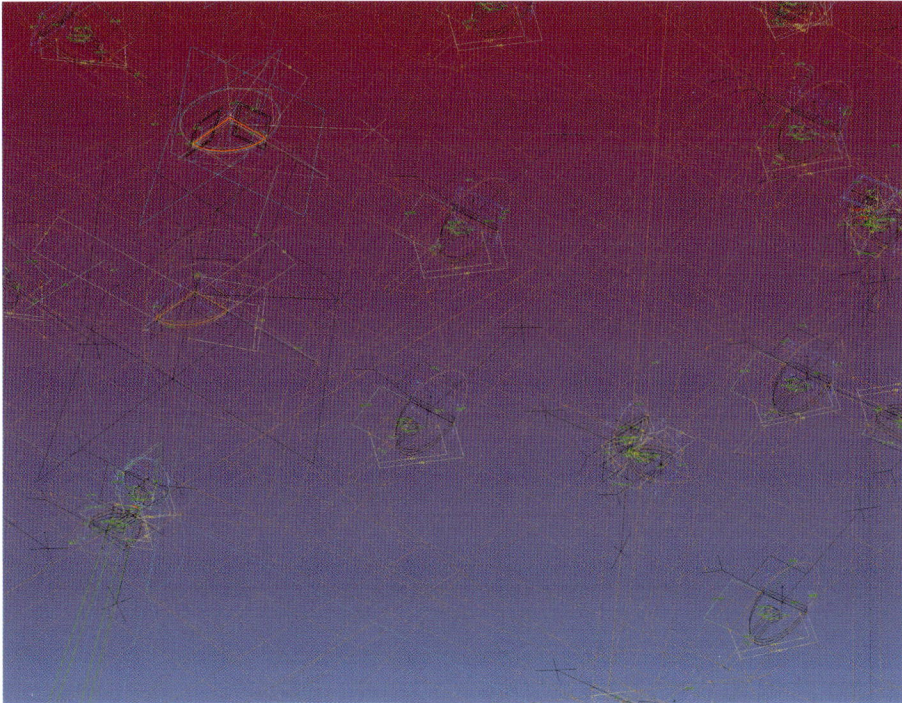

process remains what we should call a manual process because we keep on moving our mouse with our hand. Two months of detailing for a experimental pavilion is no great thing, but imagine the scale of a real building. The design process in itself would need to be automatized, and we cannot have a piece of software written for each type of design problem. The solution consists in the logic of assembly and components, which creates a second level of associativity. Instead of drawing each single piece, we build up a component model which, again, lies upon a limited number of geometrical and numerical elements that we call 'pilots'. Once this model is worked out, we create a component in the project by clicking its corresponding geometric pilots and fine tuning its numerical parameters. But the component is not an isolated geometry; it can be called 'intelligent' because it carries with it a series of tools and processes which allows the component to interact with the surrounding parts and to generate their machining process.

Geometry of connecting pieces

Digital Architecture

What is digital architecture? Concerning the shapes of the buildings themselves, the answer is that we don't know. The future of architecture is unreadable, and contemporary free forms are called into considerable question when they become a cliché and sacrifice the past to the advantage of an absolute present. Marketing strategy is the new form of tyranny but information technology can only appear as a *deus ex machina* if it succeeds in having us forget its own history. It is hoped that the above explanations will convince that digital technologies jeopardise the architecture of information underlying building and that this architecture with digits also needs to be designed. This is the task on which Objectile is currently focusing.

Notes
1 Philippe Potié, *Philibert de L'Orme, Figures du projet*, Marseille, 1996.

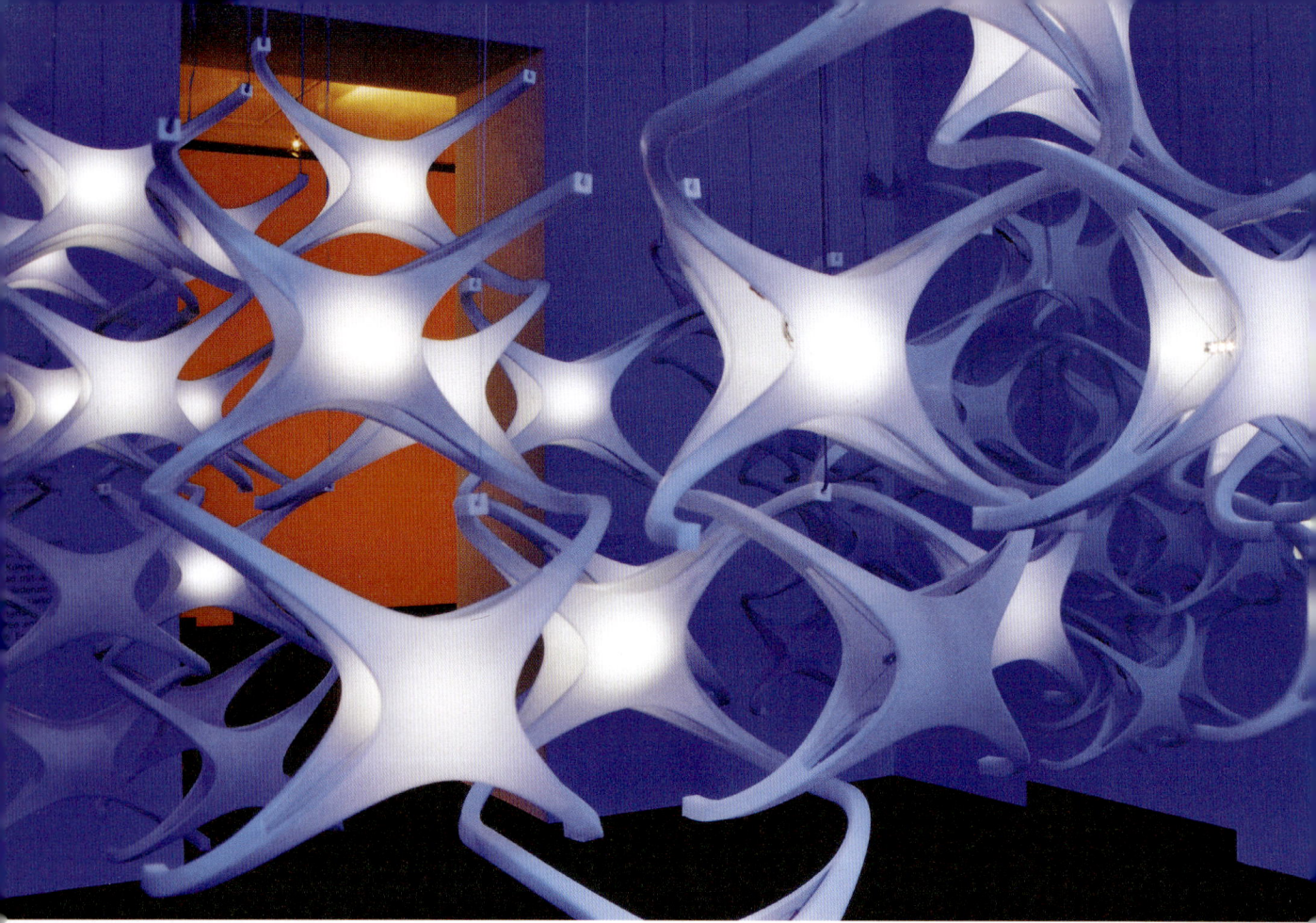

LATTICE ARCHIPELOGICS

Marcelyn Gow, David Erdman, Chris Perry (SERVO)

To render the development of a movement visible as a dynamic state is a significant action. It is not a matter of routine but fertile in its repetition, in its very monotony . . . Uecker [1]

Digital tectonics presupposes the synthesis of multiple entities. In the installation *Lattice Archipelogics* the multiple is understood in terms of *inertia*, where material manifestations of static elements yield a type of modularity that is coupled with an iterative *locomotion* or dynamics.[2] Commissioned for the exhibition Latent Utopias in Steirischer Herbst, Graz, 2002, the project was developed as a collaboration between **servo** [Los Angeles, Zürich, Stockholm and New York] and **smart studio** [of the Interactive Institute in Stockholm]. Punctuated by moments of algorithmic inertia and locomotion, Lattice Archipelogics conflates machinic and computational modes of performance with the production of a diffused atmospheric.

In the context of this project archipelogics is defined as a viscous register of the dynamic coming into conjunction with the inert, of the intertwining of fluid and solid, of particulate matter on an array of scales, of Virilio's 'grey ecology of archipelagos of cities interconnected and intelligent', and of the cumulative redundancy of movement where locomotion opposes itself to inertia or the sedentary.[3] Conceptually it occupies the convergence of two trajectories, the machinic and the atmospheric. The coupling of the machine and the atmospheric, compounded by the influence of the computational, is relevant to architectural production and practice, as these modes of operation are ubiquitous in the contemporary environment of social interactions from the urban to the individual scale. One technique whereby this coupling or interlacing of the machinic and the atmospheric occurs involves the use of computational processes. The product of numerically controlled calculation at a micro-scale, these processes can be aggregated at a macro-scale to induce stochastic permutations by incorporating external influences.

In the historical resumé of collective endeavors utilizing machinic processes for the fabrication of small-scale *environments* the atmospheric, as the instantiation of the piece, has frequently occupied a privileged position in respect to the machinic, as the means of production. The machinic aspects of fabrication are subsumed in many cases by the phenomenon which they produce. Within this architectural and art historical legacy an *environment* could be considered as something which synthesizes both formal and programmatic systems, machinic processes and atmospheric effects. The potential of the respective technologies which form these systems, processes and effects is an interlacing, a fusion or tectonic which situates the machinic as both a

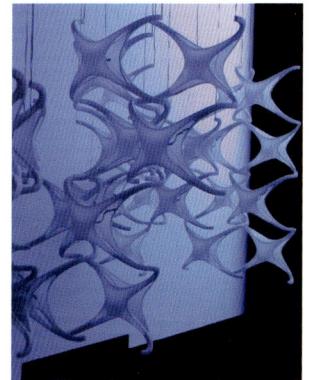

Installation views of *Lattice Archipelogics*, Latent Utopias, Steirischer Herbst, Graz, 2002

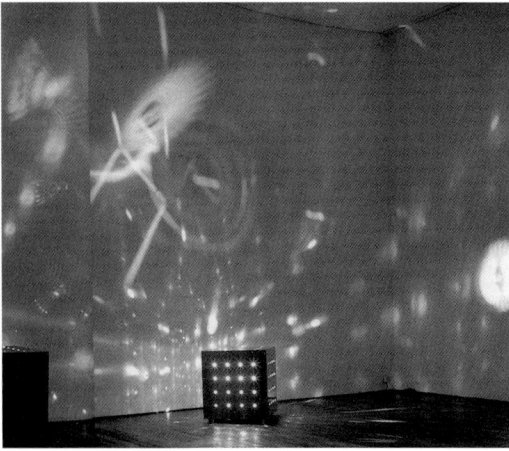

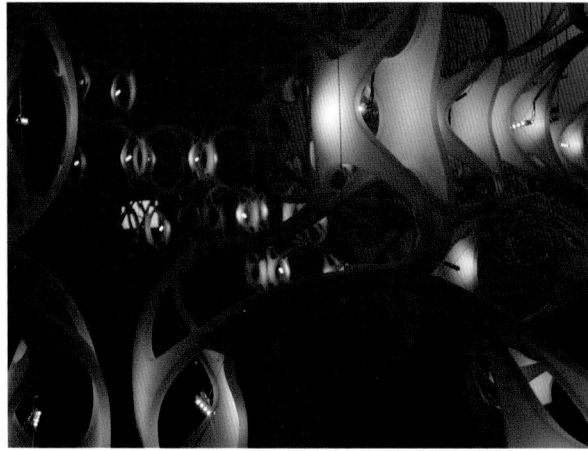

View of Otto Piene's Lichtballet 1972–2000, from Light Pieces, Casino Luxembourg, Luxembourg, 2000

Installation view of *Lattice Archipelogics*, Latent Utopias, Steirischer Herbst, Graz 2002[9]

method of production and communication. Because these machinic technologies begin to speak to one another, information can be translated fluidly across them, and imported into the system, producing an open circuit.

Cyber-technological Inscriptions

A dialogue between the machinic and the atmospheric is evident with regard to several projects that emerged from design collaboratives in the 1960s, each involved with the ephemeral optical phenomena of light. Otto Piene's *Mechanical Light Ballet*, Heinz Mack's *White Light Dynamo* and *Light Veil* from the Zero group and Superstudio's *Passiflora* are all projects that engage in the theorization and the production of environments and in the industrial design of products. These projects point to the separation of the machinic and the atmospheric, yet open the possible understanding of their combinatory logic as a broader tectonic. Within this work two directions emerged regarding the machined production of environments and the potential synthesis of light and the machinic. The environments of the Zero group, for instance, used machines to spatialize effects of light and sound, whereas Superstudio's *Passiflora* used machinic production to address issues of communication and popular culture.

The light installations *Mechanical Light Ballet, White Light Dynamo* and *Light Veil* developed by Zero in the early 1960s suggest a preoccupation with atmospheric phenomena. This tendency can be theorized with regard to the role of manufactured machinic elements and their relation to atmospheric fluxes. These installations perform as spatialized, machinic drawings where the act of environmental-scale *rendering* is a visual effect produced by the machine. Conceiving of early versions of sensors, using a combination of electronics and timers, these installations were incipient forms of numerically controlled spatial computing. A contemporary corollary to these installations would be viewing the process of computerized rendering or visualization from within the digital apparatus.

In 'Viva Zero',his introductory essay to the Zero group catalogue Lawrence Alloway points out the defaults of the systemic, articulating the tendency of these luminous environments to work from a notion of modularity: 'Zero's solution of the problem was to work within a system that can contain divergent contributions, among them light play and repetitive form.'[4] Mechanically controlled elements, often in the form of rotating perforated metal disks, proliferate in Zero member Otto Piene's mechanical light environments of the 1960s. His piece *Mechanical Light Ballet* (1960) used mechanically generated rhythmic vibration in order to channel light. The projected light ultimately functioned as an index of this vibration. Vibration in this case could be considered a transmitter of both image and energy; the mechanical acted as an enabling device for the projected light field. Zero member Heinz Mack's work *White Light Dynamo* of 1958 [screened oscillations generated by the rotation of glass disks behind plates of corrugated glass] and the suspended *Light Veil*, published in the *Zero* magazine [inflected aluminum sheets organized with geometric precision for reflective purposes] took the idea of environmental-scale *rendering* further by attempting to dematerialize the inert materiality of the environment as the carrier and distributor of light.[5] In this work light was used to organize spatial attributes and qualities, whereas the machinic properties acted as an enabling device which filtered light emissions.

Micro-environmental Landscape

Superstudio, on the other hand, cultivated an eschewal of the context for conventionally designed industrial products through the concept of the *Microenvironment*.[6] Domestic products were endowed with the potential to create environmental effects, and conceptualized as entities that could be part of a more extensive landscape. Design for the *Microenvironment* no longer addressed singular elements, rather cross programmatic issues were introduced via multiple technologies. In the design of the *Passiflora* lamp, a *Microenvironment* object for The New Domestic Landscape exhibition, electronics and industrial fabrication were rethought on a spatial scale through the positioning of light in combination with the appliance. The practice of design according to functional or ergonomic parameters came under scrutiny through The New Domestic Landscape exhibition raising questions regarding the capacity of industrial design to perform as a vehicle of communication. At this juncture, the design of *Passiflora* reconstituted the role of machined form in relation to programmatic concerns. The lamp is a cluster of plastic extrusions, particulate light confined by the strictures of machinic production. Emerging obliquely from, and thus severed by, the floor plane on which it rested, *Passiflora* used eccentricities of grounding in order to present an inversion of spatial order. The convention of overhead illumination was jettisoned by positioning the lamp as an obstacle to pedestrian circulation, stimulating alternate paths of movement in the domestic space. This machine-manufactured appliance suggested an alternate program for industrial design, one that merged discrete objects with the space of environments, reconfiguring the *domestic landscape.*

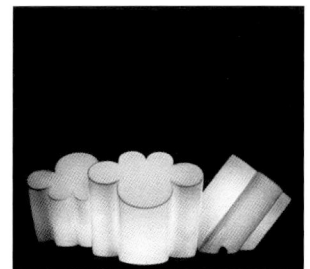

Passiflora lamp by Superstudio

The relationship between the spatial production and the programmatic implementation of these *environments* is crucial to an understanding of the extent to which machine technologies and atmospheric effects were synthesized in this work. The light installations of Zero dealt with the environment as a drawing, incorporating light effects and animation, whereas Superstudio produced objects which were integral to the domestic environment, implying the synthesis of programmatic relations with machinic fabrication.

Algo–rhythmic Environment

Servo's research on the fusion of atmospherics, machinic processes of fabrication, and computational modes of performance involves developing techniques which register and synthesize the effects of particular technologies. Sites which allow for modulation are scripted either solely in a computational context or produced as a combination of

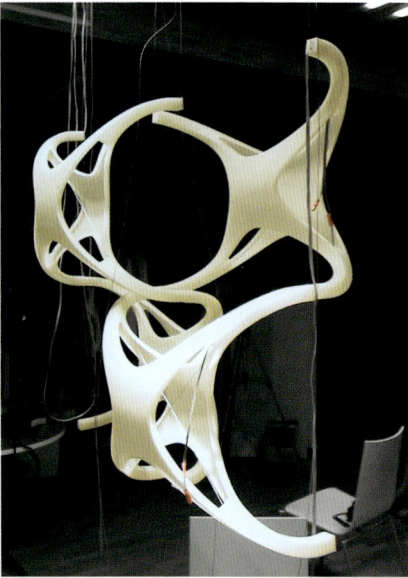

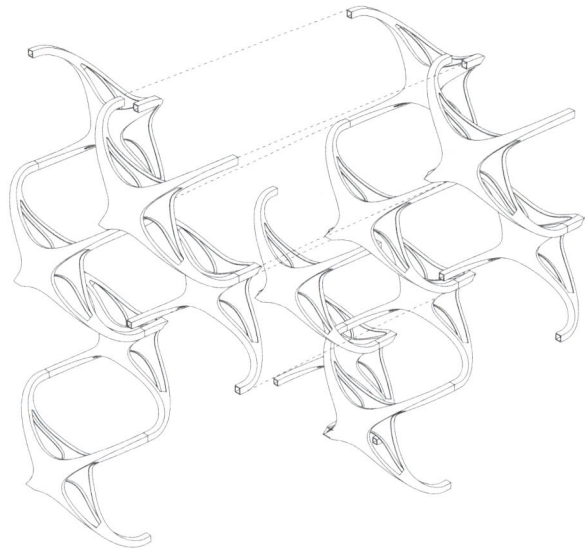

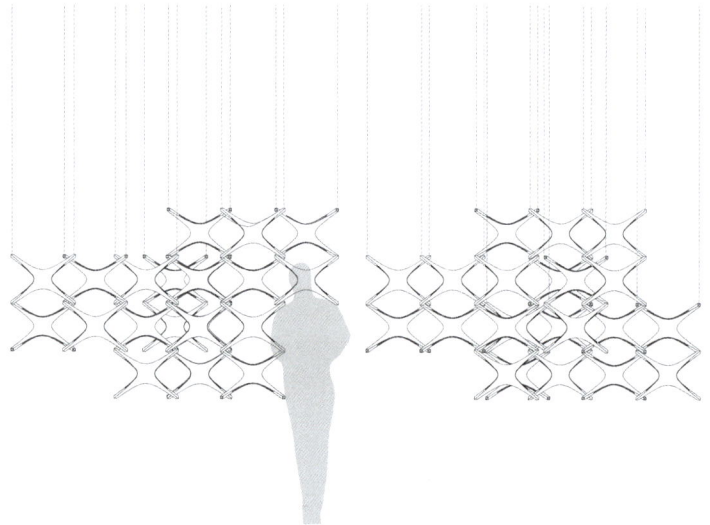

LEFT to RIGHT
**Staging view of three lattice cells at the
Interactive Institute, Stockholm**

Module assembly diagram for lattice cells

Elevation of two clusters of lattice cells

machinically fabricated environments which are mediated by a computational field of influences. These environments combine the atmospheric, the machinic and the communicative through the formulation of a physically modulated, programmed space.

Lattice Archipelogics operates as a scripting device or responsive software in which its machinic and cyber-technological attributes are precisely those which are registered through the atmospheric qualities of the piece. The project produces a digital tectonic through *elasticity* and *inscription* or spatialized drawing. Both of these operate at the scale of computational fabrication and its spatial choreography. The convention of a drawing table as the locus of calculation and design is replaced in this project by a *drawing room* as the locus of a latent cyber-technological inscription.[7] This *drawing room* is an environment which explores the reproduction of a single module with structural attributes that could link together to form a larger physical, computational and programmatic environment. This is accomplished by using sensory activated light and sound and manipulating the existing axis of the gallery space. An archive of recorded movement patterns is generated as the gallery space is populated. This is a factor not only locating bodies in space moreover it is an index of a series of social interactions which are

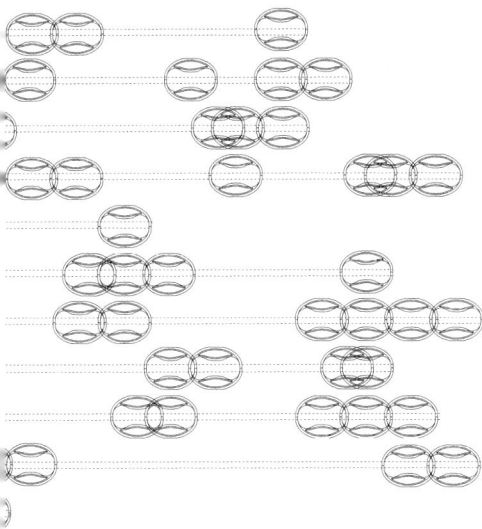

LEFT to RIGHT
Plan of schematic layout for lattice cells

Drawing of clustered lattice cells for Latent Utopias, Steirischer Herbst, Graz, 2002

Staging view of lattice cells for sensors and lighting at the Interactive Institute, Stockholm

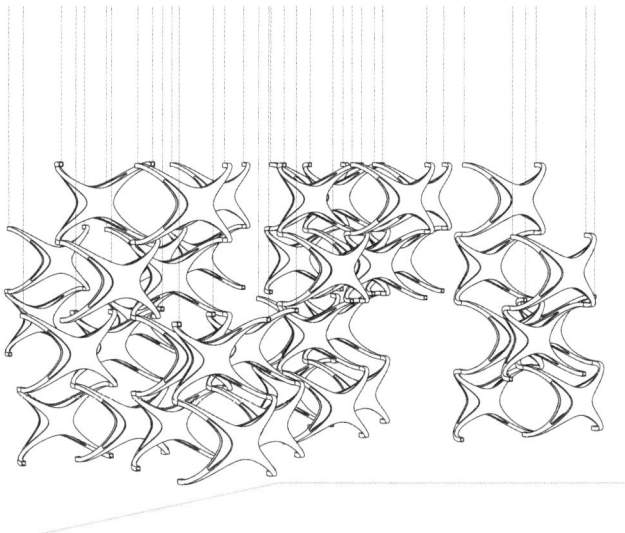

influenced by the organization of the plastic cells, creating a series of pathways and corridors. These patterns are recorded and sometimes replayed by *virtual agents*.[8]

The installation is comprised of translucent plastically deformed lattice cells and sound samples that are designed to undergo elastic deformations. The lattice cells house a series of LED illuminators which act as clustered *particulate matter*. On a macro-scale these cells form an archipelago of suspended luminous islands, on a micro-scale this *particulate matter* instantiates itself as regions of diffused light passing through the individual translucent plastic lattice cells. These luminous lattice cells are interwoven with a matrix of proximity sensors producing a dynamically responsive field. The lattice cells operate as a porous illumination device where the light levels produced at any given moment are dependent upon the number of individual elements which are illuminated. Coupled with sound, various densities of *atmosphere* are moved through the space. This archipelago of sound, and light, and its potential for dynamic modulation deals with a series of phase shifts. Conceptually the notion of *materiality shift*, for instance between solidity and fluidity, is conceived in terms of fabrication techniques, computation and programming.

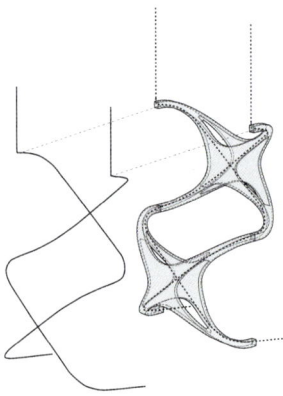

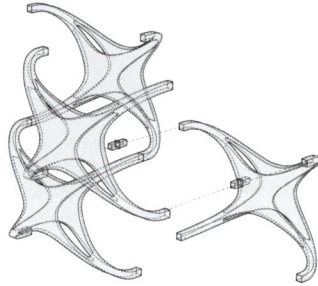

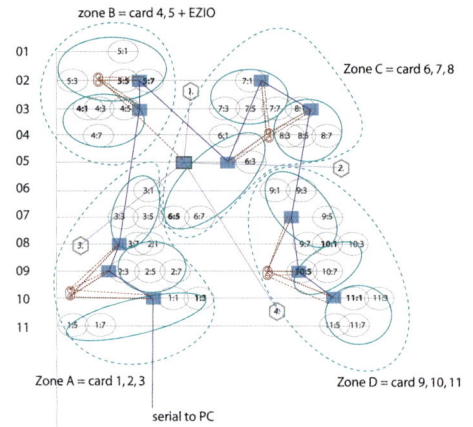

zone B = card 4, 5 + EZIO

Zone C = card 6, 7, 8

Zone A = card 1, 2, 3

Zone D = card 9, 10, 11

serial to PC

LEFT to RIGHT

Wiring diagram and joint detail for lattice cells

Diagram of the responsive field of *Lattice Archipelogics* designed by smart studio/Interactive Institute, Stockholm [incorporating sensors, lattice cells, and electrical wiring]

On a micro-scale, lattice cells are manufactured by a computational tectonic of digits manifested as a code which motivates the trajectory of stereo-lasers through a vat of fluid resin producing a deposition of sections; a sediment. Stereolithography is, in a sense, drawing materialized machinically. This *materialized drawing* at the scale of individual lattice elements is coupled with a sequence of *performative drawings*, activated by perambulation as a series of large-scale inscriptions in the space of *Lattice Archipelogics*. The *drawing* in this case is rendered as a web of sinuous edges of plastically deformed elements momentarily illuminated and then subsiding into the monotone particulate haze, an effervescent modularity. This cyber-technological inscription is reflexive, cataloguing and proliferating itself. The binary characteristics of an *algo-rhythmic* logic provides the impetus for the drawing.[9] In this manifold of interactive algorithms, drawing becomes a programmatic. Rhythm, generated by bodily motion and registered by *virtual agents*, becomes instrumental in shaping the spatial atmosphere. A three-dimensional luminous drawing resonant with sound is sketched by visitors through their bodily manipulation of the digital interface.

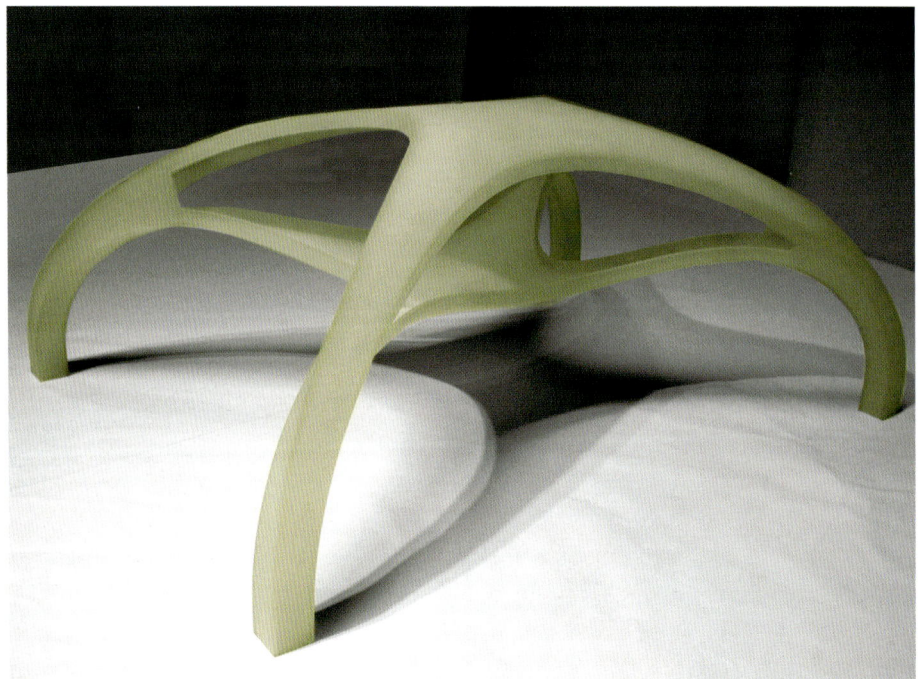

Stereolithography prototype of module [25 cm x 42 cm] for lattice cells

The inertia of the manufactured archipelago couples with *digital locomotion* whereby these virtual agents migrate or literally walk through the archipelago forming luminous deposits. This technique of digital locomotion results from the constellation of digital programming and its spatial organization which creates an algo_rhythmic interface. A dual inscription is motivated by the trajectories inscribed by occupants of the space, drawing the virtual agents through the lattice archipelago, tracing a complex negotiation of simultaneous influences. Beginning with a latent field, the movements that occur over a period of time through the archipelago are sampled, recognized as patterns, and attached to light and sound transformations in the field of lattice cells. The cumulative redundancy of these physical movements informs the sedentary state of the lattice archipelago. When left in its inert state it will sample from the catalogue of stored movement patterns to repeatedly perform them. The inscription is continuously rewritten by the locomotion of bodies in space, the trajectories of the moving digital agents and the successive transmission of light in the lattice cells. *Lattice Archipelogics* is a space where movement is subsumed by proximity, and proximity in turn generates trajectories of movement. The physical instantiation of the archipelago as a sinuous route of path systems informs this relationship between trajectories of movement and the stimuli of proximity.

Staging view of lattice cells for sensors and lighting at the Interactive Institute, Stockholm

Another aspect of digital tectonics involves the creation of a more extensive landscape imbued with shifts of materiality on a macro-scale. The lattice cell as a physical module aggregates in multiple to produce a spatial rendering. On a performative level this drawing is a self-proliferating synthesis of the capacities of the machinic combined with a programmatic input; reconfiguration of the gallery space. On a material level the drawing is an elastic fabrication or an elasticized modularity transforming the static characteristics of repetitive prefabrication. Lattice cells are designed with an inherent formal flexibility which allows for them to be manipulated according to a series of constraints producing cells that are compatible with adjacent modules. The properties of fabrication materials are considered *elasticized* by selecting a particular fabrication technique where a three-phase transformation between states of solidity and fluidity occurs: the stereolithographic prototyping of the initial form, silicone rubber casting of a negative mould, and ultimately vacuum casting of plastic for the manufactured components. The amber translucency of the stereolithographic prototype is exchanged for the particulate grain of vacuum-cast plastic, the fragility of the silicone mould mediates the flow of heated plastic cooled into a higher degree of stability and the coupling of lattice cells inscribes a sinuous path. This shifting of performance and program through various phases and scales of materialization, manifested in one instance as a fluid algorithmic, in another as inert substance endowed with effervescent properties, produces a tectonic alluding to the complex dynamics of archipelogics.

Instantiations of the machinic, as nascent spatial renderings within the ephemeral luminous environments of the Zero group or within Superstudio's *microenvironmental* grafting of program to the techniques of fabrication, allude to the potential for weaving a more synthetic set of digital tectonics. The aggregation of micro-scale computational techniques is perhaps inseparable from an informed programmatic scale. The elastic drawing room, a luminous digital sketching tool, created in *Lattice Archipelogics* can be contextualized relative to this trajectory, emerging as an effervescent, algo–rhythmic modularity.

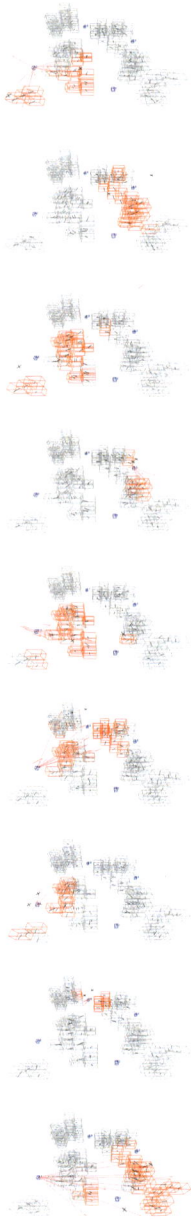

Diagram outlining trajectories of the virtual agents through the lattice cells in the responsive field of *Lattice Archipelogics*, designed by smart studio/Interactive Institute, Stockholm

Notes

1 Otto Piene and Heinz Mack, *Zero,* originally published in Germany in 1958 and 1961 (Cambridge, Mass: MIT Press, 1973), vol 3 of reprinted compilation, p. 220.
2 The installation *Lattice Archipelogics* was produced as a collaboration between **servo** (David Erdman, Marcelyn Gow, Ulrika Karlsson, Chris Perry design team: Daniel Norell, Clare Olsen, Jonas Runberger and **smart studio** (Interactive Institute, Stockholm: Ingvar Sjöberg, Olof Bendt, Magnus Jonsson, Pablo Miranda, Fredrik Petersson, Tobi Schneidler). Special thanks: Steirischer Herbst, IASPIS (International Artists' Studio Program in Sweden), KTH, Caran, White Arkitekter, SSARK Media Lab. The exhibition Latent Utopias, curated by Zaha Hadid and Patrik Schumacher, took place in the Landesmuseum Joanneum, Steirischer Herbst, Graz, 2002.
3 Paul Virilio, *Open Sky* (London: Verso, 1997), p. 59.
4 Lawrence Alloway, 'Viva Zero' in Otto Piene and Heinz Mack, *op cit, p*p.ix–xiii.
5 Ibid., pp.166–7, 189, 199. The *Light Veil* and *White Light Dynamo* of Heinz Mack and Otto Piene's *Chromatic Light Ballet* appear in *Otto* Piene and Heinz Mack, op cit. Piene's *Mechanical Light Ballet*

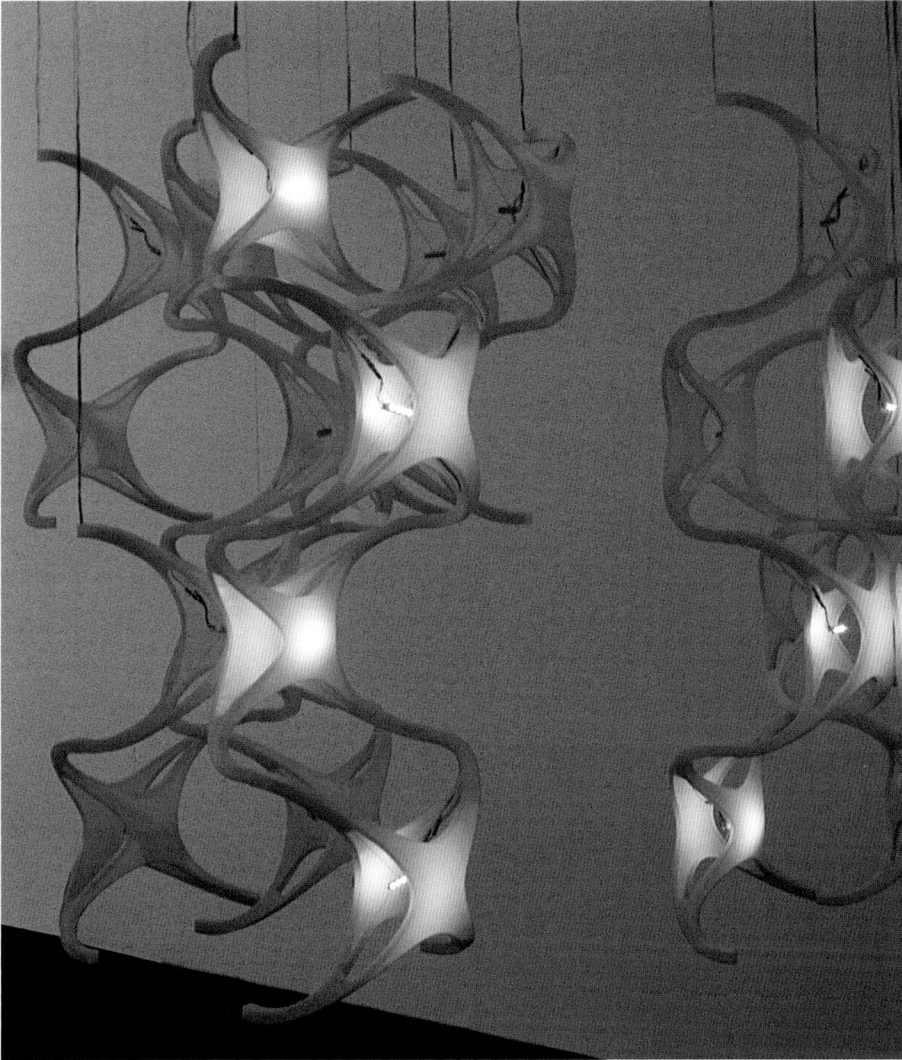

Installation view of *Lattice Archipelogics*, Latent Utopias, Steirischer Herbst, Graz, 2002

appears in *Heinz Mack, Otto Piene, Günther Uecker* (Hanover: Kestner-Gesellschaft, 1965), p.137.

6 The *Microenvironment* is a term given by Superstudio to a series of installations one of which included the *Passiflora* lamp in the exhibition Italy: The New Domestic Landscape curated by Emilio Ambasz at MOMA in 1972. Emilio Ambasz (ed), *Italy: The New Domestic Landscape* (New York: The Museum of Modern Art, 1972), pp. 100, 240–51.

7 The term 'cyber-technological' is coined from Margarida Santos in 'Otto Piene' in *Light Pieces* (Luxembourg: Casino Luxembourg, 2000), p. 59.

8 The responsive field of *Lattice Archipelogics* was designed by the **smart studio**, Interactive Institute, *Stockholm*: Ingvar Sjöberg, Olof Bendt, Magnus Jonsson, Pablo Miranda, Fredrik Petersson, Tobi Schneidler. 'Virtual agents' is the term given by **smart studio** to the active components of the software. They are defined as basic 'activity tropistic' automata, which react to the activity levels reported by the sensors, as well as to the information stored in the lattice cells.

9 The term algo-rhythmic refers to algorithmically generated feedback loops which produce rhythmic patterns..

TOP **Extraterrains at Kiasma - Museum of Contemporary Art at the ARS01 exhibition**
RIGHT **View of the Formations Installation at the Trussardi Foundation in Milan**

ARE WE READY TO COMPUTE?

Michael Hensel (OCEAN North)

Where Object and Subject touch, there is life.[1]
Johann Wolfgang von Goethe

The title of this publication – *digital tectonics* – suggests the possibility of a decisive move away from the current hype about 'the digital' that so often results in the pointless dichotomy between digital and analogue design and a careless neglect of their respective repercussions. Such a move could give way to a rigorous empirical design-based research that aims at investigating spatialities, conditions and effects produced by digital design – in tandem with the analogue spectrum of design techniques available to architecture and design and how the conditions produced effect our human social and cultural environment. The point is that a productive discourse on *digital tectonics* needs to emphasise material formations in relation to inevitably yielded cultural, social and political formations. It is important to investigate the facilitating aspect of digital technology as an integrated segment of a larger generative and design-process facilitating tool-set through which social and cultural formations might be provoked. In doing so the design process moves again into the foreground of attention, not so much because of a self-indulgent fascination with new hard and software and peripheral gadgetry, but instead with respect to developing instrumental design techniques that can serve to inject performative potential into the built environment. Indeed, as design techniques yield specific sets of conditions and effects, computational methods add to the broad scope of analogue modelling and design techniques, so as to inform interventions that engage the relational dynamic between the built environment and its inhabitants.

The hypothesis that underlies the following design-based research is that the relational dynamic between object and subject, environment and inhabitants establishes a potential space in which social and cultural experience can be located. A useful inroad to this notion is given by Umberto Eco's concept of *open works*.[2] Eco described an open work as characterised by a deliberate *ambiguity* in meaning. According to Eco, *open works* must leave the arrangement of some of their constituents to the public or to chance, thus giving these works a field of possible orders rather than a single definite one. The subject can move freely within this articulated yet ambiguous field of possibilities, which serves to avoid conventional forms of expression and prescribed interpretation. At the same time Eco points out that this is not a quest for a total laissez-faire and amorphousness, but rather that there must be a guiding directive from the designer that structures the field of possibilities in some way for the subject. While the notion of an *operative ambiguity* has been extensively pursued in dance, film and music it has remained a rather exotic notion in architecture,[3] as architecture as a control-driven

LEFT **Orca furniture piece as part of the Formations Installation**
RIGHT **Studies for the dynamic light installation on the basis of the digital 3d model**

discipline seems to be diametrically opposed to the contingent influences and generative openness and open-ended-ness suggested by the concept of *open works*. Consequently, the question comes up of whether it is possible to devise design strategies and methods which can inform inclusive design processes that provoke social and cultural formation from within the relational dynamic between built environment and its inhabitants.

Since 1998 OCEAN North has pursued the notion of a relational dynamic between the built environment and the human subject through computational and analogue modulation and articulation of material geometries and effects. An early example is the *Extraterrain* furniture project [1996], which aimed at charging a simple material surface with potential for habitation and social formations, while at the same time avoiding indications of an object-specific proper use. Various sectional geometries were digitally sampled and lofted into a non-decomposable surface in order to arrive at an abstract composite geometry free of references to any existing furniture types. Computational modelling enabled the rapid re-assemblage of the sampled geometries with the aim to build ergonomic capacity into the surface geometry. The finished piece was tested in various social events towards emergent pattern social arrangements. Unlike the soft-surface environments of the sixties and seventies, Extraterrain is made of a hard glass-fibre surface. This implies that the human body needs to adapt to the surface of the object, necessitating frequent repositioning of the body on the piece in order to seek comfortable positions. From the need for repositioning arises the need for negotiating the surface area with other occupants. The large size of the piece that enables co-occupation, together with the lack of subdivisions of the surface area into individually assigned zones, yield a need for ongoing territorial negotiations. The way the surface might then be occupied depends on the individual user's characteristics – age, weight, size, etc. and the readiness to discover ways to occupy the piece. This leads to ways of finding body positions in which the surface geometry of the object might be ergonomically suitable with respect to common sitting positions, or how new body positions might be assumed relative to the surface articulation. Geometry and positioning trigger in this way incidental individual use, with the array of individual use accumulating to collective interaction. The latter constitutes an unfolding field for social interaction that is yielded by the geometric and material articulation of the surface.

The *Formations* project [commissioned by the Fondazione Nicola Trussardi, Milan, 2002] was based on a synergetic approach that combines spatial design as an interior and installation project with furniture and product design. Responding to the theme of the *Nature* – a series of exhibitions at Trussardi Gallery – the *Formations* project drew its concept from the dynamic geo-morphological processes that shape topographic surfaces. The project consists of an architectural installation that articulates the space of the showroom, with furniture and products integrated into the spatial and formal arrangement of the installation. Two sets of horizontal surfaces, some flat and some undulating, are suspended from the ceiling and raised from the floor. They articulate a fluid spatial movement that guides the eye and yields the motion of the visitors through the space of the gallery. Integrated furniture pieces follow the same spatial movement and formal logic. All undulating surfaces were produced through CNC-milling. The primary articulation of the space follows the logic of the *Extraterrains* project in forming a programmatically un-prescriptive inhabitable interior landscape. Secondary articulation leads to objects that are nested within the surfaces. Their articulation enables the appropriation and adaptation of the object family into tableware, lighting devices and generic containers for storage of varied content. Extensive digital [CAD-CAM] and analogue [full-scale prototypes] modelling was used in order to arrive at a highly varied yet coherent articulation of the material surfaces that together make up the project. Displacement mapping of image textures were transferred into digital models that were directly CNC-milled or rapid prototyped, which opens up a new realm of possibilities where the modulation across all geometrical scales is both coherent and finally implemented in direct physical output. Rapid manufacturing then becomes an instrumental resource for the immediate testing of designs in the respective context and in direct exchange with the human subject.

AGORA was a sound-active experiential installation by Natasha Barrett and OCEAN North along a pedestrian bridge in Oslo Central Station [2002] that transcended the artificial dichotomy between auditory and architectural space. AGORA consists of five large surfaces and 150 meters of aluminium tubes, a slowly changing sound composition projected over eight loudspeakers located above, and four loudspeakers below the bridge, live electronics that turn membranes and aluminium bars into computer controlled acoustic instruments and an infra-red sensor that monitored the movement of people on the bridge as a control for the live electronics. The installation spread above, below and around a bridge, in the centre of the main departure hall at the Oslo Central Station and could be experienced by moving around and through the physical structure, by standing in the centre of the eight loudspeakers above the bridge, or by briefly sampling the space on each journey through the station.

The Agora project constituted a music-theatre work where sound, physical construction and live performance unfolded a differential experiential space that can be perceived en route as an intensified locality within the larger space of the station.

OVERLEAF

View of the sound-active Agora Installation at Oslo Central Station

PROJECT CREDITS

AGORA: Boundary Conditions
Location Oslo Central Station, Oslo, Norway
Project Type Interactive Sound Installation
Date 2001-02
Collaborators Natasha Barrett and OCEAN NORTH

Composition and Programming
Natasha Barrett
OCEAN NORTH
Birger Sevaldson, Tuuli Sotamaa, Michael Hensel

Project Members
Øyvind Hammer, Are Nielsen, Markus Høy-Pedersen, Hanne Marte Holmøy, Ambjørn Viking, Sylvia LeSoil, Heidi Leren, Dan Sevaldson, Svein Berge

Production
Rom for Kunst: Mesén as
Rigging

All Productions, Håkon Klemtsen
Formations Installation
Client Fondazione Nicola Trussardi
Location Milan Italy
Project Type Architectural Installation, Furniture and Product Design
Date 2002

OCEAN NORTH
Kivi Sotamaa, Tuuli Sotamaa, Birger Sevaldson
Project Members
Lasse Ira, Duncan Lamb, Are Nielsen, Laura Pokela, Marjukka Makela, Emilie Olivero
Sound Petri Kuljuntausta
Light Installation Reinier Van Brummeln
Material Consultant Petri Ryöppy / Kiasma Museum of Contemporary Art

Extraterrains
Project Type Furniture Design
Date 1996
OCEAN NORTH
Markus Holmstén, Kivi Sotamaa

A loudspeaker orchestra comprising twelve loudspeakers allowed the *spatialisation* of sound such that sound-fields, sound-masses, spaces and motion lines or trajectories, could be accurately located in space and perceived by the audience. *Sound spatialisation* was implemented by means of *ambisonic spatialisation*, which is a method based on flat sound waves and the encoding and decoding of sound fields and sound trajectories that can be accurately located in space. The technique can be regarded as a sound analogy to holography. *Multi-speaker sound diffusion* allowed it to take a stereo input signal and re-route it over a number of loudspeakers. The *live electronics* consisted of eight membranes that were vibrated by actuators, each connected to an amplifier and given a computer controlled audio input, as well as 6 aluminium tubes that were struck by computer-controlled hammers. Their design consisted of an electro-magnet, a hammer and lever system, and a computer 'relay' card. The membranes could be tuned to different resonant frequencies. Together with the existing architecture the installation resulted in a sonically segmented and delineated performance space. The minimized physical threshold established by the aluminium tubes was temporally intensified by the sound-scape of the installation and its exact spatialisation in time and relative to the aluminium tubes. In doing so it was possible to yield a dynamic threshold condition that intensified the space of the footbridge as a varied experience for the by-passer.

Do the above-described projects constitute *digital tectonics*? Only in so far as digital design techniques co-facilitated the desired design and construction dialogues that underlie these projects, but that is not really the point. Rather, the above-described approach to design seeks to rework the spatial concept of highly articulated interventions as a spatial politic of temporal individual and collective experiential formations. The design of highly articulated environments – facilitated by the deployment of digital design and manufacturing processes – operates through differentiation, proliferation and distribution of individual experiences in which the subject moves in an engaging way from one set of affiliations with the built environment to another. This implies the acceleration of cultural and social formation through individual and collective engagements of the human subject with a performative environment. Performativity in this respect entails differential material articulations that yield engagement. Here then, digital and analogue design techniques co-facilitate approaches to designs and interventions that make sense only in direct and dynamic exchange with their respective contexts and the way in which these interventions contribute to yield cultural and social arrangements. *Computing* could then be described as creative thinking through modelling processes – whether analogue and/or digital – that become enhanced and accentuated by a synergetic use of design techniques and technologies towards an inclusive and time-based design paradigm that engages the generative dynamic relations that make up, articulate and transform our human environment. At this point we might then finally be ready to begin to compute …

Notes

1 'Conversations with Farthey' 28.8.1827, *Goethe: Gedenkausgabe der Werke, Briefe und Gespräche*, ed. E. Beutler, Zurich 1948–60.

2 Umberto Eco, *The Open Work*, Harvard University Press, Cambridge Massachusetts, 1989.

3 see for instance, Roberto Mangbeira Unger's notion of *blankness and pointing*, 'The Better Futures of Architecture', in: *Anyone*, ed. Cynthia Davidson, Rizzoli, 1991; as well as their further explication by Jeff Kipnis, 'Towards a New Architecture', in: *AD* 'Folding in Architecture', London, 1993.

NEW DIALOGUES

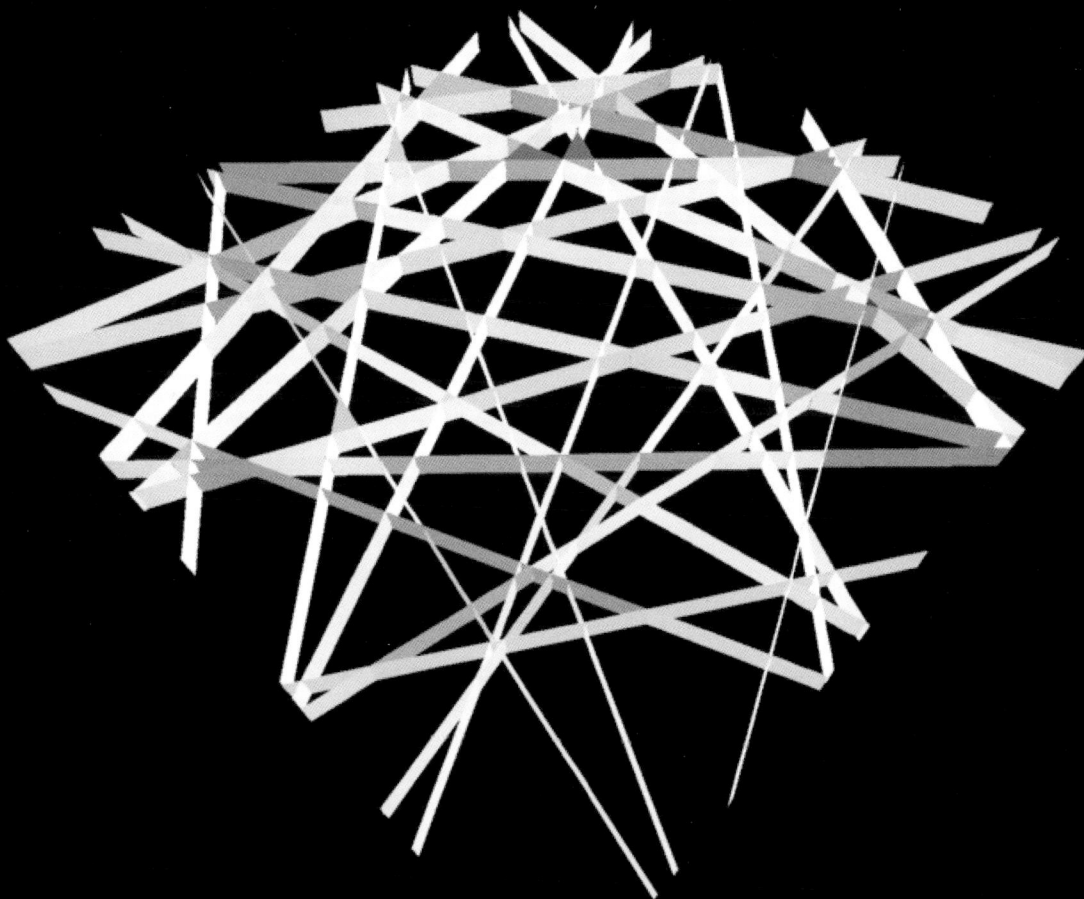

'Serpentine', Ito/Balmond.

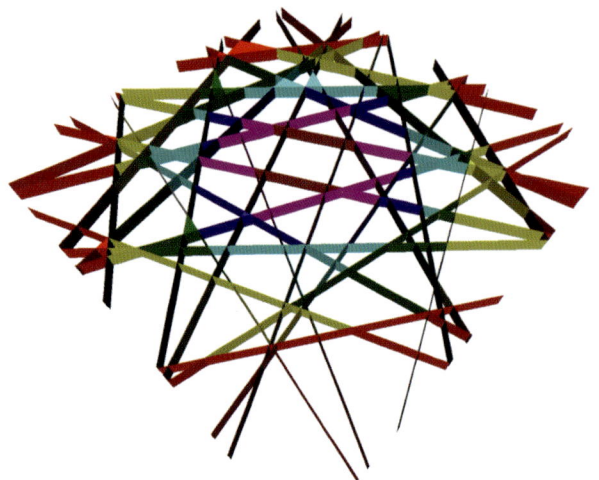

Geometry, Algorithm, Pattern

The Serpentine Pavilion 2002 – Toyo Ito and ARUP

Cecil Balmond

GEOMETRY

Geometry is an animation. It has always been so – the ideas behind Greek architecture were based on proportionate rules that took their inspiration from the relative positions of a point on a line. Imagine a dot travelling along a line and at different positions stopping to produce a measure of harmonic, geometric, or arithmetic means. At one particular point the lesser part of the line to the greater part has the same ratio as the greater part is to the whole. This defines the Golden Mean that led to the Acropolis and much of the compositional rules behind classical art. Alberti and Le Corbusier too developed their own proportionate rules for the making of architecture. With the computer we now have the power to look further into an animate geometry – using feedback techniques and algorithms. Tectonic space need not be limited to imagining structure as box like and assembled with standard post and beam constructions; it may be viewed as a serial punctuation generated by complex processes. But the investigation of such non-linear space needs its own rigours and, surprisingly, these come back to aesthetic ideas of proportion, scale, and materiality.

Initially, Toyo Ito proposed two questions:
    A – how to float a slab?
    B – how to transform the box?

A Wanting a slab to float means it loses its connection with the ground, no line shoots straight down and amplifies gravity, no squatness or robustness or claims to an assumed efficiency remain. Instead, there could be a wandering line, a kind of dreaming path.

No need for hard single contact – instead, there could be collector zones or gravity basins. Instead of descent, and the idea of a load compelled to travel downwards, what if the logic were to flipp and the 'load' ascend, upwards? The ground is given life to rise and coil up into the air – then a flat plane intersects, almost 'flying' at it, to be embedded. The movement in the roof slab is, as if, frozen. If the rising ground is translucent, pools of light may fill the space between heaven and earth, and benches and beds are fold lines. Mini program space is found within. The traditional limit of slab on columns is now forgotten. Somewhere above, the roof floats.

B With B the game is positive, negative. How much is void and what should remain of solid material? Is it an eating away of the form or a flow of large bubbles that may trap a form within?

If small holes are bitten away from a thick matrix the cuts are deep and angled,

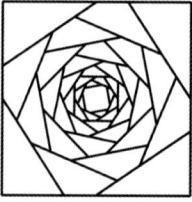

Sides : 4
Ratio 1 : 1/2
Ratio 1 : 1/3

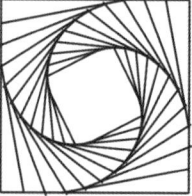

Sides : 4
Ratio 1 : 1/2
Ratio 1 : 1/4

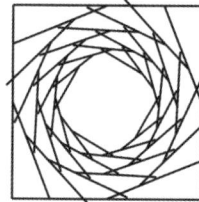

Sides : 4
Ratio 1 : 1/2
Ratio 1 : 1/5

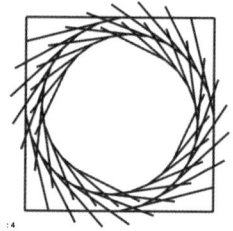

Sides : 4
Ratio 1 : 1/2
Ratio 1 : 1/8

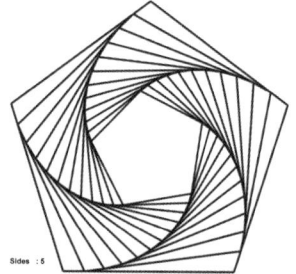

Sides : 4
Ratio 1 : 1/3
Ratio 1 : 1/8

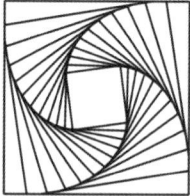

Sides : 4
Ratio 1 : 1/4
Ratio 1 : 1/8

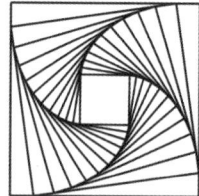

Sides : 4
Ratio 1 : 1/6
Ratio 1 : 1/8

Sides : 5
Ratio 1 : 1/8
Ratio 1 : 1/8

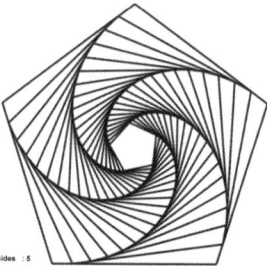

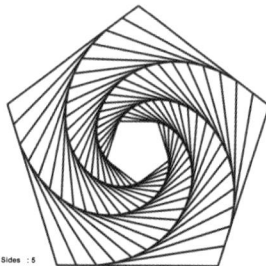

Sides : 5
Ratio 1 : 1/8
Ratio 1 : 1/8

Sides : 5
Ratio 1 : 1/4
Ratio 1 : 1/8

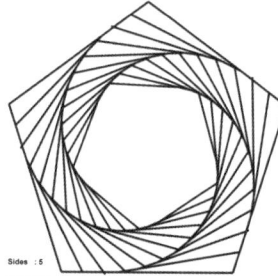

Sides : 5
Ratio 1 : 1/3
Ratio 1 : 1/8

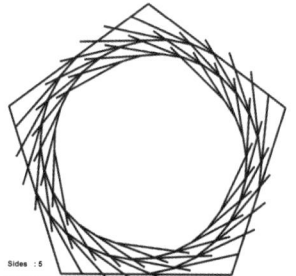

Sides : 5
Ratio 1 : 1/2
Ratio 1 : 1/8

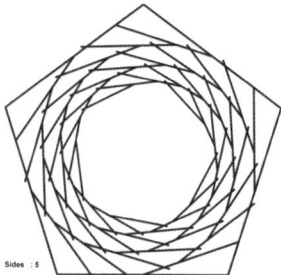

Sides : 5
Ratio 1 : 1/2
Ratio 1 : 1/5

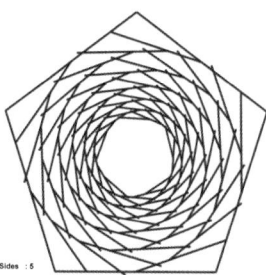

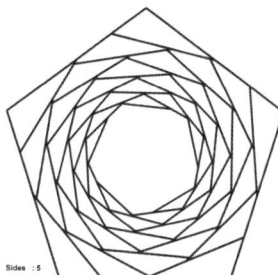

Sides : 5
Ratio 1 : 1/2
Ratio 1 : 1/5

Sides : 5
Ratio 1 : 1/2
Ratio 1 : 1/4

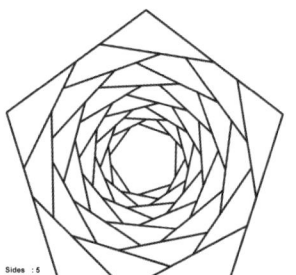

Sides : 5
Ratio 1 : 1/2
Ratio 1 : 1/3

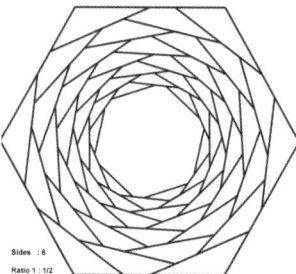

Sides : 6
Ratio 1 : 1/2
Ratio 1 : 1/3

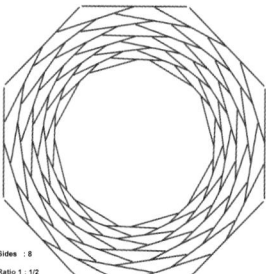

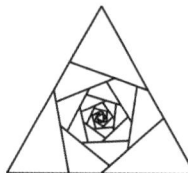

Sides : 8
Ratio 1 : 1/2
Ratio 1 : 1/3

Sides : 3
Ratio 1 : 1/2
Ratio 1 : 1/3

Sides : 3
Ratio 1 : 1/6
Ratio 1 : 1/6

adding a third dimension to the floating planes. But as the material is thinned and the holes allowed to grow, as the void increases and the solid part turns to residue or floating islands, reversal takes place. If the solid is reflective aluminium and the floor has hard and soft zones too, the pavilion becomes a capsule of drifting space. The dream of the wandering gravity line now spreads over the surface stretched by voids. Like ice floes, the solid is at risk.

Resolving A and B

The initial questions A and B Ito raised led to much speculation about form and enclosure and how to define a traditional volume. For there was much to experiment with as we investigated what could be contained or liberated simply by the drawing of pattern, and what sort of risk do we inject into the unpredictable? We chose to imagine, in the event, a cubic space made only out of vanishing lines.

NETWORK

A straight line is a constant velocity. In speed lines it streaks from nowhere to somewhere, and does not want to be stopped. But a crossing line that intersects the motion slows it down, and the question becomes, which way? A series of crossings and the questions multiply, where direction is lost, where time stops.

We may loop or zigzag or jump over intersections imposing a particular direction over others, but as the network grows the puzzle becomes more intricate, for which line came first?

Imagine such lines, as a small sample, scorched onto the earth in front of the Serpentine Gallery, and the ground trace energised to pick itself up and fold over into the planes that outline an enclosure. As the lines race over the plane, shooting down the sides at angles only to kick back through the base and rise up the other side, the surface becomes a mesh of circuits, going nowhere and yet at the same time moving towards everywhere. Normal extension ceases; we are in a time capsule. We occupy space that undermines the idea of a limit, denying hard skin to a volume.

Geometry, as a catalyst, even in this simplest condition of the straight line can subvert our notions of 'surrounding'. And since geometry is the life line of structure, its animation enlivens a piece of construction into something other than the dumb frame, making the difference in how we give metaphors to form – volume or enclosure, skin or surface, travelling margin or boundary? With such questions structure provokes a mobile sense of architecture.

ALGORITHM

Usually to construct a rectangular or square roof, lines are drawn at right angles to each other, parallel to the sides of the plan, to produce a grid of beams. This roof plane is then supported by vertical columns placed evenly around the edges. Instead of following the edges though, a more efficient pattern for the roof may be drawn by travelling across at an angle, say from half point on one side to the half point on the adjacent side. Repeating this for each side produces an inner square wholly embedded within the first, but diagonal in orientation. If the connection between adjacent sides is made more general, the start and end point of the first line may have different ratios. This puts a skew into the pattern, and once the new square is completed a virtual square is implied that goes beyond the boundaries of the original shape. Repeating the idea produces a spiral of shapes.

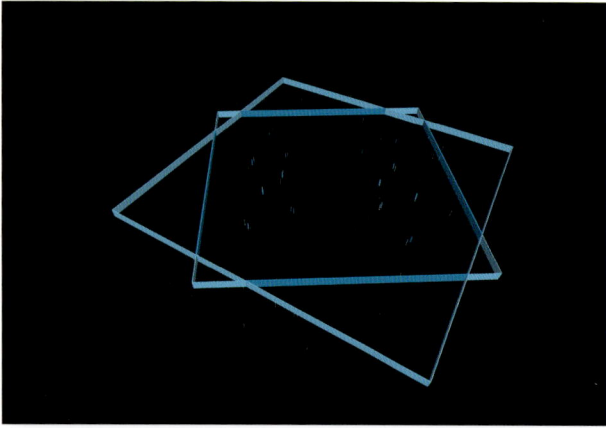

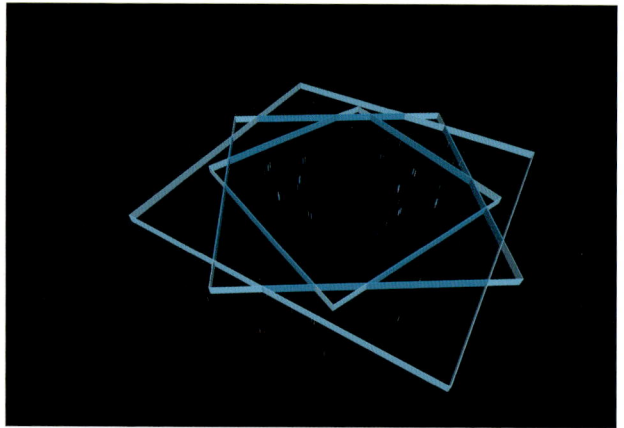

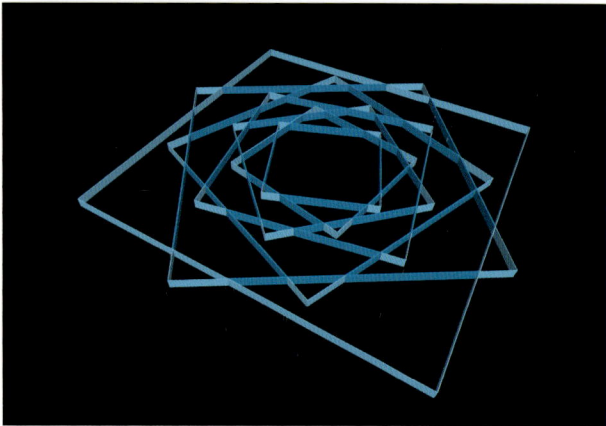

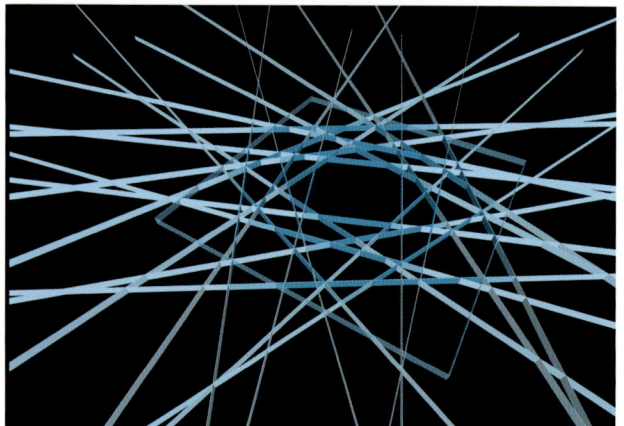

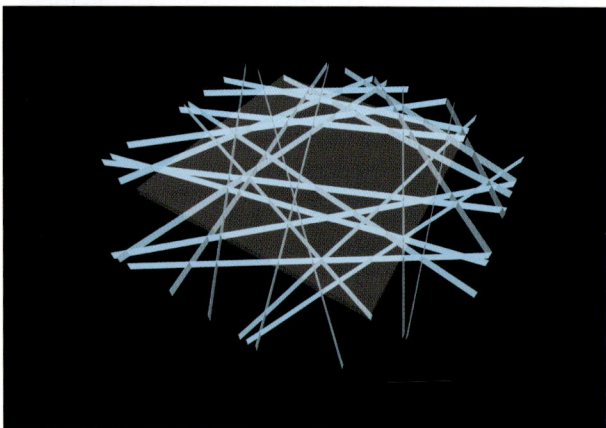

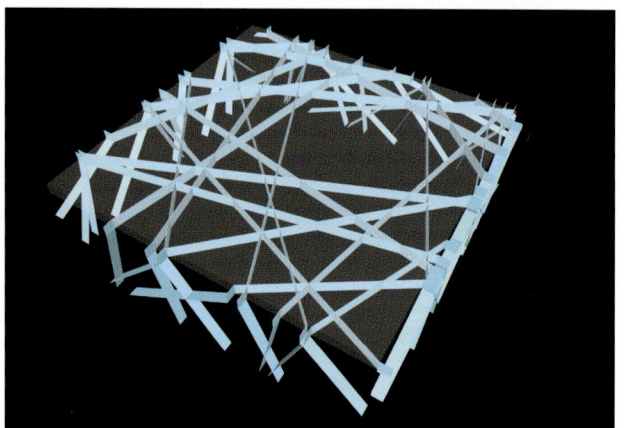

Algorithm

Construction

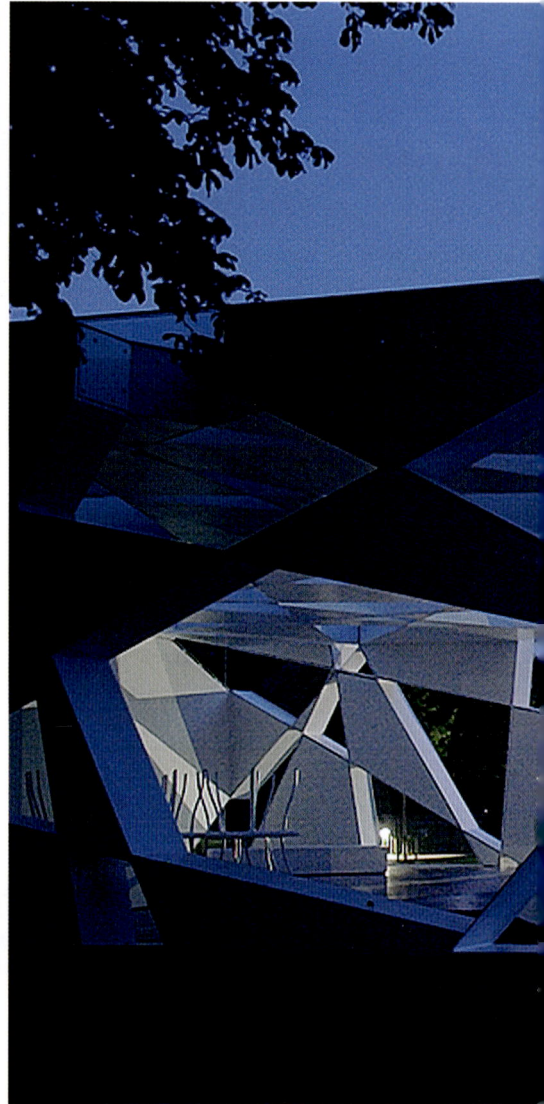

At the same time if all lines are projected forwards and backwards a dense field of crossed lines appears.

If anywhere on this two dimensional field the planes of a cube or box is laid out flat and then folded back again, the pattern picked up provides a continuous zigzag tracing over the three-dimensional form.

Daniel Bosia of Arup helped develop this algorithm, to provide us with endless opportunity in the drawing of networks that outlined the territory.

CONSTRUCTION

A minimum size of steel flat is chosen to materialise all lines.

Particular traces of the pattern are underlined and made thicker to act as structure. (We should note that normally steel flats would be judged too weak to span much distance as beams, as the thin sections buckle easily. But due to the side support made available from crossing elements in the pattern this particular weakness is easily overcome, the density offers a net of stability.)

To aid construction on site the steel flats were welded together and assembled in zones – the algorithm identifying triangular areas for panellising, as the squares rotated and reduced on the diagonal.

And it is a surprise how complexity has its own power of organisation, at one level scattered and distributed in a maze of mutual support, at another, a set of zones whose margins are essential lines of structure. One interpretation is nested within the other.

The custom of keeping things separate, to categorise, is challenged due to overlap – there is no beam or column in the conventional sense, no wall nor roof, 'in' is 'out' and vice versa. The pattern is open ended and keeps one guessing.

Credits
The Arup Team
Charles Walker   -   Project Director
Daniel Bosia   -   Project Engineer + Algorithm
Pat Dallard   -   Advisor on Analysis
Chris Murgatroyd -   Materials and Welding
Ray Ingles   -   CAD

LIVE-IT/LOVE-IT

The Mercedes–Benz Museum – UN Studio

Ben van Berkel and Caroline Bos

'Collaboration with other designers is primarily an exchange of ideas...if we can, we put ourselves in a situation where the outcome is a joint product.[1] UN Studio is 'a network of specialists in architecture, urban development and infrastructure. UN Studio organizes strategic forms of collaboration with architects, graphic designers and constructors, building consultants, service companies, quantity surveyors, photographers, stylists, new media designers and others.[2] The network idea has grown from the moment that our practice got larger[3] 'Branching out, searching, questioning...this open and explorative approach is perhaps necessary to render exciting what otherwise could easily turn into a dull activity. It is in any case a professional attitude that architects have consistently taught one other from generation to generation, ever since Vitruvius.[4] UN Studio discards the common project team approach because when you have a team, the team fixes itself around the project.[5] We asked ourselves what the end of the platonic object might mean and we decided that it had to mean that the architectural project needed be reformulated in a broader way...we now see projects as public constructions and have organized ourselves as a flexible platform organization, in which we fulfil the role of public 'scientists'. Much of the content of our work derives from these re-definitions'[6] however, 'we (still) see our relationship to design culture as fraught with tensions. To quote from a recent text accompanying our design for a mass-produced window: 'Our attention was focused on the question of the window as a product, an obtainable, happy-making, possibly prestigious, and certainly useful mass-produced object.' The questions we asked were: 'is it possible for the window to leave behind its Heideggerian heaviness and become as light, joyful and passion inspiring as a perfume bottle? On the other hand, must we contribute to turning the window into yet another commodity, and in that way add to the waste mountains of consumer society? The answer to these questions was to look for a form of newness that is directly related to factors of use in time. Traditionally, design innovation is primarily linked to new production techniques and materials. In this case, however, the novelty of the proposal is mos ly sited in operational improvements These are related to the daily handling of the window, but also to its long-term usability. The window's main characteristic is its flexibility to adapt to different demands and conditions. Thus, the design of the window prototype is based on the way the product works in time.'[7]

Live -It/Love- It describes a relationship between architecture and technology it is also an account of our design for the Mercedes–Benz Museum in Stuttgart and its use in time. This is a Museum for a legendary car, the product of a complex spirit in which

ABOVE **Computer generated view of the highway with the new Mercedes–Benz Museum**
BELOW LEFT **Sketch by Ben van Berkel**
BELOW RIGHT **Schematic diagram**

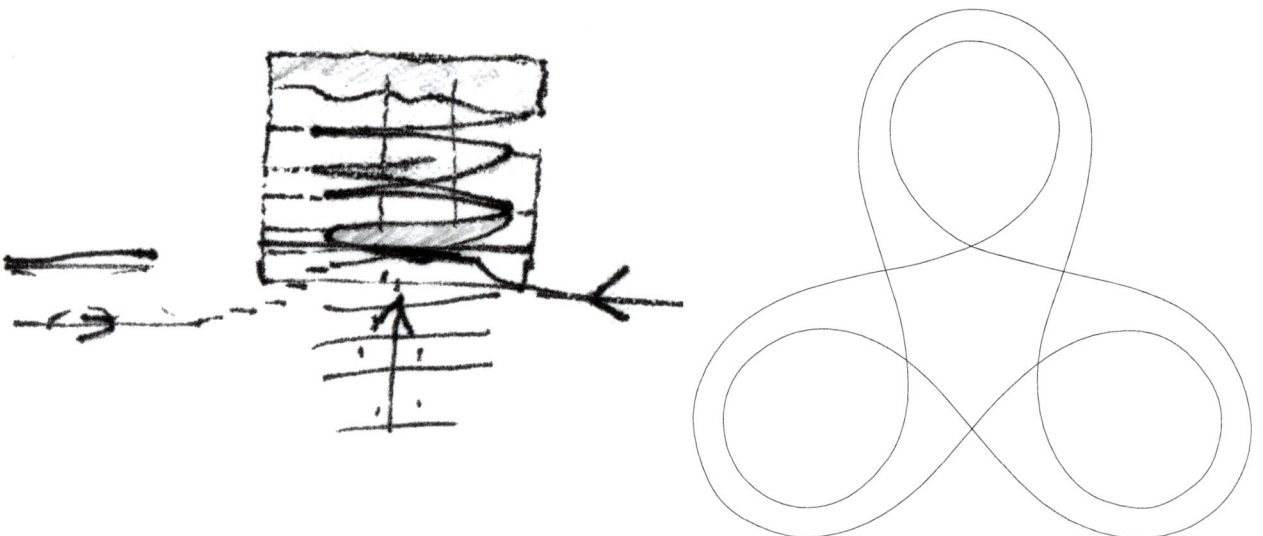

Model

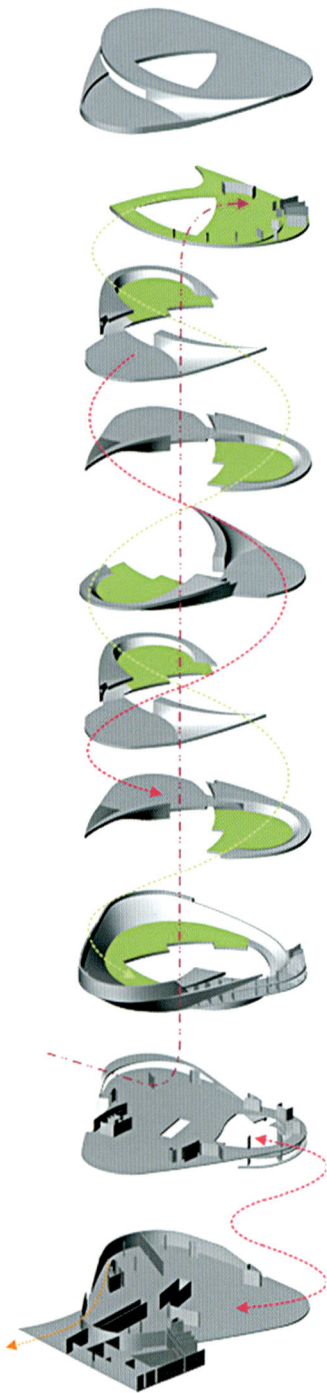

Column of floor plates

technology, adventure, attractiveness and distinction are merged. It is also a Museum for people who can move through it, dream, learn, look, and let them selves be oriented by fascinations, light and space. Lastly it is a Museum for the city, a new landmark to celebrate the enduring passion of Stuttgart's most famous inventor and manufacturer.

The vertical structure condenses the Museum program on a relatively small floor area at the location of the existing pavilion for year- old cars, leaving over half of the planning area free for outdoor programs and future development. In our proposal the entire planning site is raised in order to establish a smooth, high-quality landscaped plaza, which connects the various Mercedes activities; the Museum, the test course and the new vehicle center planned at a later stage. In this way, the landscaped plaza functions as a common plinth, differentiating the area from the industrial surroundings and emphasizing a more cultural identity.

Adjacent to the Museum are a restaurant terrace and an open arena, which can function as an open-air auditorium. This arena also offers seating for visitors of outdoor activities and events such as the annual Star and Cars show, to look at the cars as they are driven to the Test Course in a parade-like spectacle.

Transportation Trefoil – an organisation that integrates technology, visitor flows, cars and vision

The Museum program is accommodated in an intricate package in which the various exhibits, the public programs and the service and support programs are interwoven. Shifts in the floor levels challenge the symmetry of the trefoil plan in section. Spatially, the building is structured as a double helix. The leaves of the trefoil rotate around a triangular void, forming six horizontal plateaus which alternately occupy single and double floor heights, resulting in six double-height and six single height exhibition spaces. The organisation does not involve a continuous, single surface; the six plateaus themselves are level, with slowly sloping ramps bridging the height differences between them. The aimed-for effect of this organisation is to create exciting spatial constellations, enabling a wide range of look-through options, shortcuts, enclosed and open spaces, and the potential for continuity and cross-references in the various displays.

The visitor proceeds through the Museum from top to bottom. A lift moves visitors through the atrium to the top of the building; the ride in the enclosed tube provides the visitor with a virtual vertical Preshow experience as introduction to the museum. The three aspects of the collection, the cars and trucks and the Myths, are organized chronologically from top to bottom, starting with the three oldest cars at the top floor in the display dedicated to the invention of the car.

The collection of cars and trucks is shown in combination on six plateaus. The other six plateaus show the Myths and, at the lowest levels, Races and Records and the Fascination of Technology. At entry level is the lobby giving access to the Museum floors, the shop and a restaurant. Below the elevated landscape level are the Children's Museum, the Flexible Exhibition Space, Delivery and Administration offices.

The full automotive experience - the world of Mercedes-Benz

This Museum strives to respond to questions relating to the Mercedes identity, to the contemporary experience with driving and with cars in general, and to the contemporary museological experience. The scheme derives its structure from the surprising combination of these elements.

For instance, the structure enables the individual, dreamlike wandering that makes any museum visit so attractive and inspiring, but at the same time encourages the visitor to interact more consciously and dynamically with the displays by showing the items from unusual angles, perspectives and backgrounds. Thus, the strategies of display afforded by the split-level Trefoil organization stimulate change and flexibility.

The organization also encourages thematic exchanges between the collections and issues relating to the Mercedes identity, heritage, contemporary quality, technological innovation and sports. Moreover, these issues can be subtly emphasized and interlinked by spatial and contextual juxtapositions.

Depending upon the display needs, exhibition spaces are alternately open, leaving open the view to the outside, or enclosed. The variety of open and enclosed, high and lower, communicative and contemplative spaces all contributes to a lively environment through which the visitor moves easily from space to space.

In this Museum, wayfinding and orientation are intuitive and individual; the organization offers a rational framework, which the visitor is free to follow or to deviate from when attracted by a specific display, or program feature.

Enduring Passion

The difference between open and enclosed spaces is not immediately apparent from the exterior, which presents a serene, coherent appearance. We envisage a sculptural yet smooth envelope, which changes with the outside conditions, turning from opaque to transparent, taking up reflections from the outside, and even transforming in colour with the time of day, the climate, and the seasons. An innovative structural glazing façade system reinforced with carbon fibre maximizes the effect. The organization reflects the Mercedes Benz spirit in its technological intelligence; the system at the basis of the building is spatially complex, yet the repetition of elements lends the Museum a structural efficiency. Its compact form, the efficient use of daylight and energy and its large-span structure contribute to a sustainable performance. This technological inventiveness is deeply interwoven with other values and it is this integration of construction, routing, contents, orientation and light that make up the unique Museum experience.

Notes
(Montage of quotes by David Turnbull)

1 Ben van Berkel and Caroline Bos from: Digital conversation, UNFold, 2002, Nai Publishers Rotterdam
2 Ben van Berkel and Caroline Bos: UN Studio profile, UN Studio
3 Ben van Berkel and Caroline Bos from: George Elvin, Integrated Practice: Building the Innovative Architectural Enterprise, University of Illinois 2003
4 Ben van Berkel and Caroline Bos from: Digital conversation, UNFold, 2002, Nai Publishers Rotterdam
5 Ben van Berkel and Caroline Bos from: George Elvin, Integrated Practice: Building the Innovative Architectural Enterprise, University of Illinois 2003
6 Ben van Berkel and Caroline Bos from: Digital conversation, UNFold, 2002, Nai Publishers Rotterdam
7 Ben van Berkel and Caroline Bos from: Digital conversation, UNFold, 2002, Nai Publishers Rotterdam

An Aesthetics Of Calculus

Round Table Discussion

chaired by David Turnbull

Round Table Discussion
David Turnbull, Cecil Balmond, Manuel DeLanda, Caroline Bos, Greg Lynn, Mark Burry, Mike Cook, Michael Hensel

David Turnbull
While the intersection of *Digital* and *Tectonic*, of computers and construction may appear obvious, even banal, as the procurement procedures employed in the briefing, design and production of buildings around the world increasingly depend on this intersection, what is at stake here is not merely the production of buildings, it is rather the emergence of innovative modes of thinking, and of philosophical speculation with form, with technique, with space.

Two paths have opened up for architecture in the past few decades, which broadly conform to a distinction established by Deleuze and Guattari, between the near-seer and the far-seer. Each is equipped with a different viewing device – far-seers observe patterns, distributions, migrations and movements; near-seers define, categorize, and establish limits. Two related modes of practice, customarily seen as distinct, one researching the rules, algorithms, or protocols that define territories, exploring and documenting the sublime and the disturbing effects of globalization, the strange and excessive combinatorial capacities of networks . . . the second, engaged in an ecstatic exegesis of the capacities of new tools and techniques to emancipate form, liberate structure, and energize the material of architecture. The protagonists of advanced formal and material experiment may rarely communicate with the others, and both sides, rightly, believe that they are exploring and working creatively with the opportunities and implications of relatively recent changes in a global landscape defined economically, ecologically, and technologically, and especially in relation to advances in the field of computation and the proliferation of new media.

The disciplinary apparatus that our formulation *Digital Tectonics* attempts involves a crucial step, namely the abandonment of these distinctions, a reconciliation of these modes of exploration, of practice, in favour of creative collaborations that refuse any reductive definition of the discipline, weaving together pattern-seeking, form-finding, and material effects at many scales. Indeed, these collaborations that challenge conventional thinking on the roles and activities of architects and engineers may have become not only necessary but obligatory. In a fundamental sense, this step involves renewed respect for structure, the recognition that the architecture and engineering disciplines are equally engaged with the structuring of relations in space, and primary research into structural geometry.

Cecil Balmond

Some thoughts on structure, as I see it, in architecture. There was a time when the assumption of architects was of a linear space, with an explicit assumption that structure was inherent in architecture. To a large extent, apart from the very gifted engineers, who were forceful or who had a vision, architecture would go separately, and engineering could follow. I am talking here of structural engineering. What we didn't know – both as structural engineers and as architects – was that an understanding of non-linearity was growing all the time with the work of our colleagues in the environmental sciences – thermodynamics – beautiful stuff.

I started getting interested in structure in a broader sense when I realized suddenly that structure actually had all the ingredients that architecture had, if you start to look for a more radical architecture. Episode, boundary, travelling margins – these are all structural concerns, and in fact in everything that Greg Lynn was saying today I could have substituted the word structure, when he said architecture, the way that I look at it. In my team in Arup over the years now, and we have been doing this over 15 years, we have developed structural ideas that are really about generating space.

I found teaching in many architectural schools that the computer is a very seductive animal, and that fantasy is very quick to be modelled on the screen. But, more and more, as I was teaching across the world in different places, I saw a similarity growing. The worry I had was that as with the dead end that hi-tech work got into, the final modernist statement of the glass and steel box, a vanishing point of modern architecture, a cul-de-sac of thinking, that, actually we are in danger of computer-generated architecture going that way too if there was not some kind of twinning with structure in a fundamental sense. I started to see – seeing myself as a structural engineer, investigating and interrogating space, and making form – that structure is a kind of fundamental layer of how space is made, in opposition to the reductive process of Cartesian compartmentation, as an additive process that grows from a spot – a local instance – so that a point becomes a zone, a line becomes surface, plane becomes volume etc. Geometry becomes more a kind of topological animation, invariance becomes very important, a very fundamental connectivity, and if you look at any surface-making, when you move into making structure off those surfaces, you get into ornamentation and secondary values as well, so that you enter a new territory of primary and secondary. These are the ingredients that I think structural engineers who have been mathematically trained and are at home with the abstract can bring in, but we are in completely new territory with no precedent. That is a problem for many, many architects, I find, who are groomed in an intellectual tradition, of great reference and great precedent. To start anew, almost, and throw away your baggage, is really hard.

So I think that we have a fantastic opportunity here for a new kind of discipline. Looking at the work that Mark Burry was showing by Gaudí, there was someone overcoming the limits of his materialities. We too are limited by structural material, connectivity, linearity in the construction industry, and yes, there is a huge challenge here, but I think that we can meet it if we have a very close relationship of structure and architecture.

Manuel DeLanda

It was an incredible day for me because there were really no philosophers on stage – except for myself – and at the same time I saw so much philosophy being done with forms – with thinking visually. I learned so much from all the presentations about concerns. You know I am not an architect. I don't know very much about architecture, even though I teach in an architecture department. I'm more concerned with the architecture of molecules, the architecture of atoms, the architecture of animals and plants, in terms of evolutionary ideas. But today I saw for the first time a bunch of architects and engineers doing philosophy with forms, and thinking about ornament, or thinking about topology, or thinking about generative principles, such as simulated annealing, or thinking about very practical problems of how to take a surface and make it constructible. I learnt a whole lot about the capacity to do philosophy without words, in a sense, thinking visually, but at the same time very deeply about philosophical issues that are essential for the philosopher, to think about nature. And so I am going to go home obviously with a lot of stuff to chew on, and with a new respect for architecture which I thought that I had lost after so much empty postmodern textual interpretative, hermeneutic stuff, that we drowned ourselves in for the last twenty years, I see a renaissance in type of philosophy done with space, and with spatial relationships.

Caroline Bos

For me too it was also especially interesting, including presentations from engineers about their research, which is more difficult for us to relate to when it gets very abstract. I can immediately understand Mark Burry's work, as it is sited, it has an historical context. It has all these constraints that I am familiar with, whereas the constraints on the more abstract engineering research are not familiar to me, as they are often mathematical parameters. So for me they are new, and I think therefore all the more proof that we should be familiarized with this discourse far more. Of course, Cecil has contributed so much to that already by writing himself and communicating. And architects have been put in a position where we have had to communicate our ideas for a long time traditionally, and we have to open ourselves up that way. It is not easy, or some kind of ego trip. We have to really show our ambitions and our ideology, and so on. And so I think that it is very encouraging that you are putting engineers on the podium and asking them to do the same thing.

Mark Burry

I studied at a school which had an engineering faculty next to the school of architecture and there was absolutely no contact, well very little. We used to go over there and break things. I taught in three schools which didn't have an engineering faculty associated with them.

The other day we had a meeting at my current school where I made what turned out to be quite a provocative statement. I guess when you just arrive somewhere you can sort of see through the cracks. I noticed that the entire selection procedure for the school down there is based on portfolio and interview. I think the interview establishes whether you are hip as an individual and the portfolio whether you are hip as a creative thinker. I said what about the people that we need who we could have useful conversations with, what we might call specialists – architects and engineers are specialists, and it seems to me that numeracy is becoming the common denominator for their collaboration and I find it very difficult to think that architects can really reach their full potential without learning a bit of basic programming. But it is my experience that architects imagine that they don't need to have those skills. I wonder if we have been hiding behind this shield that there are other people who are numerate, who will take care of all that?

Greg Lynn

But you are not asking the architects to calculate efficient structure, are you? What we need from structural engineering and from an architectural and aesthetic theory of structure are parameters for structure other than efficiency.

Mark Burry

I think what was really behind my question was whether software is actually enfranchising engineers to be architects, and vice versa. Having taught in a Spanish school for a while, I've seen it there, the engineers come from the school of architecture. It's not a separate professional course of study. It's a very efficient environment to be in . . . I guess I'm just thinking that there must be a certain enfranchisement coming from becoming more involved in each other's specialisms.

Cecil Balmond

With free form, what you have got to realise is that every point of curvature is a structural opportunity, and that's why it is so important to work together now. The danger is that if we stick with the assumptions of structure as they are, and architects do not try to understand new structural possibilities, you end up with a post-and-beam logic underpinning free form, and you are not getting anywhere then. What you really need is a whole new logic of thinking about structural connectivity and the passage of structure. And what is good about Digital Tectonics is that it is a great medium in which to study the discreet and the continuum. That's where an area of research that I have been looking at, number, is so relevant, because numbers are abstract, and at the same time they are prescriptive. And you don't have to be a mathematician. You don't have to run differential equations, just go into numbers. This goes back to Greek times. It's an old-fashioned thing. I feel often that really I am doing very old-fashioned things. I am interested in harmony. I am interested in symmetry. I am interested in equilibrium. These are all, from a static concept, what you all understand. But if you look at them as a moving, dynamic geometry, it completely changes. Then you are into not just the dualities of opposition which symmetry comes from in the classical sense, but an inter-dependant layering of simultaneous activities. That actually is what symmetry is, and so on. It's a new thing.

I think, while listening to Manuel, the abstract meeting the visual is a very interesting new area, where an entirely new philosophy will be inaugurated. It's not just about shape. It's a deeper thing. It goes beyond that. It's about the connectivity of ideas, which move beyond architecture and engineering. But that's why in pedagogic terms there has to be a fundamental revolution in how we approach teaching, both in engineering schools, and in architectural schools.

Mike Cook

I have to very much support that. I was thinking there is something very interesting about Digital Tectonics. You know, here we are, 2002, and there is something in common with where we were in the 1970s, where architects and engineers came together over the physical model that captured the engineering logic, the form finding logic, and the architectural logic of what we were trying to do. If we call it Digital Tectonics, it's about the use of digital means to have the common ground that was there with the physical model. And I can see in that area of work, a great deal of overlap between engineering and architecture, and therefore in that area that some kind of common ground in education makes a huge amount of sense. Obviously I have to say that, in the world, may be the other world that isn't Digital Tectonics, the world of ordinary buildings may have to catch up, but at the moment the way most architects and most engineers are being trained, they are not being trained to collaborate particularly well. In architecture, technology and physics are fairly dirty words. And in engineering, aesthetics is still a fairly dirty word. So we mustn't kid ourselves. There is a long way to go. But maybe Digital Tectonics is the kind of core that might pull people in that direction?

Michael Hensel

I'd like to raise a critical issue. We've seen today beside a whole range of other things presentations that focus on mechanisms, models, technology and techniques by which we can work quite different sets of information into a project, ranging from material conditions, spatial conditions, structural conditions, and so forth; plus at some level too, speculation about an emergent aesthetic, and emergent effects. I recall even at an earlier point in Manuel's talk the possibilities of social and political repercussions. And within this context it strikes me as odd that the subject, the beholder, the occupant of these spaces that are suggested is not recognized as a part of the information.

Greg Lynn

Aesthetics links the structural, formal and political and social. What is more political and cultural than aesthetics?

Michael Hensel

Yes. But, nevertheless, our sentences often start with I, what I am interested in, not with the repercussions for the people that will be affected by our actions.

Greg Lynn

I didn't hear that. One thing is, simply, the context here of a discussion among experts, I think a lot of people didn't talk about the implication of their work socially and culturally because of that – although I think it was hit on in a lot of different ways. Economy, materials, you know. And I wouldn't make, or rather I don't know how you would make, a relationship between aesthetics and culture in which they would be ignorant of one another, because I can't think of anything more cultural and political than aesthetics. I think you communicate culturally through aesthetics as a structural engineer or as an architect.

David Turnbull

I would have said that the social and political implications were absolutely explicit all day long, in relations to themes like mass customization, in relation to the capacities of tools, who controls them, where they are. With the mega-machines of societal processes, subject to critical evaluation by people like Lewis Mumford from the 1930s to the late 60s, being restructured now through the agency of computers and mobility, and a radical redefinition of where decisions and choices can be or are made, and how space is organized.

It seems to me that Digital Tectonics is a profoundly political project. It is precisely concerned with social processes and social formations, and the status of building within those social processes.

Manuel DeLanda

I agree with your point of view. I feel we know more about society than we know about say, smaller subjects. Or of course we pretend to know, we have words like capitalism, or commodification as a process. This, of course, I'm not going to get into right now. But these are voodoo words, really. They are just words for the left to have around, and they make us seem radical. The fact of the matter is that we still don't understand the architecture of the economy. It's not just demand and supply by the invisible hand. There is an incredibly elaborate architecture and dynamics to it. So perhaps it's better in raising social issues, instead of blowing them out of proportion, where we begin using words like capitalism and so on, which are just make believe in their understanding, to be more concrete about the specific social issues we want to discuss. The ones that we were beginning to raise about the relationships between the communities or the cultures of engineering and architecture, they're deeply social issues, right?

You have two cultures, which an anthropologist would investigate and find to be completely different tribes with their own little rituals and their own little annual gatherings, and their own little journals, with their own criteria for selection of papers, and their own criteria for what counts as quality and Mike Cook just said it, the word aesthetics is a dirty word in engineering; that's a profoundly cultural comment. The words stress and strain are for some architects, dirty words. That's a profoundly social comment in the sense that there's something deeply wrong with these cultures that they have grown apart so long. I'm going to let the architects and the engineers fight it out on that one. I'm going to take advantage of being the philosopher, like Humpty Dumpty sitting on the wall, just watching them fight.

Go ahead, break a leg!

But just let me give my little two cents here on the question of the social aspect we're talking about, to get back to the subject of what was being discussed before: how do we teach mathematics [gasp!] to architects, so they could now speak to engineers. How do we teach aesthetics to engineers in a way that seems relevant to them. Not just sending an architect to teach them about aesthetics, or not just sending a mathematician to teach architects in a boring high school way, that we all went through and we didn't learn anything. We all took calculus in high school, and very few of us had any sense of the relevance of calculus, the aesthetics of the calculus. Calculus has a magical history. We all know Newton invented the algorithm, but before the algorithm, the mechanical recipe, there was a calculus that had been done all the way back to the Greeks. What the Greeks called the method of exhaustion in which you would take a square, make it into a pentagon, make it into a hexagon and see what attractor the whole series tends to, which is of course a circle, impressed the hell out of them. Because it was the first concrete image of becoming in which a particular polygon through an iterative series of increasing the number of sides approximates to a limit, a circle. So we already had the notion of a limit since the Greeks, when you read medieval philosophers, there were all kinds of mystical ideas of as to what these limits are, and of course we eventually got into problems with Leibniz and Newton's infinitesimal, because we didn't know exactly what they were, there were all kinds of mystical speculations. There are many anecdotes and interesting ways of teaching the students what the point of calculus is. Particularly if you make them understand that the actual formulae, the actual mechanical recipes, are the least important part. To know how to differentiate and to know how to integrate, shouldn't need to be taught anymore. This should be done by machines. Whereas what you should understand is what the point of it is.

Just let me try to illustrate this. I'm not going to try to specify the aesthetics of the calculus – I can imagine where it comes from; a basic differential equation – what it expresses is the rate of change, the rate of position with respect to time, which gives you speed. And the basic notion of calculus is how you use differentiation to find an instantaneous rate of change, the instantaneous speed a bullet had when it hit you in the face, you know. What bullet and what speed was it going when it hit.

The moment you change that into geometry, you change position and time by curvature, and now you're asking what is the instantaneous rate of curvature at which this surface is changing, which gives you a completely different way of thinking about space, because you don't have to embed a surface in a Cartesian coordinate system, and specify 'well, its x y z coordinates are such and such', now you are specifying it by the speed at which it changes its curvature. There will be points at which curvature changes suddenly, there will be areas in which it changes much more smoothly. This gives you a completely different philosophy of space. When Reimann invented manifolds he had no idea that Einstein, seventy years later, was going to take a four dimensional manifold and invent the theory of relativity in terms of space time. Well all these mathematicians in the nineteenth century creating these tools, they were then taken over by physicists to yield farther and farther ideas. And so, when you teach calculus this way without formulas, just telling all the fantastic history going back all the way to the Greeks, and let the students understand particularly well the mechanical recipe, the part that computers do well, because computers don't get bored with mechanical recipes, but the part that humans do badly because humans do get bored by following mechanical recipes, particularly if they don't know what the point of the whole thing is.

We must teach, not the mechanical recipes but their relevance and importance through the history of ideas, and in more abstract terms, as a kind of philosophy, the sort of space that can come from calculus that does not come from analytical geometry, that does not come from algebra. It makes it relevant to architects to understand that. Then once you've explained that, once they get the point, they'll be interested in going by themselves and finding out how the mechanical recipes work. Not the other way round. Unfortunately, we teach it the other way round. And that is the social point about our totally absurd system of education, in which they try to teach you mechanically how to do certain things instead of teaching you the relevance and importance of certain ideas.

Cecil Balmond

Well said Manuel, and I think the thing about the equations being a reductive process, is a problem, and with the new digital technologies, we can move on to integrative ideas. I'd just like to discuss briefly why the sense of aesthetics is so important. The common or simplistic view may be that engineers don't have any aesthetic sense if you equate that to object-hood, and ideas of classical beauty, but actually in an engineering company where the people are looking at formulae or stress flows, the word beauty is mentioned all the time, and anyone whose read any kind of book on being a mathematician, you know, things are just beautiful because they are. And this language of beauty runs right through the sciences. So it was always shocking for me to find when I join my architectural brethren that engineers were supposed to be dullards of the imagination. If anything, I felt the opposite. I felt architects' imaginations were restricted because they never enter the abstract fully. And they were limited by the visual.

So there is an important area here I think. I was involved in a debate recently and I was explaining my view, very boldly of beauty. I thought, well I'd better take my courage in both hands, and I said what I believe – I used an example from Arnhem, the project I was doing with Ben and Caroline and another project I'm doing at the moment with Shigeru Ban – in fact, saying that an architecture or engineering beyond the technical is what we want, because the mechanistic is done. Ticked. We don't need to fuss about that any longer. It's the other thing. It's the abstract. The edge between the abstract and the visual is where a new aesthetic is born.

Contributor Biographies

Alisa Andrasek is an experimental practitioner of architecture and computational processes in design. In 2001 she founded *biot(h)ing,* a transdisciplinary laboratory whose research focuses on the potential of physical and artificial computational systems for design. Andrasek graduated from the School of Architecture, University of Zagreb and holds a Masters in Advanced Architectural Design from Columbia University. She teaches at both Columbia University GSAPP and the University of Pennsylvania and has also taught at Rensselaer Polytechnic Institute and the Pratt Institute.

Cecil Balmond is a structural engineer with the International engineering firm Ove Arup and Partners where he has over the past 30 years worked on many prestigious and award winning projects including the Lille Project and Bordeaux Villa with Rem Koolhaas, the Portuguese National Pavilion for the Lisbon Expo with Alvaro Siza and the sculpture 'Marsyas' with Anish Kapoor. He is Chairman of ARUP's Europe Division and is currently working with Koolhaas on the Concert Hall project in Porto, the CCTV Headquarters in Beijing, and with Daniel Libeskind on the World Trade Center. His interest lies in the genesis of form and the overlap of science with art, using music, number and mathematics as vital sources. His publications include: Informal, Number Nine: The Search for the Sigma Code, Unfolding – Daniel Libeskind/Cecil Balmond, and Serpentine Pavilion – Toyo Ito/Cecil Balmond. He has been the Kenzo Tange Professor at Harvard's Graduate School of Design, Saarinen Professor at Yale, and Visiting Professor at the London School of Economics. He is currently Graham Professor at the University of Pennsylvania.

Mark Burry is a practising architect and recently took up a position at RMIT University in Melbourne, Australia, as Professor of Innovation (Spatial Information Architecture). Previously he held the chair in architecture and building at Deakin University for five years. He has published internationally on two main themes: the life and work of the architect Antoni Gaudí in Barcelona, and putting theory into practice with regard to 'challenging' architecture. He has also published widely on broader issues of design, construction and the use of computers in design theory and practice.

Bernard Cache is the leading principal of the Paris-based design and software company Objectile, which he founded in 1996 with Patrick Beaucé and Jean-Louis Jammot. Cache has acted as a senior consultant in major strategic studies on image telecommunications and digital television for companies such as Philips, Canal Plus and France Telecom. Published internationally, he has written widely on communication policy and economics as well as architecture. He has most recently held academic appointments as Associate Professor of Architectural Design and Computing at the University of Toronto, Visiting Professor at the Universidad Internacional de Catalunya, and Visiting Professor at the School of Architecture, UCLA.

Michael Cook is a practising structural engineer and a partner of Buro Happold, based in London. After graduating from Cambridge he worked with Ted Happold and Frei Otto on a range of membrane and cable net structures.before dedicating himself to various projects across the globe, including the British Museum Great Court and Imagination HQ in London and the Cultural Centre in Hong Kong.
He has a particular interest in the connection between natural structures and man-made structures and has presented papers in this field in many cities around the world.
His current projects include the Fine Arts Museum, Boston, the envelope to the new Sage Music Centre in Gateshead and a new membrane roof to Dresden's main railway station.

Manuel DeLanda is the author of three philosophy books, *War in the Age of Intelligent Machines* (1991), *A Thousand Years of Nonlinear History* (1997), and *Intensive Science and Virtual Philosophy* (2002), as well as of many philosophical essays published in various journals and collections. He teaches two seminars at Columbia University, School of Architecture: "Philosophy of History: Theories of Self-Organization and Urban Dynamics", and "Philosophy of Science: Thinking about Structures and Materials".

Mark Goulthorpe created the dECOi atelier in 1991 as a forward-looking architectural practice, whose design calibre was quickly established through winning entries in several international competitions, and with awards from cultural institutions around the world. This has been reinforced by numerous publications, international lecturers and conferences, and frequent guest-professorships, including a design unit at the Architectural Association in London and the Ecole Speciale in Paris.

Michael Hensel is an architect and has been in private practice since 1990. He is partner in OCEAN NORTH and the Emergence and Design Group.
Recent work includes the World Center for Human Concerns with OCEAN NORTH [2001–03] and the Helical Structures Research with the Emergence and Design Group [2003]. He has lectured and taught widely in Europe and the Americas, before becoming Course Director of the Post-professional Emergent Technologies and Design Master Program and Unit Master at the Architectural Association School of Architecture.
He is a frequent contributor to *Architectural Design* and guest-edits the forthcoming issue *Emergence – Morphogenetic Strategies in Design* together with Achim Menges and Michael Weinstock.

OCEAN NORTH is a Helsinki-based practice that undertakes experimental design across architecture, urban design, furniture and product design and cultural production. Tuuli Sotamaa, Kivi Sotamaa, Birger Sevaldson and Michael Hensel lead the practice, at www.ocean-north.net

Neil Leach is an architect and theorist. He has taught at a number of institutions including the Architectural Association, London, and Columbia University, New York. He is author of *The Anaesthetics of Architecture* (MIT, 1999) and *Millennium Culture* (Ellipsis, 1999); co-author of *Marspants* (Architecture Foundation, 2000); editor of *Rethinking Architecture* (Routledge, 1997), *Architecture and Revolution* (Routledge, 1999), *The Hieroglyphics of Space* (Routledge, 2002) and *Designing for a Digital World* (Wiley, 2002); and co-translator of *L B Alberti, On the Art of Building in Ten Books* (MIT, 1988).

Greg Lynn is the principal of Greg Lynn FORM and has taught throughout the United States and Europe. Before establishing his own firm, he worked for four years in the office of Peter Eisenman where he was the principal project designer on both a high technology laboratory at the Carnegie Mellon Research Institute and on a 40 million dollar university building complex for the School of Design, Art, Architecture and Planning at the University of Cincinnati. In addition to leading his design practice, he has taught and lectured around the world as the Professor of Spatial Conception and Exploration at the ETH (Swiss Federal Institute of Technology) in Zurich and as an Adjunct Assistant Professor at Columbia University. In the fall of 2002 he became an o. Univ. Professor at the "angewandte" in Vienna, Austria. In addition, he is a Studio Professor at UCLA in Los Angeles and the Davenport Professor at Yale University. His architectural designs have received numerous awards and have been exhibited in both architecture and art museums, including the 2000 Venice Biennale of

Architecture where his work was represented in the US, Austrian and Italian Pavilions. He writes and lectures widely on architectural design and theory. He is the author of Intricacy (ICA, Philadelphia), *Architectural Laboratories* (NAI, Rotterdam), *Folds, Bodies and Blobs: Collected Essays* (La Lettre Volée, Brussels), *Animate Form* (Princeton Architectural Press, New York) and the forthcoming *Predator* (Wexner Center, Columbus, OH) and *Embrylogical House* (also by Princeton Architectural Press).

Kristina Shea is a University Lecturer in Engineering Design and a Co-Director of the Engineering Design Centre (EDC) at the Cambridge Engineering Department (UK). She has taught at the Architectural Association (London) and in collaborative workshops with the MIT Department of Architecture. Her research in computational design focuses on expanding the role of the computer in engineering and architectural design through the development of computational methods and innovative environments to support performance-based design generation and exploration. She has held a postdoctoral research appointment in the Department of Civil Engineering at the Swiss Federal Institute of Technology in Lausanne (EPFL) where she helped start a new research program in Intelligent Structures and continues to collaborate.

Lars Spuybroek is principal of NOX, an architectural practice based in Rotterdam. He is a professor at the University of Kassel, and visiting professor at Columbia University, New York. His work has won several prizes and been exhibited all over the world, including the Venice Biennale 2000. He is also working on a book, the first NOX, to be published by Thames and Hudson.

David Turnbull is a director of ATOPIA and the Professor of Architecture at the University of Bath. He has also been visiting professor at Yale University and the University of Toronto. He is particularly interested in changing lifestyles and the way that individual buildings and new patterns of development respond to the impact of telecommunications and digital media.

Ben van Berkel and Caroline Bos set up Van Berkel & Bos Architectuurbureau in 1988. Ten years later they established a new firm, UN Studio (United Net), which presents itself as a network of specialists in architecture, urban development and infrastructure. They have taught at many architecture schools around the world. Central to their teaching is the inclusive approach of architectural works integrating virtual and material organisation and engineering constructions.

Dr Chris Williams is Senior Lecturer in Structural Design and Engineering, Department of Architecture & Civil Engineering, University of Bath, UK. He joined Ted Happold's group at Ove Arup in the early 1970s where he was responsible for the structural analysis of the Frei Otto gridshells for the Mannheim Budesgartenschau. Since then he has been a lecturer and researcher at the University of Bath with a particular interest in the formfinding and structural analysis of shell, fabric and bridge structures. Recent projects for which he has written software include the Japanese Pavilion Expo 2000 (Shigeru Ban Architects, Buro Happold), Weald and Downland Gridshell (Edward Cullinan Architects, Buro Happold) and the British Museum Great Court Roof (Foster and Partners, Buro Happold).